Praise for *The Moon Book*

"*The Moon Book* offers an invitation to revel in the magic of slowing down, listening, reflecting, and attuning ourselves to the cyclical forces that animate this planet—the lunar phases. Guided by Sarah, we are anointed in a new way of being, of walking in grace and vulnerability in a world designed to capitalize on our productivity; we learn that we can flourish when we align with the potency of the moon."

—Latham Thomas, founder Mama Glow, bestselling author of *Own Your Glow*

"*The Moon Book* is a treasure chest of lunar wisdom that teaches us to honor our own shape-shifting, and reminds us that we, too, can radiate in the dark. Whether you're looking to tap into ancient knowledge or manifest a more just and joyful future, this is the guidebook for you. Sarah Faith Gottesdiener generates the radical magic we need now."

—Pam Grossman, author of *Waking the Witch: Reflections on Women, Magic, and Power* and host of *The Witch Wave* podcast

"It's evident that Sarah Gottesdiener has spent a significant amount of time diving deeply into the mysteries and offerings of the moon and, luckily for us, has resurfaced with a perspective that is fresh, alluring, and much needed in today's world. A perspective of Moon as teacher, reconnecting us to a world without patriarchal, industrialized control over our cycles, instincts, and true selves; inviting us to return to intuition and wildness. A perspective of Moon as life goals, leading by example with her boundaries and honesty. A perspective of Moon as mystic, 'orbiting around a language beyond a language,' casting her luminous spell over us each night in myriad ways. This book is a beacon of healing, illuminating our inner realms through ritual, introspection, and more. For someone who recognizes how challenging it is to encapsulate the wonder, sacredness, and spiralic nature of moon magick into words, Gottesdiener has certainly done a magnificent job of doing so."

—Chelsea Wolfe, musician, witch

"Sarah Faith Gottesdiener is a kind, gentle soul who understands the deep connection to celestial energy and is a mindful guide through the lunar phases. She offers readers a journey into the wisdom that *The Moon Book* offers with in-depth knowledge and inspiration for both novices and experienced practitioners. This is an essential book for the spiritually curious and those seeking connection with the moon."

—Shaman Durek, thought leader and author of *Spirit Hacking*

"*The Moon Book* brings us into the alignment that is already within us, our inherent worthiness, and how we can use the power of the moon to return to it when we forget. Sarah's own connection to the sky and to herself makes her the perfect guide for this inner work, the work that is vulnerable and messy and in the shadows, Sarah takes our hand to bring us into the light—both working with the changing light of the moon itself and the changing light within us. This book is a must for witches new and old who want to understand themselves better in service to people they love and the collective with the magical support of celestial waves."

—Marlee Grace, author of *How to Not Always Be Working* and *Getting to Center*

"*The Moon Book* is the perfect guide for working with the energy of the moon while navigating life in the twenty-first century. The best way to mix your magic with intersectional feminism, activism, and self-awareness."

—Erica Feldmann, owner of HausWitch, author of *Hausmagick*

"Filled with wisdom, depth, and sweet, reassuring warmth that spills through every page, *The Moon Book* is the book every mystic, witch, feminist or anyone who wants a deeper understanding of self needs. Whether you've been working with lunar cycles for decades or are completely new to this sort of cyclical work, Gottesdiener offers a new perspective and incredibly comprehensive look at the ways in which working with the Moon can change your life and your magick in the best way possible."

—Gabriela Herstik, author of *Inner Witch: A Modern Guide to the Ancient Craft* and *Bewitching the Elements: A Guide to Empowering Yourself Through Earth, Air, Fire, Water, and Spirit*

THE
MOON BOOK

Lunar Magic to Change Your Life

SARAH FAITH GOTTESDIENER

ST. MARTIN'S
ESSENTIALS
NEW YORK

First published in the United States by St. Martin's Essentials,
an imprint of St. Martin's Publishing Group

THE MOON BOOK. Copyright © 2020 by Sarah Faith Gottesdiener.
All rights reserved. Printed in the United States of America. For information,
address St. Martin's Publishing Group, 120 Broadway, New York, NY 10271.

www.stmartins.com

Grateful acknowledgment is made for permission to reproduce from the following:

"Who Am I to Feel So Free" lyrics written by Every Ocean Hughes.
Song written by JD Sampson and Every Ocean Hughes.
Record: Talk About Body. Year: 2011. Record label: IAMSOUND Records

The Library of Congress Cataloging-in-Publication Data is available upon request.

ISBN 978-1-250-20618-3 (paper over board)
ISBN 978-1-250-22233-6 (ebook)

Our books may be purchased in bulk for promotional, educational, or business use.
Please contact your local bookseller or the Macmillan Corporate and Premium Sales
Department at 1-800-221-7945, extension 5442, or by email at
MacmillanSpecialMarkets@macmillan.com.

First Edition: 2020

10 9 8 7 6 5 4 3

For my grandmothers' grandmothers,
who are beloved strangers I carry inside of me

For my grandmothers, Eleonor and Shirley,
who showed me what was most important

For my mother, Marsha,
everything I am, anything I do that matters, is because of you

Contents

Why the Moon?

Because she's the world's celestial anchor. Her gravity stabilizes earth on its axis. She's both predictable and wild. Because she's got a rhythm all her own that mirrors the seasons. We find our own rhythms when we look to her as a guide. Because we can feel her inside of us. Coaxing us to connect, forcing us to remember. The earliest people obeyed her orbit, and that lineage is still within us. It mirrors our own rhythms and cycles, our energy and our emotions. These observations remind us of our humanity and our true nature.

Because she represents our interior: the unseen, our receptivity, our psychic abilities. The power of our water. The vitality of our love. The entirety of our complexities that can't be packaged and sold. Because La Luna lights up the night, illuminates the darkness of the subconscious, where the deep mind lives. In astrology, psychology, and some magical traditions, the moon represents the subconscious. The subconscious is a source of our yearning and fear; it is where the stories and motivations behind our conscious behavior reveal themselves. When we decide to program our subconscious, we change our beliefs. When we change our beliefs, our behavior changes. When our behavior changes, our life changes.

Because moon work helps us tap into our deepest patterns and aids us in reflection and release around them. She is a tool to help us discover our unique truths and our specific needs. She helps us connect to and unleash all unique wisdom we possess.

Once upon a time, this planet lived by the moon. Our calendars were lunar. We planted by the moon, made decisions in harmony with the seasons and the constellations. Over time, through war, violence, and colonization, the shadow solar life—productive, binary, externally focused, competitive—came to dominate. Industrialization removed many humans from nature. Lunar life receded. Instead of placing value in our intuition, in the unknown, in cycles and mysteries, we deemed them scary and thus nonexistent. What one could not explain, one could not control. What could not be controlled was demonized, exploited, extracted, locked up, killed. Indigenous people. Black people. Queer people. Trans people. The feminine. The wild woman. The witch.

But she's back. That bitch, that witch, she's back. The season of the witch ascends again, and the moon has always been our emblem: since Hathor's crown, since Sappho's lyrics, since the first stone temples were built to worship Hecate's sorcery. Witch on broom, flying across a full moon. Cauldron in a clearing, night shadows dancing, potion charged for healing. Because she is here to remind us that everything sacred returns. (That's because it never left.)

Because we are here now to dismantle white supremacist patriarchy—and we must do so together. With our mindset, our conversations, our actions, and our collaborations, a new wave of soft power, change, and magic is being brought forth. For all people who know and long for a different way, forged of compassion—anyone who has felt othered, punished, policed, or anyone who has been abused or marginalized for simply being who they are.

The moon is a love letter to our wildness. It's a reminder of our resilience in the face of subjugation. It's a promise to recognize the power inherent in the collective feminine. Our soft power: power with, power within, not power over. Developing and defining our own magic is feminist art. Tapping into our personal power and channeling it for the betterment of all is feminist art. Helping others work with their own gifts, supporting one another, reflecting another's beauty back to them is feminist art. The moon reflects and transforms sunlight. We reflect ourselves back to one another and behold collective transformation.

Since the beginning of time, artists have tried to translate her particular light into an understandable language. Yet she somehow still summons us to the page, the instrument, the easel. The moon inspires, perhaps because her cycle acts as a blueprint for the creative process. There are dreams, visions, inspiration; we are in a new moon phase. A spark becomes a flame; we roll up our sleeves, seduce material out of thin air; we gain momentum, we build; we embrace the energy of the waxing moon. After practice and repeated effort comes culmination and embodiment. We celebrate, we share, we shine brightly. Others witness our glow. We are under the possession of the full moon phase.

Because magic is real. Moon magic is potent. When we follow along with her cycles, it aids our goals and dreams. Our power is channeled effectively when we mirror the processes of nature. Cycles of rest next to cycles of harvest lead to moments of embodiment, which turn into time spent clearing and reflecting. When we experiment with our own definitions of success, when we respect our own flow, we find ourselves pleasantly surprised by what transpires.

Because time is not linear and neither are our lives. Following the light of the moon goes against the binary of either/or. Beyond duality. It encapsulates the spiral; it acknowledges the death that precedes rebirth. When we are attuned to this natural process and can navigate our own processes accordingly, we are able to deal with change masterfully.

Moon work results in the exploration of different paradigms, endlessly generative options, and greater integration and understanding of the levels and layers of our conscious states. This book will provide you with a framework on how to utilize the entire lunar cycle holistically. You will be invited to explore the main phases of the moon, and will be offered various suggestions on how to work with each one. We will also introduce ways to develop a relationship with your own cycles—energetic, personal, and emotional—through the lens of the moon's phases. I encourage you to do this work for a while, just for you, without a lot of other outside input or influences. Give yourself the time and space to tune in to your own flow and energy patterns. Create your own personal relationship with the moon.

This book is written from my perspective, which is a feminist, queer one. I cannot separate my politics from my spiritual beliefs. What I share here stems from my life experiences over the past twenty years as a magical practitioner, a teacher, a student, a professional psychic and tarot reader, and an artist. My perspective reflects my background as a white cis woman, and all the conscious and unconscious privilege that identity holds. I do not write thinking that readers will resonate with every thought or sentence presented. Part of the most important work we can do is to think critically for ourselves and explore what resonates and works for us. Take what you like and leave the rest.

This book is written in the hopes that it will support you in helping you to remember exactly who you are, exactly what you want, and show you how to get there. I hope to provide you with a variety of tools to help you as you walk confidently along your own precious path. You are incredibly powerful. You are fundamentally worthy. I seek to provide you with a lunar guide to show you how much you are already connected—to your cycles, your gifts, your intuition, the magical world, and the web of the cosmos.

What Is the Moon?

THE MOON IS A SATELLITE

For millennia, humans have gazed at the night sky and asked themselves the same question. What is the moon? The answers have varied—at times literal, sometimes metaphorical, often spiritual. Often these answers have led to more questions.

The moon is the earth's only natural satellite. Johannes Kepler coined the term in the early seventeenth century, from the Latin *satelles*, meaning "companion" or "guard." Formed at least 4.5 billion years ago, the moon is about the same age as the earth. General theories of how the moon was created all involve impacts, though scientists are still trying to figure out the exact genesis of our cosmic companion. The "giant impact" theory hypothesizes that the moon was formed when an object struck earth. The matter that came off that impact, over time, accumulated to become what we now call the moon.[1]

The moon is our closest celestial neighbor. The same side of the moon faces earth. This could explain the moon's comforting familiarity to us, as her repeated visage has slowly been etched in our minds. The moon completes one orbit around the earth in approximately 27.3 days, which is called a sidereal month. Because the earth is also moving around the sun, it takes additional time for the moon to complete one whole phase, to realign with the sun, from new moon to new moon. This is called a synodic month, and for us on the earth, it appears as 29.5 days: approximately the length of a month. The moon's elliptical orbit rotates counterclockwise. At times it is quite close to us, other times much farther away. This is how we get "super" and "micro" moons. One month the full moon looks show-stoppingly huge. The next, it appears as distant as a lover departing.

The moon is made up of a variety of different matter, some of which is shared with our planet. Igneous rocks, feldspar, and iron are some of the types of material found on and in the moon. One of its minerals, olivine, is found both in the tails of comets and in the upper mantle of the earth.

There is no atmosphere on the moon. Aside from intermittent moonquakes, it is a still and quiet place. The footprints left behind by the astronauts more than fifty years ago will stay forever. The moon is sensitive, just like you.

Humans have projected pictures on the surface of our satellite. These turn into stories, myths, deities. The numerous peaks and valleys on the moon create the appearance of a hazy face, complete with Mona Lisa smile. Some have interpreted these marks as a rabbit, or a buffalo, or a frog, or a man. These were created by large impacts of asteroids and meteoroids hitting the powdery lunar surface over billions of years. The moon's geographic phenomena have their own nomenclature, created by Giovanni Battista Riccioli in 1651.[2] The basins and plains on the lunar surface that appear darker are the maria, which is the Latin word for *seas*; the singular is *mare*. (The earliest viewers of the moon thought these lower elevated plains were seas, but the moon's surface, to our knowledge, contains no water.) Their names are beguiling and evocative: Serpent Sea, or Mare Anguis; Sea of Cleverness, or Mare Ingenii; Sea of the Edge, Sea of Serenity, Sea of Crises.

Similar to the maria are the lacus: smaller basaltic plains. (*Lacus* is the Latin word for "lake.") There is the Lake of Luxury, which resides near the Lake of Forgetfulness. The Lake of Hatred, or Lacus Odii, is on the same latitude as the Lake of Happiness, or Lacus Felicitatis. Intense dramas alongside pools of contentment; such is life in the lunar realm.

There are smaller, similar features called sinus (Latin for "bay") and palus (Latin for "marsh"). These include the Seething Bay, the Bay of Rainbows, the Marsh of Sleep, and the Marsh of Decay.

The moon is not a circle. Like the earth, the moon is shaped like an egg. The cosmic egg figures in many ancient creation myths. The moon is about 33 percent smaller than the earth—its diameter is slightly less than the distance between Los Angeles and New York.[3]

What are we looking at, when we look up at the moon? A reflection of the sun from across the universe. The moon does not generate its own light. It is a very dark gray, with some green due to the olivine. The moon appears bright white, silver, or yellow, or red, or even slightly blue sometimes, due to the way light changes moving though our atmosphere. Most folks have particular moon memories: a full moon that seemed to follow them as they walked home alone one cold winter night, or stare them down through their bedroom window as they unsuccessfully tried to sleep. A full moon disco ball as backdrop to the perfect summer dance party. The unique angles, reflections, temperature, atmosphere, season, and weather conditions make each appearance completely unique, enhancing our experience with the element of surprise.

The moon is responsible for the gravitational force of water on our planet. It affects all the tides—not only the ocean, but the lakes and rivers. Not just the water on the surface of our globe. All the water *on* the earth and *in* the earth. That includes all the water in plants, animals, and humans. People consist of up to 60 percent water. The moon influences all the water inside of you.

The sun's gravitational pull also has an effect on the tides, but as the moon is closer to the earth, its influence is much greater. The moon's gravity affects the earth so much that the earth itself may rise as much as a foot when the moon is directly overhead.[4] The moon stabilizes the earth's axis. Without the moon, the earth would shake more, and shift on its axis in unpredictable ways. This gravitational relationship regulates our seasons. If the moon didn't exist, seasons would be irregular and the weather more extreme. Days would be much shorter; life on earth would be very different. The earth's only companion is a helpful one.[5]

The moon helps crops grow. Humankind originally planted and grew their crops by the moon. Many still do. Lunar gardening uses the phases of the moon, the moon's path, and the moon's sign, to sow, plant, and harvest vegetables. This system was developed thousands of years ago and is still used today. There are various "elemental days" that correspond to what astrological sign the moon is in: An earth day corresponds to roots, water corresponds to leaves, air corresponds to flowers, and fire corresponds to fruit/seeding days. Moon calendars for gardening are based on astronomy, not astrology. They use a sidereal zodiac to determine recommended times to plant, harvest, propagate, and sow.[6]

Human's evolution is partially linked to the moon. Our bright satellite helped humans see at night, while they traveled, worked, and worshipped. The moon helped humans keep track of time, which led to the proliferation of agriculture, which led to the formation of organized societies.

Acknowledging the moon in this way brings us back to our bodies, our lineages, our life. It reminds us of our bodies' natural intelligence, its circadian cycles, our other responses and rhythms. We observe the moon's changing light reflected in the seasons, in our gardens. We connect to the tides inside of us.

THE MOON IS FOR EVERYBODY

No one owns the moon. This world is so extractive, though, it's only a matter of time before the moon becomes just another place to pillage and destroy. The 2015 S.P.A.C.E. Act (Spurring Private Aerospace Competitiveness and Entrepreneurship) is allowing U.S. citizens and industries to "engage in the commercial exploration and exploitation of space resources." In other words, any corporation can mine the minerals of any planet, asteroid, or satellite. Any corporation can drill on Mars, can drain the moon of its fabled stores of subsurface water. Profit above all.

Already, our globe can barely contain the emptiness disguised as greed that courses through it. Even the men who landed on the moon left trash on her. People still regularly litter her surface, routinely crashing probes on the moon at the end of unmanned lunar exploration missions. All in all, we've left upward of 400,000 pounds of debris on the moon. Tossed in the Sea of Tranquility, strewn about in the various lunar maria are twelve pairs of moon boots; several Hasselblad cameras; a plaque signed by Richard Nixon; 96 pounds of urine, excrement, and vomit; multiple hammers, five American flags, and much, much more. Because the moon has no atmosphere, these objects will never decompose or be blown off.[7] Nowadays, with lunar tourism on the horizon, it's not so far-fetched to imagine a universe filled with candy wrappers, plastic bottles, and diapers floating past one's spaceship window.

This is the trash that we leave on the holy face of the cosmos. This is the extractive way we are taught to treat sacred nature, and our sacred natures. This is the extractive way we are taught to consider relationships. The extractive ways we try to use and sell magic. The moon has watched us this entire time. She was overhead as Alexander the

Great pillaged; she circled us during the Tiananmen Square protests. She has always been a muse, beaming her rays of inspiration down on poets from Rumi to Rilke to Audre Lorde. She watched as the buffalo were slaughtered, wiped almost entirely from the plains of Turtle Island; she was overhead as the Trail of Tears left an entire land almost empty of its stewards. A full moon shone down on the last moments of the Stonewall riots, beer bottle missiles glittering in the night. The moon shines upon us still as coral reefs disintegrate and as we protest seemingly endless injustices and as we continue to figure out ways to love one another without destroying ourselves. She will continue to shine even in our absence. The great moon, mother of the heavens, does not belong to us. She exists beyond human time. She does not care. That doesn't mean we shouldn't care about her.

If you are involved in any spiritual or justice work, then you know: We do this work for a future we can't see. For a future, quite frankly, we may *never* see. We know not to underestimate the power of one person's intentions and repeated actions. This is a long, heartbreaking road, but one that must also be pleasurable, beautiful, and connection-filled. Part of our responsibility is to heal the wounds of those who came before us. To love something is to want to protect it, to save it, and to share it. Love offers us a way to live on after our bodies are no longer.

The moon belongs to no one and the moon belongs to all of us. For each of us, she is a cosmic crystal ball, helping us to see, encouraging us to pause, cajoling us into wonder. Even in this age of ultra-futuristic special effects and uncanny simulations, a bright moon still makes us gasp as though we've stumbled upon a favorite celebrity. She prompts us to point up at the sky mesmerized, pull the car over, change plans, stay in, go out, gather with like-minded strangers and friends. For millennia, the moon has inspired and guided humans—pyramids and sculptures and songs and entire religions and ancient cults and fashion collections have all been created to worship and pay homage to our guardian of the night. The moon belongs to no one. The moon is for everybody.

THE MOON IS OUR ANCESTORS

To be a scholar of the moon is to study the entirety of human history. How we have behaved and what we have valued is reflected in the various ways we've interpreted the moon. Through the ages, her powers have been revered, then rejected, then utilized anew. The passage of months and years were archived through observing her. She's been a partner to our fertility and to the earth's fertility: our food, a tether to life itself. Later, the moon became a force of evil, the source of witches' power and women's wildness, an instigator of hysteria, something to be feared. The history of the moon overpowered the herstory of the moon. Her knowledge became folk knowledge, passed down over the centuries through mostly oral traditions; information disguised in myth, tall tales, songs, and recipes. But the Goddess never left, she just went underground. Only to show up and return to those who need her most.

All of humanity has looked up at the same moon and wondered. About the meanings of life, love, mystery, and all matters of existence. From Cleopatra to Cher. The full moon has been watched by our grandmothers' grandmothers' grandmothers, and all the ancestors whose names we will never know. They sat under the moon and cried, just like we have. Assimilation may have wiped out some, or all, of our ancestral connections: access to our mother tongues, our ancient rituals, certain recipes. Slavery and colonization have wiped out bloodlines, magical traditions, folk medicine, and languages. The moon is one tool that we can use to discover more about our ancestry, and to uncover traditions, rituals, and other practices our ancestors may have utilized.

The ways our ancestors understood the moon resides in the language used to name it. The English word *menses* comes from *mensis*—Latin for "month"—and is also the root of the word *menstruation*. The proto-Indo-European common root of "moon" and "measurement"—*me, ma, men*—also includes "to measure," "mind," and "mental."

Many cultures named full moons; these names spoke to place, season, what was growing, the environment and more. For example, in North America, the Algonquin people named the autumnal equinox full moon the "Corn Moon" and the January full moon the "Wolf Moon." Later, *The Farmer's Almanac* inaccurately and problematically popularized the full moon names from the Algonquin as being the same for all Native American moon names. However, there are over 573 Native American tribes in North America. Many have different names for each full moon and month.[8]

Full moon names are time capsules of what people held precious. They describe specific periods of time, place, and ritual, and mark activities and traditions as well. For the Cherokee people, March was "Month of the Windy Moon," or *a nu yi*. May was "Month of the Planting Moon," or *a na a gv ti*. By reading these descriptors, we have record of what was happening in the American southeast. The Gaelic lunar months were mostly named for trees, as Celtic spirituality believed trees held healing and magical powers: January corresponded to the Birch Moon; mid-February, the Rowan Moon; mid-March, the Ash Moon. Some Chinese full moons were named for highly revered sacred flowers: April is the Peony Moon; June is the Lotus Moon; September is the Chrysanthemum Moon. Moon names as poetry, moon names as ritual reminders, moon names as a kind of home.

There are endless myths, parables, and stories of the moon. A Yiddish tale of two brothers recounts them attempting to steal the moon by capturing it in a bucket. But they can't, and learn that one must not steal what is not theirs, especially when they already have their own light.[9] Some explain why the moon appears the way it does. In the Jataka tales—Indian literature devoted to stories of the Buddha's past life—the Buddha is a hare who selflessly offers himself up as a meal to a hungry Indra, who is the Lord of the Gods. The kind hare is memorialized in the face of the moon.[10] Some are origin stories for the earth and its seasons. Demeter-Ceres, the goddess synonymous with grain and fertility for the Greeks and Romans, reaped with her moon-shaped sickle. Tlazolteotl, the Aztec Moon Goddess, gives birth to herself.[11]

If you have knowledge of the geographical region your ancestors came from, you can do some research. What stories did your ancestors share of the moon? How did they honor the moon? What were their names for the moon? Try to find out what they ate, what herbs they used, and any other traditions or folklore, if you feel called to do so. Lunar-associated traditions are an easy place to begin to gain more information, as almost all cultures had their own relationships with the moon.

This isn't to say you can't make up your own names, your own stories.

Our ancestors live inside us. They are our bones, our hair, our blood, our talents, our sorrows, our resilience. In honoring the moon in both old and modern ways, we honor ourselves and our ancestors.

THE MOON IS A MIRROR

The moon is a mirror. The sun shines light on the moon; the moon reflects that light onto us, illuminating our intimacies, shadows, and secrets. It is a symbol to help us find personal and collective meaning. Whatever symbol the moon becomes merely describes the seeker. How we speak of the moon, what we see in the moon, and how

14

we work with the moon shows us much about ourselves. She strips away our pretenses and delivers us back to ourselves as we gaze into our reflections.

The moon mirrors our natural spiral processes. Our lives aren't ever static, even if we worry they are. We cycle in and out of various phases in our lives, contracting and expanding, building and shedding. The moon dies, frequently. The moon sheds her shadow in order to be reborn. Sometimes, we too must rebirth ourselves in order to gain a truer version of the self. As we tune in to our own energetic patterns that so often mirror the moon's, the self-knowledge gained facilitates transformation. Accepting *all* the impossible or challenging or amazing things about yourself forms the golden glue Kintsugi for embracing the imperfect complexities of life. We are many things at once. Our pain leads to our pleasure, our mistakes move us toward humility. This is one way to attempt wholeness: living with the moon's varied reflections.

Observations are magical. The Talmud says: *We don't see things as they are, we see them as we are.* We are all mirrors. Who are others, if not mirrors of our own perceptions, fears, hopes, and dreams? The moon illuminates the ways in which we need to receive love. This forces us to think about how to offer others care and compassion. We are asked to *reflect on* others' needs, their love languages, their yearnings, and what they need to feel safe.

The ability to reflect is magical. In a world that emphasizes power *over*, reflecting is a gift. To think before one speaks is always a genius idea. Time put aside weekly, or daily, to reflect, to come back to ourselves, is a priceless practice. The pause becomes a place to truly see.

Part of lunar living is to be in a constant state of cleaning the mirrors of our psyche, our emotions, our inner landscapes. In order to stare into a clear looking glass means being in the present moment, unencumbered by the dust of the distorted stories of the past. To clean the mirror is to be as honest as possible: projections and delusions must be wiped away. To clean the mirror is to attempt to keep our perspective loving and our reflections in service to our evolution.

THE MOON IS OUR WATER

The moon dictates our inner tides. She tugs at all the water we hold: our blood, our sweat, our tears. Our amniotic fluid, our spit, and our milk. In witchcraft and tarot theory, water traditionally correlates with psychic ability, flow, intuition, our emotions, spirituality, nostalgia, and memories. In ancient times, priestesses built moon shrines at the mouths of springs, on the banks of lakes, in caves that sheltered secret pools, to guard and access their healing waters.[12]

Water is a force powerful in its versatility. It sinks massive ships, caresses seahorses in its cerulean depths, and travels down through the soil to offer sustenance to the roots that weave through the fabric of earth. Many people are not comfortable with fluidity. For them, the black-and-white rules are the only rules and their way is the only way. Rigidity is mistaken for safety. Water reminds us we are fluid. We are mirrors of the ocean, of the rivers, of the rain. When we own and practice fluidity, the experience of the spectrum of our existence turns technicolor.

When we ignore our emotions, when they become unbalanced, our actions turn dangerous. When water gets too cold, it freezes; it is completely impenetrable. Too hot, it scalds. Sweet sprinkles quickly become a thunderstorm; a warm spring turns into a boiling cavern. When our water is supported it is free to flow. Safety, boundaries, and other appropriately chosen vessels allow us to float easily on the rivers of our lives. We do not discount our psychic abilities, and we act on them just as we would with "tangible" or logic-based responses. Acts of care, love, pleasure, and beauty that heal others and ourselves are revered. The mysteries of our world are appreciated as much as the mysteries within.

Below the surface lies the subconscious, driving the patterns we enact and repeat. Within the basement of our subconscious are the old belief systems we've constructed in order to keep us safe: our ego, repeating the same reassuring stories. When doing the transformative, watery work of the moon, we will come up against the parts of our ego that are harmful. These are the parts that keep us punished, in scarcity, and underperforming. We will reencounter the parts of ourselves that were forged long ago, maybe not even by us. These will need to be examined, integrated, and in some cases, released.

Carl Jung famously stated that "until you make the unconscious conscious, it will direct your life and you will call it fate." Our emotional patterns can point us to what exactly needs to be healed. Through practice, we can learn how to engage with our emotions without allowing them to overpower us. In doing so, they become sources of information. We come to understand we are not our emotions, any more than we are defined by one short moment. Our intuition also correlates with our subconscious— our knowing that lies beyond language, beyond critical or analytical thought. In the realm of our subconscious also lies our past: those beliefs and experiences that influence our reactions and behaviors in the present moment. The moon is a bridge between the subconscious as past and the embodiment of the present. Moon work offers us keys to open the doors of both our subconscious and our consciousness. This work allows us to understand what our responses are about, where the root source of that response began, and what we need to do in order to transform those response patterns that direct our lives in unwanted trajectories.

Noticing our larger patterns and cycles helps us integrate different facets of our consciousness. With practice, we easily access the direct line between our consciousness and our subconscious. This builds trust and greater self-intimacy. This fosters our belief in our innate ability to transform.

THE MOON IS FEMINIST ART

The moon is feminist art. Her phases take us outside of the binary; both dark and light simultaneously, she plays with our perceptions. Like the moon, we naturally move from one state to another. Our soul still emanates while our behaviors shift, and our identity discovers new realms to play in. We get to hyphenate until we can no longer count the hyphens. There are no limits to our becoming.

The act of art making is alchemical. Art saves lives. Nature is art. Both heal in multiple dimensions.

On the vast canvas of our evening sky, the moon is the closest symbol to us of the divine feminine. We can utilize the moon to examine what the feminine encompasses, and how this can be expanded upon and evolved. (Venus, the only other cosmic body who appears to have phases, has also been assigned a feminine gender by ancient peoples and astrologers.) Over time, there have been a lot of assumptions made around the feminine and the moon both.

The moon's pronouns are whatever you choose. The moon isn't picky or attached like that. There have been feminine moon goddesses and masculine moon gods and larger lunar energies that exist beyond gender. The moon is for all genders: trans, cis, non-binary, or however else one chooses to identify. If we get our periods the moon is for us. If we don't get our periods the moon is for us.

That said, there is an undeniable connection between the moon and the menstrual cycle. Beyond the twenty-nine-day similarity between the lunar cycle and human menstruation cycles, there are theories that the moon helped regulate those cycles. This supported procreation, which helped us proliferate on the planet. Most people's periods do not line up consistently with a lunar phase; they fluctuate.[13] Electricity, screen exposure, medication, and stress may affect our hormones and pineal glands much more than they did thousands of years ago.

The period/procreation and lunar connection led to a widespread correlation between the moon and the feminine. This also contributed to perception of the moon as a malevolent force—tied to the witches, the stormy emotions, psychic wildness, and birthing abilities, access to which so many feminine folks naturally have. In many Neolithic societies, it was the moon mother—the goddess or goddesses who symbolized the moon—who was the most important or central deity to worship. Over time, most matrilineal societies were conquered by patrilineal ones. The matriarchal deities had to be subjugated accordingly. Gods are reflections of us tiny humans and the powers we crave, the fears we hold.

With increased colonialism and the rise of the patriarchy came the rise of the binary. With the rise of the binary came domination over women and femmes, which was enacted through violence, rape, menstrual shame, and other denigrations. The patriarchy destroyed the moon mother, and replaced her with the sun god, which then became a Christian God. Remnants of our former matriarchal lunar practices still hide in plain sight—the father, the son, and the Holy Spirit: the trinity that reference the three phases of the moon, the three heads of Hecate, the holy triumvirate that prances through a plethora of Goddess cultures.

Magical practitioners across the globe have always continued to worship the moon. Most recently, we've seen this with the rise of goddess-centered pagan religions, beginning in the 1960s and extending to the present day. Some of that has surfaced in popular culture, in Internet listicles about why this particular new moon is important, in tweets bemoaning the potent emotions around a full moon. *The moon made me do it.* All this digital popularity has its origins in religious reverence, in covens—in the ancient lunar worship that has been going on since the dawn of time. Many folks continue to awaken to their own spiritual interests, turning away from a patriarchal and white supremacist–induced, prescribed, religious dogma. Practicing nature-based, intuition-led lunar mindfulness is part of this spiritual recovery.

Some of the ideas and practices of the New Age goddess culture that emerged in the 1960s, which still has influence now in certain spaces, have been transphobic. It is difficult to imagine members of oppressed groups (cis women and cis lesbians) deciding to oppress others, but is understandable. Traumatized and oppressed groups will often try to find control wherever they can, will often enact violence on a projected "other." That is one symptom of internalized abuse. Hate-led people deciding that they alone can deem who a "woman" is—and that it is based on gender assignment at birth, and genitalia—is a practice that must end. This sort of thinking is just as patriarchal as the idea that women's magical identity is based on their life stage (maiden, mother, crone); their ability to give birth. A gender essentialist rhetoric is harmful and untrue. Having a biological womb doesn't connect you to the moon any more than it does someone who doesn't. As the doula, writer, and activist Latham Thomas says, "Your intrinsic worth has nothing to do with your ability to bleed or give birth."

The moon affects us no matter what body parts we have. We are all made up of water; we all hold shadows and light. All of us feel the moon, relish her silvery glow on our skin, carry her songs inside of us. When I speak about the moon being feminine or femme, this is beyond gender. I am referring to an energy, a quality, a philosophy, and a relational structure that values mutual care, aid, safety, and nonhierarchical and nonviolent interactions.

The link between the moon and the divine feminine is in constant evolution. The divine feminine is not one gender. The divine feminine is all races, abilities, all body types. Men and non-binary people can embody the divine feminine. Not every woman may feel comfortable embodying the divine feminine. The divine feminine is a place of fertility and fecundity—the place where we create from deep down in our soul. The place where expressions flow freely. It is what we love, and how we love. This is Empress energy. The divine feminine can be fierce and fearless and juggle ten tasks one day, and go to her therapist and cry over takeout the next. The divine feminine is vulnerable, joyful, thoughtful, sexy, sweet, takes others along with her. She wants to do the best she can, not out of a fear-based drive, but out of a spiritual calling born out of a rendezvous with the transcendent.

Feminism is part of reimagining the divine. As we evolve, so does our feminism. A feminism that does not include BIPOC, sex workers, trans folks, non-binary folks, disabled folks, sick folks, poor folks, working-class folks, undocumented folks, and folk from any and all backgrounds is not feminism. The divine feminism invokes a form of feminism that is radical—one that is not interested in perpetuating the struggle to gain equality with men.

A divine feminism seeks to deprogram from abuse. We don't want to mimic the patriarchy; we don't want to preserve the violence of white supremacy and capitalism. There is something else entirely different to invest in. The cultivation of communities based on trust, mutual respect, and deep listening. The centering of pleasure over robotic productivity, generosity over competition. Gardens where everyone can thrive, places where everyone is thought of. Spaces to cheer each other's accomplishments, because someone else's success does not diminish our chances. This is about developing an abundance mindset. We want to find our way back to our natural states of being. This is about creating new ways of existence in the world that are complex, messy, personal, and intersectional. We wish to revel in the generosity of *power within* that is found in our witchcraft and spirituality. To remember, connect, create, and adapt our own unique forms of magic and belief.

Witches, Magic, and the Moon

WITCHES

The moon and witches have been tied together throughout history. Witches follow the moon for timing of all sorts. Many witches will only cast spells with, not against, their interpretations of a lunar phase. Witches who make herbal remedies will frequently harvest and process their medicine to coincide with lunar cycles. The phrase "drawing down the moon" refers to an ancient practice of a priestess or witch standing with arms up, underneath the moon, to draw that energy inside of their bodies. The participant then becomes the moon, or channels its energy, lit up by its magical charge.[1]

A witch is many things. A witch is untamed; wild; full of rage; ready to cry in public; generous with her gifts; able to communicate with nature and spirit; able to heal bodies with acupuncture needles. A witch locks herself in a room with a pen and comes out twelve hours later with an indescribable masterpiece. A witch with a stained lap of elderberries receives a download and creates a fortifying elixir. A witch fucks however she wants, whomever she wants, whenever she wants. One may find her foraging in the forest; caressing crystals in caves; climbing trees for a better view of the egrets; holding her breath for long periods of time under the waves that crash against a gradient-soaked horizon. Witches are in classrooms teaching children algebra; in grocery stores carefully stacking produce just so; taking temperatures in busy clinics; on movie sets wearing oversized rhinestone-encrusted sunglasses; in abortion clinics holding clammy hands; dawdling in parking lots swiping left on their phones; seducing the crowd from strip-club stages; shuffling tarot decks across from people with burning questions. There's a witch wherever you are.

Witches name themselves. Green witches, kitchen witches, glamour witches, hedge witches, color witches, Fae witches, art witches, sex witches, moon witches, doula witches, word witches, astro witches, queer witches, fashion witches, herbalist witches: these are just some of the ways that I've heard witches describe themselves. Witches are brujas, are wizards, are priestesses, are seers, are root workers, are sorcerers. Witches are Muslim, Jewish, Buddhist, Christian, Wiccan, and questioning. Witchcraft is a sprawling and vast belief system in which there is room for all different ideologies. Witches don't need to insist on being right, or belittle forms of witchcraft different from their own. There is no wrong way, and no one way, to witch.

Witches are terrifying to the patriarchy. Magical people invent and embody their own definitions of power. This is why the patriarchy fears them. This fear has led and continues to lead to control, punishment, and violence. To this day, witches are still persecuted. Witch hunts were and still are used for control over marginalized folks' bodies, knowledge, labor, and land. Indigenous people, Black people, Brown people, people of color, women, and gender-nonconforming people have been the predominant targets of violent campaigns and are who have suffered most under colonization.[2] The war against witches is and has been an attack on nonconforming and noncompliant folks.

We alone can reclaim the power of our magic. As witches, we must disentangle ourselves from the stigmas that have created shame around our superpowers. Being empathetic, sensitive, kind, caring, fierce, psychic, or intuitive is wonderful. Feeling things deeply, having relationships with animals, plants, the elements, guides, fairies, spirit, the spirit realm, or certain ancestors is a blessing. If you possess particular gifts, it is for a reason. If you are a channel, a medium—however that looks—there is nothing wrong with you. You are just as you were intended to be.

As we reclaim our identities, we must also take care to scrutinize our magical practices. Question if we are stealing or appropriating, and stop if we are. Question what sort of language and framing we are using in our communities and how these might need updates (for example, using "white" to describe good and using "black" to describe bad). Using spiritual bypassing as an excuse not to examine our own practice or behaviors for any racism, classism, ableism, transphobia, misogyny, and other systemic oppressions that unfairly burden so many in our collective. If you are a writer or teacher, are you properly citing and referencing the origins of your ideas and concepts? Do you give credit where credit is due?

Be conscious of the role of commodification in your practice. Capitalism has a way of confusing the accessories of the thing with the thing itself. In this case, the thing is magic. Magic is priceless and it cannot be bought and sold, only shared and experienced.

MAGIC

Magic is sorcery. Power. The ability to change the course of events using supernatural forces. The ability to change one's consciousness at will. Magic is the art of living well. Magic is a feeling and an action. A noun and a verb. Delightful, intense, intriguing, enchanting. A sparkly quality, something out of the ordinary. A state of alignment and groundedness. The art of energetic mastery.

There are numerous types of magic practiced on the planet. The magic I present in this book is nondenominational. That means there is no specific god, goddess, goddexx, or other deity you have to believe in. You can weave your own customs, practices, and philosophies in with the suggestions provided. You only need to believe in energy, nature, motion, change, beauty, connectivity, relationships, the basic principles of cause and effect. You have to believe in yourself.

A magical practice will be as varied and unique as the practitioner. Some witches are very particular about timing and correspondences. Others are very disciplined in their ceremonial and spell structures. There are witches whose work is heavily influenced by their ancestral lineage; and since not everyone has that access, there are some witches who are creating their own lineage, derived from their learnings in this lifetime. Some work with deities; others do not. There are those who solely cast spells for their own benefit; others cast spells only to serve others and the collective. Some do a mixture of both. Many witches are solitary practitioners. Others engage with magic in community, with a coven, in a temple, or in another organization.

Engaging in a daily, consistent spiritual practice alongside your magical one will build your discipline. The more disciplined you are—mentally, emotionally, and behaviorally—the more effective your spells will be. Discipline is used to bring core sensitivities, talents, and desires out of the ether of dreams and into the material. Your discipline is derived from returning to the source of your values, loves, interests, intuition, and dreams.

A consistent complementary morning and/or evening practice brings you back to yourself and creates space in which you can process and reflect. You might try a minuscule but mighty routine: Take five minutes to center yourself in the present moment. Pull a tarot card and journal about it. Add a grounding meditation or some focused breathing. Adapt your practice as needed: some days you may have no more than a few minutes to spare; other days you may wish to spend an hour or more with yourself. Improvisation is a key part of any magical practice. Most likely many days your spiritual practice merges with your life, because a spiritual practice is a life practice. You use the tools and habits you've cultivated to stay aligned, focused, and centered through rough patches.

Seasoned witches know that magic is about mastery of mind and mastery of energy. Both are necessary. Both require consistent development. Practice having mind and energetic mastery while moving. Then practice having both while moving and no longer reacting to external situations based on limiting beliefs and unhealed wounds. Then notice the correlation between your mind, emotions, and internal reactions while also cultivating an interior baseline of self-awareness and compassion. This is some wizard-level magic, yet it requires not one crystal, not one candle. This practice does require commitment, willingness, patience, and discipline.

This is what I call being in alignment. What your mind is thinking is directly connected to the words you use. Your words are connected to your actions. Your actions reflect the ideals you hold around your self-actualization. This sounds simple but is quite difficult. When we are in alignment consciously and consistently, we are living spiritually. This is also magic.

A magical practice must be a place where one feels seen and supported. If a magical practice doesn't resonate with you, then do not do it. You can always augment and revise spells or philosophies that you come across, including the ones in this book. An inherent part of magic—and life—is making it all up! A spiritual practice is creating something intimate and specific to you, your beliefs, your needs, and your perspective.

Within the safe container of your practice, you can try to make new kinds of art, figure out your own interpretations of tarot cards, spend time learning how to make your own magical tools, get to know your body in loving and sensual ways, and work on refining your energetic mastery. You are allowed to change your mind, your goals, and your desires. As you experiment and evolve, you'll keep some practices and leave others.

A magical practice must be an exchange. Many spells require ingredients, such as crystals, plants, herbs, and candles. Personally, I enjoy a practice where a little goes a long way. I have a sweetgrass braid that a friend gave me that has been used for the last five years. I burn a little at a time. I have cast spells with nothing more than a tea light, a bowl of water, a paper and pen, and some dirt. Spells don't need any ingredients at all to be effective. Invoking the elements is powerful. Calling in the energy of deities, angels, guides, and other celestial helpers requires nothing but focus. Go outside into the forest. Make the river part of your spell. Infuse the stars into your whispered desires.

A magical practice opens a doorway into the realm of endless possibilities—a place we had almost forgotten but that still pulses inside our veins. Magic offers us a lifeline back to the most essential parts of ourselves: back to our hibernating hopes, back to earnest longings we had wrapped in recycled newsprint and thrown into the corner of our psychic closet. Magic provides a way back to the desires the external world rarely grants us permission to feel, let alone congratulates us for voicing.

When we enact magic, we wander down the pathways of our imagination. Once, we had imaginary friends we would play with for hours. Once, a twig became a wand, imbued with electric volts of dragon fire. For many of us, that vital, fertile imaginative part of us got bulldozed over by needing to survive, by heartbreak, by obligations, by trauma. Magic is a place where we can resurrect our innovative dreamscapes and reencounter the sheer wonder that accompanies an awakened life.

In a magical practice, the only failure is not trying.

MAGICAL PRACTICE AND THE MOON

As I teach it, lunar magic is magic that is specifically co-created with an entire lunar cycle. The energies of the different phases of the moon are worked with consciously and intentionally. In spell work, in ritual, and in the external world through actions and behavioral change. While the majority of practitioners use lunar timing, they don't always work with and make magic throughout the entire lunar cycle. They may cast one spell and leave it at that. The lunar magic I use and teach involves working with all of the moon's phases over at least one cycle around one goal or desire. Even if I am not casting a spell a week, I am taking actions around my goal every day. I might cast just two spells at opposite times of the lunation. In between, I am observing and working with my energy, taking steps to shift my behavior, naming my blocks and transforming my relationship to them, and much more. This all works in conjunction with the energies of each phase, as well as my own energies.

Lunar magic is the most effective tool I have found for actual, long-lasting manifestation results and effectual magic. It is holistic; it asks us to take a 360-degree approach to our goals. Every lunar phase asks us to engage and approach our desire in a different way. The external and internal are addressed. Our mindset shifts; we reprogram our subconscious; our actions are energetically and magically amplified. Even if we take one different action, let go of one limiting belief, or change one behavior for each lunar phase, results will be seen. Through an entire cycle of the moon, we are committing to our goal—and our self—over and over again. This ends up creating fundamental transformation within us, which leads to profound, enduring change.

Some practitioners treat the moon as a deity. They think of and treat the moon like a divine, supernatural god or goddess. Your worship of the moon could include prayer, honoring actions, making offerings, and time spent in gratitude for her. You can also ask the moon, like any goddexx, god, or goddess, what it wants or what it would like. Then, do it, as a symbol of your devotion.

Others work with her energy elementally. The moon becomes an ingredient in your magic. As discussed elsewhere, the moon traditionally corresponds with the feminine—psychic and intuitive gifts, the home, et cetera. Some practitioners use lunar energy as an additional boost to their spell. They might cast their spell outside on a Monday, day of the moon, or when it is in its home and astrologically favored signs of Cancer and Taurus, in order to harness potent lunar energy.

When making moon magic, one might wish to solely focus on traditional magical correspondences of the moon for their altar. Those are items from the sea: coral, crab shells, sand, seashells, seawater, and pearls. There are the animals of the sea: whales, dolphins, narwhals, sea lions, otters, mermaids, pelicans, eels, seahorses, selkies, penguins, or your favorite aquatic creature. Some crystals that correspond to the moon are selenite, silver, clear quartz, lapis lazuli, celestite, and moonstone (with the various types of moonstone corresponding to particular lunar phases: black moonstone for the dark moon, pink moonstone for the new moon, and white moonstone for the full moon).

Some plants that correspond to the moon are seaweed, mugwort, motherwort, passionflower, poppy, moonwort, and blue vervain. Any plant life that grows in water, such as lotus and water lilies, correspond. Flowers that bloom at night correspond, as do white and silvery plants: queen of the night, datura, moonflower, jasmine, evening primrose, lavender, and sage. Fruits and vegetables that tend to be juicy, like melons, aloe, and cucumber, also correspond.

The colors that correspond to the moon are silver, white, all shades of blue, gray, and black.

Of course, the moon corresponds to all water. The rivers, ponds, brooks, waterfalls, hot springs, ice sheets, lakes, rain, sleet, and all forms of H_2O on this planet. This also includes recordings of water sounds: whale song, crashing ocean waves, and gurgling mountain streams. All the fluid we hold: tears, blood, and other body fluids, as well as our lymphatic and reproductive systems, correspond to the moon as well.

Each specific lunar phase will have its own specific energy for you. This is an opportunity for you to explore your own correspondences as they correlate with your energies or intentions. Part of a magical practice is creating your own correspondences: You might have a perfume that reminds you of the waxing moon, all earthy tones and frankincense. You could make a playlist that gives you dark moon vibes—the sounds of feminine rage and faraway futures. In each specific moon phase chapter, I've added suggested correspondences. Try working with those, or use them for inspiration to create your personal symbolic bank.

You may wish to call on the moon as a helper or spiritual guide for times in your life where you would like to enhance a particular quality that she traditionally corresponds to. Emotional mastery, emotional health and well-being, spirituality, going with the flow, vitality, psychic ability, intuition, giving and receiving love, the divine feminine and the divine femme, travel, parenting work, inner-child work, magic of all kinds, wholeness, and embodiment practices are some themes the moon corresponds to. The moon could be one of your sovereign deities for your entire life, or you could dedicate a period of time to work with her specifically.

SPELL WORK

A spell is an intentional act utilized to effect change.

The act itself is a creative ritual that may include elements, symbols, and communion with source, spirit, ancestors, or specific deities. When one casts a spell, one declares one's desire and consciously harnesses different energies in order to provide support and boost momentum around one's focus.

A spell is intention + energy + action. Within the spell working, your own energy is also fundamentally transformed. A spell is an initiation into another way of being, another way of behaving, another way of believing.

During a spell, you are programming yourself to be in energetic alignment with that which you desire. You are reprogramming your mindset: the beliefs and words you use around yourself and your goals. You are using emotionalized thought to create a powerful field of motivation and attraction. Emotionalized thought is mixing positive and strong emotions into your thoughts and energy so that they gain strength. When we consciously and intentionally connect the heart to the nervous system to the subconscious, our personal paradigm shifts. A spell needs some kind of transformative aspect, energetic movement, or mindset shift. This is vital, as it reorganizes your baseline imprint.

An important aspect of spell work is the change that occurs by the process of casting the spell itself. Spell work is transformation work. When you decide to cast a spell, you are committing to change and you must transform yourself accordingly. In deciding to cast a spell, you are accepting that unpredictable change will come as a result. The decision to cast the spell is also a commitment to step into the unknown.

Part of the art of spell casting is paying attention to your own internal messages and willingness to grow. A spell will boost or enhance actions you are already taking in the material realm. A spell can also activate a focused desire. The spell acts as the beginning, a rose blooming from the inside out. At times, you let your intuition guide you; you might feel called to cast a spell that comes from a place deep within, without completely understanding why.

Record what you do in a journal. Some witches call this a grimoire, or a book of shadows: a place where one notes all of the details of their magical workings. Write down the day and time, any ingredients, your poems or chants, and any other pertinent info. Include any insights or messages that came through during or after the spell. Leave a couple of pages blank, so you can write down what happened weeks or months after your spell.

Spells and Intention

Before we cast a spell, however, we must possess an unwavering belief that what we want will come to pass. An intention is transferred into solid knowing and clear action. This is why we undergo honest reflection around our desire before we commit to a spell.

Before casting a spell, spend time reflecting and getting clear on your intention. What do you want, and why? Our spell is a symbol for a deeper desire, a true core healing. Honestly interrogating our motives before doing spell work brings us into a deeper engagement with our desires. If our first impulse is to cast a spell for more money, we need to ask ourselves why. Is it because we equate money with freedom? Perhaps it is because we long for safety and security. Maybe we have conflated how much money we make with how valuable we are as a person. Questioning our motives adds clarity to our intentions. Before you cast your spell, figure out what your motives are. Get clear on what your beliefs around your desires are, and how you need to shift them into greater alignment with this desire. This will aid you in the subconscious programming and reprogramming that is integral to spell work.

In the beginning of your magical practice, it might make the most sense to experiment with spells that will have a tangible outcome. There isn't a hierarchy to types of spells: a new place to live, another job, or a bigger salary are all worthwhile spells to cast. So is banishing shame, attracting healthy relationships, or embodying courage. You may wish to go the route on getting your material needs met, then focus on spells for healing or on clearing other blocks. Casting spells that serve as umbrellas for both, and that will affect your life in immeasurable ways, is a smart strategy. Spells for peace, grace, flow, protection, love, or bravery all enhance the overall experience of one's life.

Below are ways to help clarify the motivations of your spell work. If you can answer these questions clearly and honestly, you will receive greater results.

Does your spell address the core root of your desires?

If you are working quick-fix spells, there is a slim chance that the foundations of what you need to make happen will be addressed. A good guide to follow is to focus on creating lasting structures, habits, and foundations that will serve you for years to come, not stopgap measures born out of desperation.

What resistance do you have to your desire? Does it make sense to cast a spell around clearing out those blocks first? Would your time be better spent doing focused subconscious reprogramming?

Sometimes, we have to begin with shadow work. Clearing and unblocking spells are always a great place to start, spell-wise. Knowing what makes the most sense, order-wise, is key.

Is your desire coming from a place of anxiety, desperation, reaction, or control?

If so, calm down first. Make your first priority your mental health. Be clear that your spell is not coming from murky motivations. Your spell work should not attempt to control others or enact revenge. Cast your spell from a place of clarity.

Do you think your spell will solve all your problems?

If you think your spell will result in a "happily ever after" scenario, those are the wrong intentions. Spells don't fix everything forever. Spells do not absolve internal and external work.

How will you raise or transform energy?

Be clear on how you will change and raise energy within the spell. Be clear on how your energy will shift in various ways in your daily life.

Are you trying everything in your power to make your desires unfold?

A spell can't do all the heavy lifting. Start by working toward your goal as much as possible. Belief is the foundation of a spell. Start a little outside of where you are already. A spell can kick off a time period of doing the work in the tangible realm. It can also boost the work you've already been doing. It can create more support within your efforts. But nothing will happen if you continue to sit at home, staring at the television for six hours a day instead of working on your dreams.

Are you truly ready to step into the outcome of the spell?

Be ready to be changed. Be ready to take responsibility for your greatness. Be truly ready to receive. Be ready to collaborate with the universe and what it will bring. That might mean ending certain habits or relationships that keep us comfortable or unhappy.

Will you be able to recognize that your spell is unfolding?

Outcomes can show up in subtle ways around us. These little shifts connote the activation of a spell. Sometimes we can be stuck in our everyday routines and not notice. Make a promise to yourself to notice how your spell is unfolding. This could show up as casting a spell for love, and then getting lots of invitations—where you might meet someone! Small signs could crop up in your periphery; be sure to turn your head. Commit to noticing the positives and synchronicities waving to you on the other side of a spell.

How will you know your spell was successful?

Be as clear as possible in your expectations while also being open to outcomes that you simply have no way of anticipating. The analogy I use is planting sunflower seeds. When you plant them, you expect to grow sunflowers, but you aren't picky about how many, or what exact height or color they will be. Tune in to the sensations and energy of what you want. Release certain toxic expectations of how you want your desires to appear that might hinder you from receiving some unexpected beautiful outcomes.

How is your spell ultimately for the good of all?

Ultimately, your spell is for the betterment of the entire collective. Abundant-feeling people spread abundance. When we feel agency and self-trust, we inspire others to access their own. Even if you are enacting a binding or banishing spell, being clear about the positive outcomes is important.

A spell is a promise between yourself and the universe.

A spell is a declaration of the soul.

Ingredients of a Spell

Most spells include similar ingredients. There are representations of the elements: fire, earth, water, air. Candles, crystals, plants, tinctures, water, bells, chimes, incense, art, meditations, Reiki, visuals, breath work, chants, intentional movement, and paper and pen are some of the materials used. Certain spells require other unique and specific ingredients as well: an ancestor altar, for example, could include photos of your deceased relatives, items that belonged to them, symbols that remind you of them, or offerings of their favorite food. And then there are the ingredients of emotionalized energy, affirmations, and desire.

Infuse as many qualities as you need into your energetic cauldron.

Spell structures tend to follow a basic formula. There is the preparation, filled with spell crafting: cleaning and preparing the space, and sometimes a ritual bath, shower, or meditation. One grounds and calls the elements in. The circle of protection is cast. Then within the circle, the spell work begins. This usually involves the lighting of candles and the stating of intentions. Inside the circle is where your energy work takes place—such as raising power, meditation, and whatever additional divination or other activities you will be doing. Energy is raised and transformed, and you feel the shift within. Then, you disperse the energy and ground. Give thanks and gratitude. The circle is then opened. Any spell cleanup happens. If yours is a multiday spell, leave your altar up. If you are leaving the vicinity, put out the candle. Depending on the type of spell, you dispose of your ingredients in your trash, or in a trashcan outside of your premises. Folks will save certain ingredients used as talismans or reminders.

Sacrifice and Surrender

There are always aspects of sacrifice within the crafting of a spell. Sacrifice is needed to transform energy. When you cast a spell for enhanced focus, you'll have to sacrifice a number of things to get there. You might have to let go of the belief you can't be focused. You might have to let go of the habits you hold that keep you unfocused. Part of these sacrifices must be clearly defined. Work on changing the energy in your body—so that when you think about all the benefits of elevating a focused mindset, your body tingles and associates focus with reward, or a new identity. If deity work interests you, call upon one that you feel comfortable invoking to help you. This could be Saturn, the planet of boundaries and discipline. If you invoke a specific energy, goddess, or deity, you will also have to honor them by doing what they ask, or giving them offerings.

Before the spell, you'll have to clarify exactly what a successful result would look like. Are you starting with five minutes of meditation a day? Set yourself up for success. You may have to put your phone on "do not disturb," or install an application that keeps you from surfing the Internet if these distractions impair your focus. After the spell, bring your intention into the real world with your actions. Be clear on what beliefs or behavior you will be sacrificing and transforming for the new.

Spells also require an aspect of surrender. You want to be specific, but not too specific. For example, when calling in love, I always advise clients to call in a lover that sees you exactly as you need to be seen, and will love you exactly how you need to be loved. This works more effectively than if you put all your focus on a particular person, or "type of person." Surrender also comes into play while waiting. Let go of the grasp, the grip, the urge to control. Invoke patience, trust, and cheer. While we wait for results from our spell work, we carry on with our lives and move forward in the direction of our spell's intention, as if we have received a letter that it is already on its way. We must meet our future with actions, belief, and aligned energy.

How to Know If Your Spell Is Successful

There are different ways to define a successful spell. One is that consciousness and energy have been raised and circulated, creating movement and attraction for you around your desire. Blocks have been cleared, resolve has been solidified. A belief has been firmly planted within. You feel different: mentally, somatically, or emotionally. You leave the spell different in some way.

Another way a spell can be successful is that, inside the container of the spell or in its aftermath, potent information may surface in your waking or dream worlds. Untapped memories may rise to consciousness. Imagery may enter your mind. Sensations may travel across your body. Spirits or ancestors may enter with guidance. You could feel elation intense emotion, or deep gratitude. Insights may arrive that help you move forward. More information may be revealed, such as why you had been stuck, or where you are resistant, or what to do next. Solutions could chime in: the right person to contact crosses your mind, the next step solidifies.

A general indication that a spell is working is that something changes in some fashion. This usually takes a couple of days, weeks, or months. If your spell is really ambitious, it could take longer: I've had certain spells take years to fully come to fruition.

If you truly do not feel like your spell worked, that is where a grimoire or journal comes in handy. Look back and see what ingredients and wording you used, and what happened during the spell. Think about what you can revise or tweak. Feel free to try to cast another spell. Change or clarify your words, ingredients, timing, or get closer down to the root of your desire. Be sure to have waited awhile. Give your spell time to unfold. Look for patterns: Do you keep wishing for the same thing, over and over, and it doesn't happen? That could require therapy, or time spent invested in uncovering blocks, beliefs, or behaviors that stop certain wishes from coming true.

When we first make magic, and we cast a successful spell, it can be shocking. Sometimes we can't believe it. It gets chalked up to a coincidence. Do not do this! Have gratitude for your magic. Recognize that you did that. Magic is absolutely real and it absolutely works. Be open to this fact! If the spell work and magic is around internal change, you could second-guess or doubt yourself around the subtle yet irrefutable shifts that are occurring within. Witch, if you are casting spells, for the love of the Goddess, expect them to work! It isn't a fluke. *You* are responsible for the transformation happening in your life.

A successful spell is a cause for celebration! Enjoy it. Thank any and all of the elements that helped you. Make an offering. Practice gratitude. Do something meaningful that facilitates more support. Send more ripples of goodness out into the world.

Up-leveling Setbacks Are a Very Real Thing

So you've cast a spell and you've gotten what you've wanted. This is the time we integrate. We recognize results. Our desires are celebrated. We adjust to the beauty of blessed change. It's also a time we may experience a phenomenon I call "up-leveling setbacks." Sometimes when we get the thing we want, we may be surprised to find that our feelings in the wake of that success are strangely negative. You might feel guilt, shame, disbelief, or hollowness. It's akin to manifestation postpartum depression. That's an up-leveling setback.

Why does this happen? Humans have been taught to fear change. Our nervous systems sometimes interpret any change, even good change, as a threat. Our limbic system can interpret ungrounded territory as a crisis. And in times of crisis, the first thing that our mind, our nervous system, and our ego want to do is to go back to a familiar zone. This is where it feels safe. The known, even if it is painful, feels more secure to the ego than the unknown.

Identify a couple of your core negative self-talk patterns that are surfacing as a result of your success. Give them a name: imposter syndrome, undeserving, fear of failure, fear of success. How does this new identity or expansion you are now in directly challenge any of these? Try to shake off those old fears, leaving them like a snakeskin shed on the side of a long desert road.

Then there is the hedonist's ladder we are all inclined to want to keep climbing. We want something, we get something, then we want something else. (Many pop songs have been written about this!) Relax into your good fortune. Rest. Practice integrating accepting, and believing for a while.

Small Spells and Living Magically

Small spells are everyday magic. This is magic you create in tiny moments. Stirring a little bit of honey in your tea to remind you of sweetness. Conjuring up the right words to incorporate in an email that turns it into a spell of appreciation. Moments spent in visualization, creation, meditation. Do something every day to bring you back to your core energy. Connect to your intuition, your breath. Notice the signs and symbols that enter your world.

Everyday magic can include cleaning, rearranging furniture, or hanging up symbolic art. It can include wearing certain colors, adorning yourself in certain scents. Everyday magic includes doing something generous and kind for someone else, for no reason. As much as you can, ask: How can I make this person's day a bit brighter? How can I make my world a more accurate reflection of my dreams? Then do that. It is understanding we are all here as part of a woven web, together.

Spell work, magic, and living magically are all in service of your healing, your growth, and your evolution. The end goal of doing spiritual and self-improvement work is to eventually be able to help others. To help the planet, our earth, our water, our air, our sky. The creatures and the other living things that are just as alive as we are. To heal deep pain and damages our ancestors have unknowingly placed upon us, in the hopes that our wounding of others becomes minimal. To support and help the environment that has been damaged by greed and ignorance. To join together to overthrow injustice everywhere. To become—with our own behaviors, speech, and actions—examples and inspiration to those around us. This is our responsibility as witches, as dreamers, as artists, as healers, as creators. As conscious human beings on the only planet we belong to with the only lives we've been blessed with.

"Ultimately, magic is about living," Robin Rose Bennett reminds us.[3] Only you can define what living magically means to you. Align your actions with your values. Align your days with activities and sensations that remind you of possibility, serenity, connection, and what you value. Count your blessings and they will multiply. Magic is your birthright, and you are magic.

Living in Moontime

While the earliest civilizations operated around a lunar calendar, and some cultures still do, the Gregorian calendar does not. The "moonth" and the month are almost never in sync. A new moon might appear at the end of the month, a full moon right at the beginning.[1] The Gregorian calendar has become a tick-tock container that prescribes when to clock in and when to clock out, when to sleep and when to work. This rigid, mechanistic scheduling is neither healthy nor natural. The lunar cycle is less prescribed, more personal. It's the way so many of us experience time. Dipping into peaks and valleys; sinking into what we feel, what we need.

The Gregorian calendar prioritizes productivity over all else; as a result, we are constantly "behind." Exhausted. Not enough. Feeling guilty for a nap, for an early reprieve from work. Solar time is binary; we've been trained to be either "on" or "off." When we connect with our natural intelligence and observe our natural cycles, our quality of life and time drastically improves. Time becomes abundant and holographic, healing and reconciliatory. For example, a three-minute meditation sometimes feels like an hour.

The moon is both an internal and external timer. It helps us tell spiral time. Our energy bodies, creative processes, and healing cycles all correspond to the moon's cycles. The moon can serve as a tracker for our dreams, our self-development, and more.

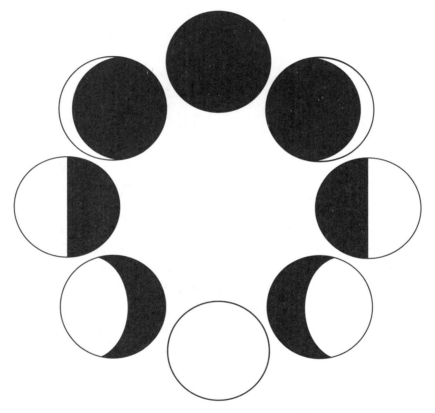

The actual moon orbits counterclockwise, not clockwise as shown. This diagram reflects the perspective of the Northern Hemisphere.

Look at the diagram of a lunar cycle. It is an illustration of the largest celestial body in our solar system—the sun—dialoguing and engaging with the celestial body nearest to earth—the moon. This is a visual that represents motion, time, perceptions, interpretations, energy, and relationships. The past, present, and future are intertwined. Moonlight is reflected sunlight, traveling to us from the past, eight minutes from its initial reflection. The earth—us—is the bridge of perception that connects the interaction of these luminaries. As you gaze at the diagram of the lunar cycle, take note of all that you see. There is symmetry and fluctuation. Balance and movement. Expansion of light and loss of light. Waves rising and crashing, the inhale and exhale.

A belief of evolutionary astrology is that zodiacal archetypes evolve through their opposite sign. Integration is found through embodying and engaging with the archetype that is furthest away from one's natural state. Look to the lunar cycle. What phase do you most intuitively feel drawn to at this time? Now look to the phase directly opposite of it. What could this phase teach you? How could working with the themes of this phase help you to embody your most intuitive self?

There are eight distinct phases of the moon that Western astronomy recognizes. Other cultures have different interpretations. Hawaiians observe the approximately thirty days of the lunar calendar with an understanding of each day, with thirty different moon names that are divided into three ten-day periods.[2]

The nine phases that I discuss are: New Moon, New Moon Crescent/Waxing Crescent, First Quarter, Waxing Gibbous, Full Moon, Waning Gibbous, Last Quarter, Waning Crescent, and Dark Moon, also called the Balsamic Moon.[3]

New Moon
This is the first day of a lunar cycle. For many folks, the "new moon" is still the "dark moon." There is 0 percent illumination. This is a phase for planting seeds, tending to the underground, intentions, new cycles, imagining, initiation, dreaming, envisioning, hope, rest, renewal, recharging.

Waxing Crescent
The waxing crescent is approximately two to six days old. It is between 1 percent and 49 percent illuminated. This phase corresponds to beginnings, optimism, creating better habits, tangibility, action, breaking the surface, visible new life, starting a process.

First Quarter
The first quarter moon is approximately six to nine days old. It is at 50 percent illumination. (The day before and the day after may still look and correspond to first quarter energy and themes, though technically the first quarter is the exact halfway mark of the lunar

42

cycle.) This phase is conducive to choices, pivoting, changing course, refining, balance, overcoming hurdles and blocks, discipline, will, healthy habits, boundaries.

Waxing Gibbous

The waxing gibbous moon is approximately six to thirteen days old. This is between 51 percent and 99 percent illuminated. It can facilitate health, healing, energy, fertility, luck, abundance, expansion, growth—particularly in the tangible realm, sensuality and self-care, and achievement.

Full Moon

The full moon is approximately thirteen to fifteen days old. This is at 100 percent illumination. The day before and the day after might also be energetically felt and utilized as a full moon. It corresponds to the harvest, ripeness, blooming, celebration, sex, creativity, embodiment, amplification, emotional release, emotional information, consciousness work, psychic ability, intuitive work, divination, ancestor work, any efforts you need a magical boost around.

Waning Gibbous

The waning gibbous is approximately fifteen to twenty-two days old. The moon is between 99 percent and 51 percent illumination. The light on the moon has now flipped over to the left, in the Northern Hemisphere. This is the time of the second harvest, reveals, downloads, dissemination, release, and sharing inner wisdom.

Last Quarter

The last quarter phase, also referred to as the third quarter moon, is approximately twenty-one to twenty-three days old. The illumination is at 50 percent. This is the counterpart to the first quarter moon. This phase is associated with balance, cross-roads, uncrossing, recommittal, surrender, "behind the scenes" work, subconscious or "below the line" work, organization, research, and internal processes.

Waning Crescent

The waning crescent is approximately twenty-two to twenty-seven days old. The light now fades from 45 percent to 1 percent illumination. This time corresponds with cleaning, clearing, banishing, diving deep, and going within. The entire waning moon phase facilitates all growth around internal work; when the light of the moon fades, many of us can process and connect to self more deeply. As the light of the moon fades, our inner knowing grows.

Dark Moon

This is the traditional end of the cycle. The moon is in its last three days. It is between 27 and 29.5 days old. This is traditionally the time of deep rest, release, turning inward, the void, the destruction before creation, connecting to other worlds and other states of consciousness, peace, acceptance, banishing, cutting cords, death, endings, bold visionings, brave new worlds.[4]

Look again at the lunar cycle diagram. What now jumps out at you? What are you intrigued by? Do you see things differently?

The Lunar Cycle as Seasons

The lunar cycle is a visual metaphor for the seasons of our lives. Looking at the entire cycle, we can intuitively tell that our lunar-suggested rest time would be from the third quarter to the new moon. However, you may find that this is the time where you have the most energy. I will write this repeatedly, because it bears repeating in this world of restrictions and prescriptions, and one size fits all advice, and "shoulds": Do what feels right and what works for you. Become your own authority. Discover your own patterns. Create your own permission slips. Moon work is about tuning in to your patterns and needs, and attending to those accordingly.

The lunar cycle is a visual metaphor for our earth's seasons. I am using the Northern Hemisphere as my reference. (If you are in the Southern Hemisphere, this is flipped, just like the lunar phases.) The new moon is from very late winter to early spring: when the light is much more apparent, but the earth is still not quite entirely thawed. Springtime, with its green shoots starting to poke up from the earth, and the tiny buds on the tree, simultaneously so verdantly alive and yet still so fragile: that's the waxing crescent time. At first quarter, there's no turning back: fragrant blossoms seduce us outside. The bees pollinate, fastidious and focused, and we wish to follow suit. This is around late spring leading up to summer solstice.

The full moon is around summer solstice, headed into midsummer. This is the time of the first harvest. Abundance is evident, receive it. Folks are pulled to go out, to show up, socialize, and celebrate life. However, your mood might not match the season. Many folks feel the summertime sadness. While the world buzzes around us, we may feel forlorn. Feel your feelings. What comes up could be useful information for getting resourced.

The season that correlates to the waning gibbous is late summer to around the autumnal equinox. This is the time of the second harvest. A period of simultaneous slowing down and preparation. Our gaze starts shifting toward the end of the year: that which we've been trained to mark as our collective finish line. For some of us, our inner flame is relighted, reminding us of what we'd like to heal, produce, or move toward accomplishing.

The time that correlates to the last quarter moon phase is between the equinox and Halloween. This could feel like a time of reckoning and turning corners. Of dedication or rededication. Our energy is urging us to turn inward, to reflect on the past and sift through it.

The waning moon correlates to the time just before the winter solstice. Most of our days are spent inside, and so our awareness and attention is affixed to our interior. We cleanse and clear. The promise of another cycle allows us to take stock. At night, we can see the stars more easily. The great beyond beckons. We get cosmic.

The dark moon is that time from the solstice to the first months of the Gregorian calendar. Technically not the dead of winter, but it can certainly feel that way. Spring is coming, the light in our days is growing, yet our bodies may not yet believe this. This season asks us to dream in the dark. We could feel called to plan, to strategize, and to imagine ideal futures.

These are cycles of birth and death, destruction and resurrection. These cycles mirror the spirals of time we all experience: dreaming, incubation, beginnings, learning, trying, doing, building, fruition, illumination, becoming, sharing, reconciliation, shedding, decay, death, transformation, healing, and visioning into the great beyond.

There are no "good" or "bad" moon phases. Every single moment can teach us something important if we are paying attention.

The Lunar Cycle and the Wheel of the Year

Let's compare the lunar cycle and the Wheel of the Year. The Wheel of the Year is a series of seasonal celebrations that celebrate the equinoxes, the solstices, and the midway

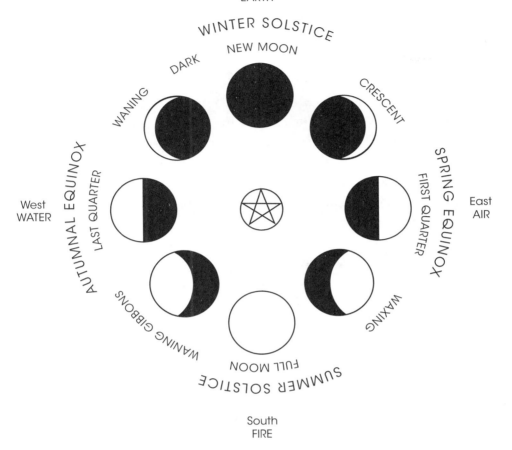

North
EARTH

WINTER SOLSTICE

NEW MOON

DARK

CRESCENT

WANING

SPRING EQUINOX

FIRST QUARTER

AUTUMNAL EQUINOX

LAST QUARTER

West
WATER

East
AIR

WANING GIBBONS

WAXING

SUMMER SOLSTICE

FULL MOON

South
FIRE

Please note that the moon orbits counterclockwise, not clockwise as shown.

points between them. The Wheel of the Year is a Neo-Pagan invention. It was first introduced to mass modern consciousness by Jacob Grimm in 1835 in his book *Teutonic Mythology*. In the 1950s and '60s, modern Wiccans and other Neo-Pagans adapted it for their religion.[5]

There is evidence that all around the globe, cultures honored the cycles of the earth, the sun, and the moon. Before, and after, monotheism was introduced, nature-based living and worship was what most Indigenous peoples were guided by—as a way of life, as a spiritual practice, and as a religion.

There are the remnants of Indigenous practices in the holidays that Christians celebrate. The holy days that some peoples observed were colonized and Christianized.

Samhain became All Soul's Eve. Yule became Christmas. Ostara became Easter, and so on. Almost every Christian holiday has a Pagan or Indigenous root. Of course, there are Christian and Catholic witches who combine their various practices and beliefs beautifully. In the West, over time, communing with the earth, with multiple deities, with various aspects of nature, was taken over by the patriarchal theory that there was only one God to whom we were to answer. The chorus of different aspects and different relationships with different deities and natural states connoted an engagement, a dialogue. Living with a relationship to nature, to the elements, to the seasons, to the zodiac, to the phases of the moon is one way to regenerate one's own intuition and reconnect with a very ancient, very human rhythm. Adapting and adding to these practices creates ancient futures.

In the Northern Hemisphere, Western Pagan and Wiccan traditions, eight Wheel of the Year Holidays are celebrated. They are:

Samhain:
October 31–November 1. Dark moon. Ancestor work, internal work, intuitive work, shadow work, grieving, banishing, releasing, binding, protection.

Yule:
December 20–23. Usually corresponds with the solstice. New moon. (Dark moon in some practices and traditions.) Rebirth, cosmic consciousness, intuition, divination practice, summoning hope, optimism.

Imbolc:
February 2. Waxing crescent moon. (New moon in some traditions.) Sprouting, healing, new beginnings, rebirth, thawing, planting seeds, dreaming.

Ostara:
March 19–22. This corresponds with the equinox. First quarter moon. Renewal, growth, abundance, turning the corner, health, generation.

Beltane:
May 1. This corresponds to the waxing gibbous. Sex, love, fire, creativity, celebration, connection, community.

Litha:

June 19–23. This correlates to the summer solstice and to the full moon. Accomplishment, celebration, gratitude, joy, blooming, teaching, self-empowerment.

Lammas/Lughnasadh:

August 1. This correlates to the disseminating moon. Second harvest, abundance, unions, work, investments, bounty, relationships.

Mabon:

September 21–24. This correlates to the equinox, and to the last quarter moon. Gratitude, harvest, balance, discipline, shifts, clearing.[6]

The Wheel of the Year may not resonate with you. It does not with me, as I am not from a Celtic background, nor am I a practicing Wiccan. It doesn't make sense for everyone to adhere to a system that does not resonate for any number of reasons. I utilize the solstices and the equinoxes, as well as holidays from my own background in my practice. Look to your culture for guidance, or observe the holidays you feel called to celebrate. What I do like about the Wheel of the Year, which is why I included it, is its focus on certain energies and themes that flow with nature. There is a similarity between the Wheel of the Year's rituals and activities, and an entire lunation. Incorporating seasonal and earth-based practices into your praxis is living in concert with the cosmos. These holidays reflect the quality of light we are exposed to, the temperature, what is growing, and what is dying. It could be a fruitful project for you to develop a more localized "Wheel of the Year" based on the natural cycles of where you live and what you value. Find a system that works for you. Create your own rituals. Forge your own traditions. That's all holidays are, at their root.

Working with the Seasons: Making Up Your Own Practice

Many people make New Year's resolutions. A couple of years ago, I began making "seasonal resolutions." New Year's resolutions felt too vast and overwhelming; it was hard to choose just one thing. At the beginning of each season, I started making intentions for that season only.

This shifted my life. By tuning in to my energy levels and following my focus seasonally, my life became more manageable and enjoyable. I wasn't fighting against myself, I was listening to my needs. Three months is a less daunting time frame than a year. Commitments are more easily made and kept. If the season passes, and you still want to keep moving forward with your habits or goals, do so.

Obviously, we can't quit our jobs and obligations and burrow under the covers with soup tureens for the entire winter season. We do what we can. Maybe we take on less during the winter: go out less, conserve our energy. Go to bed an hour earlier. If we are sick, disabled, or chronically ill, we center our needs, no matter the season.

If we are working with the moon to make magic, we tune in to the lunar phase that correlates with the season. Our dark moon work and new moon work may be potent around the winter solstice. If we are interested in spells and actions for discipline, strategy, and new growth, we focus our efforts around those themes from March to June, the time that correlates to these themes. The crescent moon–waxing moon time period would be a particularly good time to focus on magical efforts. Following is a list of suggested activities for each season.

Fall:

Harvest, abundance, work, projects, lineage and family tree/ancestry work, health (especially scheduling in ways to take care of your health—doctor's appointments, finding walking buddies, etc.), structuring and restructuring, getting organized, learning/education, mentorship, clearing out, wrapping up loose ends, "fall" cleaning, living "with the season": eating more soup and baking, less screen time, going to bed earlier.

Winter:

Inner knowledge, divination and journeying work, interior work, shadow work, banishing, ancestral work, destruction/creation, grief, death, emotional healing, fortifying, dreaming, visioning, tending to the light inside, spiritual practices, living "with the season": slowing down, taking on less, resting more, self-care practices, connecting with loved ones in person, eating to fortify the immune system.

Spring:

Sowing and planting seeds, love, fertility of all kinds, collaborations, growth, new projects, new relationships of all kinds, communing with nature, sex and sex life, risk and rewards, nurturing, living "with the season": waking up earlier, eye toward productivity, new aesthetics, greens and raw foods, bolstering and fortifying the body.

Summer:
Accomplishment, contracts, good luck, celebration, prosperity, joy, travel, community, tending to all your gardens, consciousness and identity work, birthing of all kinds, creativity of all kinds, expansion, emotional healing, consciousness exploration, living "with the season": being outside more, connecting with nature, relationships, relaxing, exploring new places—both outside of you and inside of you.

These are some suggestions. Make the process your own. If this structure inspires you, plan a few "seasonal resolutions" to experiment with over the next few months.

MOON MAPPING

 Part of working the lunar phase in a holistic fashion is planning. In the classes I teach on the moon called Moonbeaming, the first step I advise everyone to do before working with the moon around a specific goal, is to strategize and plan. I call this moon mapping. This is where we begin.

Moon mapping is that process of pairing the appropriate actions with the most supportive lunar phase. Writing down blocks and challenges, and then making plans to address those, is important. Anticipating roadblocks and figuring out why these are happening, and how to move through them, is imperative. Getting in a calm space and figuring out a realistic plan has to happen. Any magical practice is about discipline, connection, and building belief. We must name and commit to what we will be doing emotionally, mentally, physically, spiritually, and magically that will support our efforts. Each lunar phase corresponds to the 360-degree quality of your process. On the other side of our desire is what we fear. Moon mapping works with all aspects of a goal.

Planning ahead is useful to folks with trauma, as it offers a sense of security. When we plan ahead, we prime the subconscious to be in an accepting state. Any large change is an accumulation of repeated thoughts, actions, habits, and beliefs. The repeating pulse of the lunar cycle keeps us motivated, on track, and in alignment.

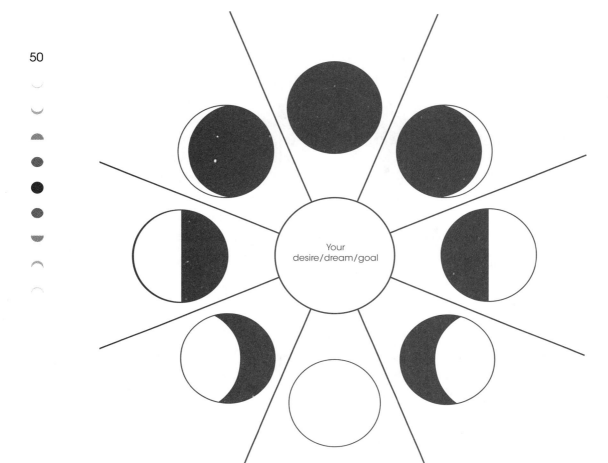

This is an example of the moon map I use. To download your own, go to themoonbook.com.

Let's discuss a moon-mapping example with a past Moonbeaming client, who wanted to transform their relationship to abundance: from a scarcity lens to an expansive lens. The first step was writing down all the clear goals around this. "To create a relationship to abundance where I feel like I have enough. This would include having six months of savings in the bank, working less, and being able to spend more time on doing things other than my day job that bring me joy."

Next, blocks or fears around this are named. "I'm afraid that if I work less, I'll be destitute. I'm afraid I'm not 'good enough' to let myself experience joy for no reason. Collecting six months of savings seems really daunting. I don't know how to do this."

Then, we go beyond these blocks and fears into the subconscious beliefs and behaviors that lie underneath them. "I have to be perfect, and because I'm not perfect, I do not deserve to make more money. I spend money both as a form of punishing myself, and as a numbing/soothing device. I am afraid to experience joy regularly."

Habits are addressed. "I've become undisciplined and accustomed to a dull life that is rinse and repeat. I need to tap into my motivation and tap into my discipline." The student is prompted into naming exactly what that looks like in action.

Now we envision a best-case scenario. After that, we would get even *more* specific. Our moon mapper would begin working backward from their goal. How could this person work on their discipline and their self-esteem? What subconscious beliefs would have to be transformed, and how? An undercurrent that came up for the person doing this process was that they didn't feel deserving of being joyful, happy, and abundant. They knew they would have to address this in various ways, including therapy.

Through the moon-mapping process a lot will come up. Painful emotions will surface. That's normal. It is also very normal to experience the domino effect of looking at a goal, seeing all of the other pieces that need to be addressed, and feeling overwhelmed. The person is now thinking about self-worth, discipline, and willpower. They are also thinking about joy, pleasure, play, creativity, and how that intersects with self-worth and money. Anyone going through these themes would most likely not expect to see the entire outcome they want in a single lunar cycle: this could be a seasonal, or even yearlong process.

After all this unpacking, you might want to rest for a few hours or a few days. Figuring this all out is mentally and emotionally exhausting! From a calm and rested place, you would then moon map. You would plan actions to take for each phase of the moon, based around your goals. For example:

New moon: Cast a spell for safety around healthy expansion of all kinds, define and cultivate abundance and joy, look for therapists.

Waxing moon: Meet with a financial planner or knowledgeable friend, figure out a budget that would include a savings plan, schedule thirty minutes three times a week for joy that does not revolve around money, look at where and why money is spent on so many "extras," decide on a therapist.

Full moon: Cast an "enough" spell, where permission is granted to take up space tending to pleasure, just as you are.

Waning moon: Freeze credit card, eliminate a couple of "extras" that aren't needed such as cable and some takeout, do a ritual to say good-bye to the part of yourself that believes you can't feel safe and abundant at the same time, allow yourself to make "bad art" joyfully, have first therapy session.

Dark moon: Begin a forgiveness meditation practice, make space for grief, rest.

Next new moon: Begin work around a more expansive creative practice, figure out how to negotiate a raise at your job, and/or start looking for other employment that will appreciate your creativity and pay you more.

Our friend would make a plan that would also keep them accountable on a day-by-day, week-by-week basis. An important part of moon mapping is locating what needs to change in the everyday. A lot of our actions reinforce our limiting beliefs. A lot of our actions are habits that feel scary to change at first, but over time, with repetition, are replaced with better habits. Many of our reactions originate from the subconscious, which in turn begin as limiting stories we tell ourselves. Part of this work is writing new stories, imagining different outcomes. This needs to happen every day. Even a few minutes is a fantastic start.

When we make a moon map, it will inevitably have to be revised. Life rudely scribbles over our best-laid plans. Through engaging with this process we may wish to go deeper into a specific limiting belief, or we may be compelled to go down another path. Revise and adjust your actions and spell work as needed.

I often get asked: Where to begin? Check in with yourself. There are times where what you will be focusing on might be really "small," but you really must start there: beginning a morning practice, or completely cleaning and organizing your home. There are other times when you are ready for deeper transformation and to make large life shifts happen. Putting yourself out there after a painful breakup, deciding to have a child, leaving and healing after being in a cult, focusing on managing anxiety or trauma, coming out, undergoing a gender transition, moving across the country, getting diagnosed with a chronic illness and adjusting and learning how to manage it, or starting a business are all examples of these sorts of huge life processes that may not have a definitive ending. When we begin one of these larger processes, we need to understand that this is the beginning of a longer, winding cycle. It may take months or even years of diligence and devotion to witness the results of our efforts.

I encourage reaching out for additional support, such as to a group, a therapist, an accountability buddy, or a life coach or other professional that has additional expertise. Going to support groups, sliding-scale therapies, or taking affordable workshops from reputable sources can also be an alternative. You could also create a low-cost "curriculum," where you find and read books, dialogue with friends, listen to podcasts, and journal a lot around the subject. This is free and works best for those who are self-directed.

The moon-mapping example shared begins at the new moon, but remember that the lunar cycle is a Double Dutch circle that one can jump into at any time. In any spiritual system, the goal is evolution; there is no beginning or end. I encourage folks who are interested in working with the moon magically or spiritually to experiment with starting their process at different phases. Beginning at a full moon or waning moon has been extremely useful for myself and others. (I actually prefer starting at those phases.) A go-to practice in magic or personal coaching is starting with the blocks you have. That would mean starting at either the waning moon/last quarter moon, or at the first quarter moon: the times for clearing away, and the times of the lunar cycle that traditionally mark a crisis of consciousness or faith, a pivot, or the ability to be able to see all of the challenges and positives of a certain situation. Begin at the time where you feel the best, or that correlates most strongly with what you need. Follow your intuition and instincts.

LIVING IN MOONTIME

Living in moontime means rejecting the toxic solar imperative. To be "on"—productive, producing, exerting, competing—the majority of the time is not natural. We live in a capitalist society that isn't going to be revolutionized tomorrow. (Not that we can't work toward that.) There are jobs to get to on time and bills to pay. Living in moontime isn't necessarily about going off the grid and living in the forest. It is about paying attention to our own cycles. Understanding what our needs are and meeting them. Buying less into a system that wants you to mindlessly consume, to be detached from your intuition and your body, or to feel as if you have no agency. Living in moontime is to know yourself well enough to be adaptive to life, to accept change, and to develop and use your own set of resources.

Cycles of the Moon, Life's Cycles

The same patterns and themes surface in our lives many times. They come back around continuously. Birth, growth, death, rebirth. What we need to heal, what gifts we must bring forth. These spirals make up the trajectories of our entire lives.

Our willingness to evolve transforms cycles of mindless repetition into spirals out into freedom. Our mind, our habits, our lives can get trapped on autopilot. The moon above our heads is a reminder that lessons come back around until they are learned. Without awareness, patterns automatically get repeated. Then we wonder why our life feels the same. We wonder why the same things keep happening to us. We wonder why we aren't getting the results of our dreams.

Every hardship and challenge can ultimately be received as a gift for us to reclaim our power. Every heartbreak can be a reminder to move forward with love. A reminder to acknowledge the bullshit, understand our wounds, yet not let our core goals and visions become compromised. To keep our most sacred selves sovereign. To remain heartfelt and conscious even though the machine threatens to break us down. To stay connected to our highest ideals and deepest intuition even as society tells us to do the opposite. This is part of living in alignment.

There are larger circular and spiral patterns of time, space, and energy outside of a moon cycle. There are the transits the planets make. There are the smaller and more specific energy shifts and flows within a day. There are the larger patterns of our careers or family dynamics. There are the greater rhythmic patterns of our lives: the years we need to coast, the years we need to push. Identifying what larger pattern or phase we are in can help us adapt. If you feel like you are in a waxing moon phase, maybe you can and you will work more. If you feel like you are in a dark moon phase, more rest, shedding, and introspection is needed. If one is in a new moon phase, maybe this is a time period of going for it and welcoming in the greatest, most fascinating, and vibrant outcomes imaginable.

Living in moontime requires us to tap into our intuition. To pay attention to the messages that come in. We touch base with our core energy: try to understand it, be curious about it, take care to hold it like water. Living in moontime is honoring your true self: not squashing it down, ignoring it, neglecting it. To stop forcing it into prescribed boxes that were invented for someone else. Living in moontime is also being considerate to the truth that many other folks are trying their best to live in their own moontimes too.

Moontime Is a Spiral, Moontime Is a Circle

Raise your head to stare at the full moon in the night sky and you perceive a glowing circle hanging over the horizon. A circle is an endless line. A protected space. Witches cast circles to create a protected portal of possibilities. It is an act that invokes our own center, and the center that is in all things, the center that sits in the middle of all the elements, the perfect blend of balance and energy. Dark and light, day and night. A center is a circle.

Draw a circle in your mind. Where are you in the circle? Do you need to step into the center?

We sit in circles to reinforce the idea that we are all equal. That all our wisdom is valuable. Sitting in circles feels familiar. We see everyone we are creating the space with. A circle is at once an activated line and a never-ending loop. From the center of a circle all is equidistant. We walk in the circle of a life labyrinth. Lose the loop and then circle back around. The medicine wheel is a circle. Circles connote wholeness and fulfillment. It is infinite: no end and no beginning. Ancient Greeks thought of the circle as being the perfect shape. The universe does not produce perfect shapes; only pure mathematics does.

Our existence is spiralic. Proof of this is in the blood and cells of our grandmothers' grandmothers that make us, us. When something we've done years ago ends up coming back around to grant us an opportunity, a chance we thought we'd lost, we are reminded of spiral time by way of synchronicity. Seeds of wishes planted long ago become cheerful green starts, waving to us from the past's future—a wish fulfillment we had almost given up on. Healing is spiralic as well. There isn't an end goal. There isn't a finish line to cross, a certain amount of therapy appointments to go to, a time when we will no longer feel discomfort or pain. Our healing needs to take the time it needs to take.

Lunar technology is some of the oldest out there. The Gregorian calendar is just one invention. Before it the moon cycle *was* time. There were never black moons or blue moons; there was never a need for forcing our rituals into a random Tuesday night. The seasons *were* time. Honoring the season and our cycles brings us back in touch with our natural existence, our natural intelligence, our essence.

The uptick in interest in the moon, in astrology, in ancient or alternative healing modalities also speaks to the non-linearity of time. The algorithm of the goddess/goddexx, of our ancestor's practices, finds its way back to us, again and again. Remembering, rediscovering, reenergizing, reemerging: that is moontime too.

To live in this way is to bend time. We heal the past from the present. We go back into the past and clear things up. Apologize to our past selves. Understanding that time expands and shrinks, goes back and forth and around and around and knots and unknots and gets unraveled. It speeds up and slows down. The choices we make today may drastically affect our future, and the futures of others. We must do what is most needed in the moment. That in itself is bending time. So, take your sweet, spiral time. It belongs to you.

Moontime is feminist praxis. It is something we work with, not something we have power over. Collaboration, not competition. A deeper power, not a higher one.

Moontime is a different way in. It asks us to go very far inside in order to find our way back out. Moontime allows us to step into wholeness. Times of aching, of grief, of sorrow, of frustration prepare us for flow, for joy, for resurrection and connection. Rest prepares us for activity.

There are greater, more political implications for living in moontime. Living in spiral mode means being able to hold more. Acknowledging our complexities widens our compassion. Loving and accepting the most painful truths about ourselves grants us more space. Separations are dissolved. We tell the freezing cold parts of us, "Come inside, thaw out. We see you and we love you. It isn't your fault. Come inside the circle of heart-led acceptance." When insecurity, exclusion, and competition go away, violence does as well.

To live in moontime is to create healthier paradigms. Yes, and, both, also. We exist not solely in opposition. There isn't a race, there isn't a reason for punishment. There aren't only winners or losers. We are here to learn from one another.

Living in moontime means remembering to rest because evolution is exhausting.

It is up to us to reclaim our own spiralic, holographic, multilayered existence.

Living in moontime requires the ability to create and partake in new paradigms. All the best magic does.

How to Live in Moontime

Follow the phases of the moon.

Track your energy.

Accept your own rhythms as reality.

Decide to soften. Breathe. Notice. Listen.

To your imagination, to your inner stirrings, to your mythologies.

Create new stories and share them.

Pay attention to what comes through in timeless moments.

Make space to remember what you've always known.

Make the shape of your life an accurate reflection of your heart.

Promise to never abandon yourself: your dreams, your gifts, your moonlight.

Define your anchors. Lean on them through change.

New anchors to make their way into your life.

Be in conversation with exciting, mysterious things.

Let the experience of mystery be your teacher.

Honor the experience above all else.

Always remember that you are a blessing.

Even on the endless hard days. Especially on those endless, excruciating days.

Your existence is a gift, and the risks you take, the love you make, the worlds you
 protect and save, the vulnerabilities and courage you enact will serve the
 collective long after you are gone.

Sing a song to the moon.

Let the moon share songs with you.

Ways to Work with the Moon

PRACTICE MAKES A PRACTICE

The most important piece of any spiritual path is to have a consistent practice. This means time invested every day engaging in activities that support your self-care, your intuition, your self-development, and your compassion. A spiritual practice enhances your connection to spirit or source, however you define that. A practice isn't usually glamorous. Some days it is just you and a notepad, scribbling sentences in the early morning with fuzzy, unbrushed teeth. Your practice won't usually offer you immediate reward. Some days it might feel boring or pointless. You might be too tired, sick, or overwhelmed. Create a flexible, experimental practice that can be tailored to your circumstances. It is recommended that you commit to your practice no matter what.

Over time, as you connect with yourself more and more, your practice will guide aspects of your life in both subtle and profound ways. A consistent practice fosters growth. The accumulation of consistent efforts adds up. All the tiny rivers of love eventually flow into your heart's ocean. The enlightened self offers up knowledge that can only be found through inquiry, through continued exploration, through the decision to take your own hand through the marathon of your life. Think of a practice as a master class in the discovery of your true self and your soul.

Western overculture does not always emphasize the benefits of a spiritual practice. And yet, every single thing we care about, we practice. Every single thing that we think will give us rewards in any way, we spend time doing. The benefits of a consistent spiritual practice include a huge investment in our future, as well as a positive influence in the greater world. The payoffs are priceless!

A lunar practice is a spiritual practice. A spiritual practice is praxis. It is walking the walk. Identifying and naming your values, then actually living those values out in the world. Placing importance on your desires, and living a life that prioritizes them. Doing the right thing, not the easy thing. You get to make your practice all your own. There's no "wrong" in a lunar practice.

Beginning Your Lunar Practice: The Basics

The first suggestion is to start a lunar journal. That is a notebook where you write the date, what phase the moon is in, and how you feel. Note your emotional state, your physical state, and anything else that is coming up for you. You could write down patterns or thoughts coming up. If intuitive messages are coming in, if you feel motivated or inspired or stagnant or despondent, write that all down. If you can't see the moon, due to weather or location, you can use a lunar app, check online, or keep track simply in your notebook. Begin by using your lunar journal specifically to track the moon and what your energetic states are during each phase. After a while, you can modify to fit your needs.

Do this for at least one lunation, if not longer. Over time, you will start seeing patterns. This will look different for everyone; it may not correlate to a traditional lunar cycle. For example, perhaps traditionally during the new moon you feel anxious, and during the waning moon you feel clear and motivated. This is important information to have! Other factors determine our moods and energetic levels: if we menstruate, whether or not we have chronic illness or mental health issues, our sleep patterns and what we consume, our stress levels, external situations, and more. The wonderful thing about keeping a lunar journal is that it also ends up keeping track of our lives. We can look back and see what we were going through. Hindsight helps us connect the dots.

Define what your lunar practice will be for. Name your intentions and motivations. It could be very simple: to track your energy, to find out which phase of the moon is most enjoyable or difficult for you. Your intentions could be tied toward focusing on goals or dreams.

Next, make a lunar altar. This is a space to specifically call in and work with the energy of the moon. An altar is also the space where you create your spells. It is where you sit when you journal or meditate. If you don't cast spells, your lunar altar is a safe space to connect with yourself. You could decorate your altar with the colors of the moon, put other traditional lunar correspondences on it, or decorate it with personally meaningful objects.

If you already have an altar, it is good to make another one specifically for honoring the moon. Try this for one lunar cycle, at least, to initiate your journey—especially if you are going to be making magic for the entire lunar cycle. If you decide to keep your lunar altar up, you can keep the set-up the same, except for maybe making new offerings to the moon, and cleaning it once in a while. You can also switch it up for each phase.

Next, spend focused time with the moon. Sit underneath her even if you can't see her, and tune in to her energy. Meditate. Moon gaze. Have a staring contest with her. Talk to her, ask questions. Pay attention to what the moon wants to share, what messages are there, how she wishes to communicate with you. Lunar language comes from within. Close your eyes and tune in to *your* energy. Pay attention to the reflections that the bright one offers up.

If it is possible for you to do so, go on nightly moon walks. Even if you can't see the moon, try to feel into that energy. An outdoor meditation, on your porch or in your yard, is beautiful as well. Put a mason jar of water outside, to be charged with moonlight.

You may wish to connect to the moon creatively. Paint pictures of her, write love letters or songs to her—like so many other artists have! Listen to music that reminds you of the moon; start a lunar playlist. Read poems about the moon. Research and reading might be part of your lunar practice as well. Read science books about the moon, attend astronomy lectures, and watch documentaries about it. Create a relationship that is meaningful for you.

I frequently get asked if I am always casting spells, creating rituals, in every single lunar cycle for each phase. Of course not! My life is busy. Probably like you, I am not constantly seeking out goals to conquer. In the beginning of my practice, I absolutely did stick with a strict cycle for many moons. This was important for me to do because it taught me discipline. It taught me about my own specific energy, and how I best work with the energy of the moon. It taught me a lot about myself, and my magic.

After reading this section, you might want to spend some time thinking about where you'd like to begin. Consistency is key; it may take several weeks or months for you to build connections and insights, or to figure out what practices will provide resonance and benefit. Even five minutes a day in a spiritual practice end up being just over thirty hours in a year!

You and the Moon

Your relationship with the moon is meant to be an intimate one. Everything is a relationship. Relationships are ever evolving. When we take that approach to life, there are always different options and choices. Your relationship with the moon can begin with looking up what phase the moon was in when you were born. This can teach us a lot about ourselves. You just need your birth date to look it up in an online search.

Once you find this out, check in. Does that "feel" accurate? When you are tracking your energy and emotions, take note if there is anything different. If you don't know your birthday, that's okay. You can note which lunar phases you feel the best around in your lunar tracker.

What phase the moon was in when you were born could determine a number of things. It could determine what time of day you feel most conscious or productive. Each lunar phase rises at a particular time of day.

Your natal moon could also give you more insight around what your natural tendencies are, where your challenges lie, and how to use your inherent gifts to their fullest potential. The idea of the lunar personality was brought to my attention by the astrologer Dane Rudhyar. In his book *The Lunation Cycle*, he goes over his interpretations of the types. I've developed my own definitions, which I'll share with you now.

If you were born during the new moon (the day of, and the three days following it), you might be naturally optimistic, hopeful, and love a fresh start. Beginnings aren't difficult for you, but endings could be. Be careful not to hang on to the remnants of a dream that is past its expiration date. New moon types are innovative, inventive, and brimming with ideas. They generally have no problem with sustaining hope and cheer, but have a harder time with discipline and practicalities. Follow-through can be a challenge. Find ways to bring little sparks into the everyday so as to stay motivated.

There could be a number of false starts in a new moon person's life before they find the right path. Luckily, a new moon type does well with brushing themselves off and trying again. The time of the full moon could be balancing for this lunar type.

Those born while the moon was a waxing crescent to just before first quarter may feel most at home when they are in pursuit—goals, relationships, ideas, or the next "thing," whatever that may be. Expansion and growth need to be evident in a waxing crescent type's life in order for them to feel fulfilled. They may wish to steer the ship; others' authority could be difficult for them. Recognition and positive feedback is important for them to continue feeling mobilized; these types can fall prey to compliments, or rely too much on outside feedback. These are action takers and solution makers. Waxing crescent types feel at home when they are doing something different. They love to explore new spaces internally and externally. They are generally focused on the future, yet need to reflect on their past in order to learn from their mistakes. The time of the waning crescent provides them with the respite they need.

Those born during the first quarter moon could experience tension around making decisions. When first quarter moon types harness their remarkable ability to see all angles of a situation, their wisdom is unmatched. There is usually some kind of obstacle that they perceive or that is actually in their way to getting what they desire. This is the moon phase that correlates to a crossroads; shadows and light must be in balance. Lessons constructively processed create remarkable resolve and resilience. If you are a first quarter moon babe, structure and organization can help you keep going. Find ways to remind yourself that the glass is actually half-full. You know more than you give yourself credit for. Balance can be found through tuning in to the qualities of the last quarter moon.

Those born under the waxing gibbous moon will most likely have lives of external accomplishment, because external accomplishment is important to them. They are happiest when the fruits of their labors are easy to see; patience isn't always a strong suit. They seem to possess endless reserves of energy and drive. Challenges for these types include feeling true contentment, as well as defining "enough." If you are a waxing gibbous natal moon, define what contentment, success, and happiness mean to you, especially outside of the external. Being in the present moment and remembering to appreciate what you have is a practice to cultivate. Schedule in rest frequently. Sink into the waning gibbous, and its energies and qualities, to find balance.

Full moon babies generally have no problem being seen and no problem leading.

They want to share, to shine, and they want to connect. Being understood and being seen accurately is an important value for these types. In order to feel whole, they need to explore and experience the multitude of their gifts. It is through experiencing the variety of life that they can access wholeness. A challenge for these types could be over-investment and over-giving, which lead to depletion and resentment. Boundaries are especially important for those born under a full moon. There can be a tendency to mirror those around them, sometimes unconsciously, sometimes for approval: if you are this lunar type, themes of identity may take an especially prominent place in your life path. Full moon babies tend to be empathetic, so they need to be careful about the company they keep and the energy allowed into their space. A dark moon or new moon phase/activities can help to balance their energy.

Those born under a waning gibbous moon are incredibly observant and very skilled at communicating bigger picture ideas. Learning fulfills you. Connecting different dots—which you are naturally astute at—lead to new concepts and techniques. Your natural ability to take a lot of different ideas and weave them together into new forms is not a gift to waste. Service to the collective will give your life meaning. Prioritize your own needs, especially those related to abundance and recognition, as much as you give to the cause/group/lovers. Connecting to many others, in a more public role, may also be part of your path. Lean into the hopeful self-care of a waxing crescent to shed some of the pragmatism and disappointment that sometimes bogs you down.

If you were born under a last quarter moon, you may feel similar to those born under a first quarter moon, with a twist. Instead of focusing on the waxing moon themes of growth and expansion, you may be preoccupied with updating existing systems. Dane Rudhyar refers to last quarter natal moons as "the reformer."[1] You are here to change systems: whether it's your family constellation, how the world perceives your chosen vocation, or the culture itself. You are discerning and tend to have strong instincts on how to improve just about anything, and how things work best in general. You may have to work on self-doubt and anxiety around your intuition, which is your secret power for a lot of the projects you birth and the journeys you take. Let others in. The first quarter phase can be a time for you to connect to feelings of optimism.

If you were born during the waning crescent moon, you could feel most comfortable behind the scenes. Research, education, and intense study may be activities you excel at. Waning crescent moon babies can be more private and interior, needing more space and time to figure out their emotions and thoughts. Time spent alone is refreshing and recharging—this is where you connect to nature and receive downloads. You may have a career where you influence and reach many, but most of the work you do is in solitude. (Think: writers, painters, researchers, coders, online business owners.) A theme of your life may be reconciling your past with your present self. Show yourself as much empathy and compassion as you do others. The waxing crescent moon can be a time of balance for you.

The dark moon personality is anyone who was born in the three-day period before the new moon. This type tends to be rebellious and interested in bringing innovative ideas to the collective. You often feel misunderstood. This is because you are a visionary and often are answering to a future that others can't comprehend. Part of your path on earth is to birth radical new ways of living and relating. This is often met with challenges, particularly from the status quo. When in alignment, dark moon types are brilliant and brimming with inspiration. Give the projects you dream of the focus and seriousness they deserve. Be careful not to isolate or settle into despondency. In order to function as your truest self, you may have to lean heavily on spiritual practices. Cultivate a few very close relationships with like-minded, trustworthy people. Death and rebirth will be a constant theme in your life. So will intense, extreme endings and beginnings. You must become comfortable mastering change. The time of the full moon or the waxing gibbous could be a time to bring balance.

Knowing the phase that the moon was in when you were born can help you explore where these themes will support your interests and patterns. The opposite phase to your natal lunar phase could feel deeply uncomfortable or incredibly balancing. For example, if your natal lunar phase is the new moon, then the full moon would be the opposite. (Check the moon cycle diagram on page 40 for yours.) Try basking in and expressing the energy that is opposite to you.

You as Moon

Using the phases of the moon to describe the life cycle one is currently in is helpful to make sense of the bigger picture. Reflect on what lunar phase you are currently in. Are you feeling on the verge of an accomplishment? You may be in a waxing gibbous/full moon phase as you get closer to your goals. Have you just begun an activity that is invigorating and is altering your relationship to self? You could be in a new moon phase. If you feel deeply uncomfortable, and ready to destroy some area of your life in service of profound recalibration, you are most likely in a dark moon phase!

You can work with the phase that resonates with you in various ways: as an overall archetype of the energy you are harnessing, as a reflection of who you are in the current moment, as guidance on how to go more deeply into the themes of this phase, and how to find the best ways of supporting yourself. You can research goddesses, deities, and myths that correlate to the themes of each phase. You can place charms, talismans, colors, and other symbols of that phase around you, to remind you of what to stay focused on.

Our lives are complex, and there could be a number of things going on in your life that reflect different states. A relationship could be just beginning (new moon), while a beloved pet has just died, and you are grieving (waning moon). My advice to you—if you are interested in figuring out what "phase" you are in—is to touch base with both your emotions and energy and go by *how you feel overall.*

Knowing what phase we are in also helps us to be aware of what we might need to balance our energy and not go into extremes. If we know we are in a full moon phase, we know that is going to require a lot of energy. This could invite us to double down on our boundary work, focus on getting enough sleep and hydration, and figure out how we are going to take advantage of all that we've been working toward.

In general, the phases in our lives do follow the order of the lunar cycle. If you are in a dark moon phase, then that will most likely be followed by a new moon phase. If you are in a waxing moon phase, that will be followed by a full moon phase. These particular energetic phases can last months or years.

We can work with this knowledge *and* work with the current lunar phase. If you are in a dark moon phase, dealing with a breakup and letting other things go, then the entire waning and dark moon phase can support that process. The focus around the lunar cycle could be about grieving and healing from loss: knowing you need to focus on internal work can help you design your days. At the dark moon, perhaps you create a ritual that releases all attachments to the past relationship. Because that energy is already potent within, the dark moon may be a particularly helpful time to release. This could last for one lunar cycle, or longer. When you feel called to move on, you can consciously mark that with a ritual or spell.

Honoring the Moon

When you decide to commit to a lunar practice, also commit to a way that you will honor the moon. Like any precious relationship, it must be a reciprocal one. If the moon is helping us, we figure out how to help it. There are plans to extract water from the moon: we can try to stop that activity. Think about all the correspondences of the moon. Water, womxn, femmes, shape-shifters, empaths, children, fertility, home, hearth, reproductive rights, the protection of all the vulnerable of the earth, plants—all who are nourished, nurtured by water or who live near it—reside in the realm of the moon.

We can leave offerings to the moon both in our magical workings and in our every day. Think about choosing activities to reinforce that connection. Maybe you donate every month to Planned Parenthood or another caregiver that provides low-cost abortions. Maybe you fundraise for an organization addressing Black mothers' mortality rates, or commit to stop buying plastic, or find ways to focus on clean water efforts locally or in polluted areas.

In a magical practice, I'll do spells once or twice a year to protect the moon and thank her. I'll give money to clean-water efforts, and to protect threatened and endangered sea life. One way I honor her is by teaching about her and utilizing her energy and messages to help others. Another is by consistently donating money to organizations that support the lives of systemically oppressed and marginalized folks.

The Moon and Your Menstrual Cycle

The lunar cycle is the same length as an average menstrual cycle: approximately twenty-eight days.[2] Many people call their periods "their moon." The shape of the moon, round and visibly growing larger, reminds us of a pregnant belly. During a menstrual cycle estrogen rises and falls; another tidal-like interior experience that reminds us of our own natural inner risings and our inner crashings: womb as moon.

There are some men who get periods, and there are many women who do not. There are many non-binary folks who do and do not get their periods. Linking periods with femininity and wombs is understandable, as some women get periods and give birth. But there are many women who do not get their periods for varied reasons: some are pregnant, some are on birth control, some are trans, some have had hysterectomies, some have been through menopause. Assuming that all women get periods, and that only people who get their periods are women isn't true, and isn't inclusive.

If you don't get your period, that doesn't make you any less connected to the moon. And if you do get your period, and it doesn't sync up with the moon's cycles, there is nothing wrong with you. Studies have shown that the majority of people who get their periods are not synced up to the new moon.[3]

Our periods are natural and beautiful. They need to be supported, not shamed. We see the inherent misogyny in how our culture treats periods. There is the lack of comprehensive treatment for them by the medical field. If you menstruate, learning about this part of your bodies is imperative. Observing the rhythm of your period, and your estrogen levels, against the lunar cycles is one way that many become more attuned to the body's cycles.

If we get our period, and we find that we are more in sync with our hormones than the lunar cycle, it is important to take both of these pieces of information into account. For extensive information about your period and ways to work with it, I suggest Maisie Hill's *Period Power*. In the book, the idea of a menstrual cycle as a season, with the start of our period being winter, is discussed. If one of your goals is to become more aware of how your menstrual cycle impacts you, then take a deep dive into that aspect of your body, using lunar tracking as part of your process.

The Moon and Humanifestation

The moon is a natural guide to any and all of our goal setting. Throughout this book, I outline various methods and techniques to work with the moon in this way.

Sometimes in teaching, and throughout the book, I use the term *humanifestation* as a play on the oft-used word *manifestation*. I like to use it to center all humans and to differentiate it from stereotypical New Age ideas around "manifestation." (The word *manifestation* also makes me think of "Manifest Destiny," which is the opposite of the process I share.) I also like using the terms co-creation and creation. Lunar humanifestation posits that resting, trusting our intuition, and letting help in is part of the process. Learning to float is as important as surrendering is as important as working incredibly hard is as important as calling in abundance is as important as being generous is as important as learning to love oneself. Listening can be as important as doing. All of these activities that guide us toward a rhythmic and holistic life exist within the spectrum of humanifestation.

We must also take into account structural oppression and understand that many "love and light" discussions of "manifestation" do not acknowledge racism, transphobia, classism, ableism, and other systemic challenges so many face. Some parts of our life conditions are not just "choices" we can "positively think our way out of." Acknowledging hardship, discrimination, mental health issues, and structural oppression is not about "bad vibes," it is about living in reality.

Lunar creation also emphasizes desires that aren't necessarily deemed valuable by our dominant culture. This is growth that does not always look like stereotypical growth. Turning down opportunities that appear amazing, but that are not in alignment with one's integrity or intuition. Focusing on emotional healing, prioritizing health, unraveling self-harm. Stepping into embodied self-love, creating and maintaining appropriate boundaries, or recovering from addictions are all examples of valuable work. Open yourself up to the ways that inner growth fosters outer blooming.

Co-creation with the universe requires your commitment and your devotion. Through the cycles, we learn how to dream, how to dare, how to try, how to accept, how to trust, and how to surrender. Everything we need is already within us. It is just a matter of staying connected with our intuition, our will, and our curiosity. It is just the practice of staying with ourselves, of not giving up, of tapping into our patience and resilience. The universe will meet us where we are, and help us. First we must meet ourselves.

Moon humanifestation is different from the mainstream consumerist promises about manifestation, even though the moon will certainly help you get big external results. And also: Getting the material thing you want will not solve all your problems. It won't stop you from ever having to do any work on yourself. It won't stop painful things from happening. Moon manifestation knows we are always in process, so might as well go deep.

Moon Magic

The majority of this book discusses magic, spirituality, and ritual in a variety of different ways, through each cycle. The way I teach lunar magic is holistic. We are looking at the entire lunar cycle and working with the qualities of each particular phase accordingly. This is all covered in this book, complete with suggested spells, tarot pulls, activities, and journaling prompts. After becoming comfortable with your own practice, create your own kind of lunar magic. Find your own ways to connect to the moon, your magical practice, and *your own particular form of magic*.

The magical traditions I have been taught reflect a European Neo-Pagan tradition. The other lunar tradition I practice is a Jewish one. That is part of my ancestry, and the Jewish lunar tradition is strong. I have attempted to make this book as nondenominational as possible, so that you can weave in your own traditions and practices that resonate with you. In general, every single culture uses the elements: water, fire, earth, air. In general, every single culture meditates, prays, burns dried plants to clear and connect, burns candles, works with items from nature such as crystals and bones, and uses talismans made of objects special to them to do their spell workings.

The Moon and Astrology

In astrology, the moon is a luminary: a personal planet that corresponds to one's personality, relationships, and one's particular life path. In ancient Western astrology, the moon was seen as malefic, but most modern astrology treats the moon as benefic, depending on what sign or house it is in. In traditional Western astrology, the moon is related to mothers, parenting, and caretaking. It describes our emotional needs: how we've learned to get them met, and how we have to practice figuring out what we actually require to feel safe, nurtured, and seen. An astrological perspective of the moon is one where the moon also represents our unconscious as well as our subconscious. The parts of us that are mysterious: our shadows and underlying motivations lie in this realm. The moon represents the parts of us that only our most intimate see. Our vulnerable side, the private sides of our personality that we let out when we feel comfortable, correspond to the moon. The femme and feminine, our sweetness and softness: these also are influenced by what sign and house our moon is in. The moon also corresponds to our memory, our moods, our emotions, and our bodies.

In Western astrology, the moon is a symbol of the past. This can also result in conservatism or an overdependence on tradition. It evokes nostalgia, and our memories, both blissful and brutal. So much of our present is tied up in the past. So much of our current experiences and responses are shaped by past events. To truly move forward is to clear out the harmful attachments to the past. To heal is to not allow the hardships of the past to negatively influence present behavior. To heal is to take the lessons of the past and use them as compost for verdant future gardens.

In Western astrology, the moon corresponds to the sign Cancer and rules the fourth house of the zodiac.[4] The fourth house has to do with parenting, your perception of how you were cared for from childhood, family history, ancestors and ancestral inheritance, past lives, the home, self-care, instincts, what you need to feel safe and secure physically and psychologically, as well as establishing a home and putting down roots.

When interpreting one's chart, aside from your moon sign, astrologers also take into consideration the house your moon is in. The different houses inform how the moon is revealed and expressed. There could be other aspects, such as sextiles, trines, or squares, that could affect your moon. Another astrological lunar theme is your north and south nodes; this refers to an aspect of your personal destiny.

Magically, we can work with whatever sign the moon is in to correspond with our spell work. For example, if the moon is in Virgo, then spells around work, growth, security, spiritual tending, and devotion could be cast. You could do spell work around healing digestion and the liver, as those are some of the parts of the body that Virgo is associated with. You could do work around worry, anger, or anxiety, as those emotions are linked to those body parts.

Over time, you can figure out how you feel when the moon is in certain signs. The easiest to deduce how the moon signs land with you, in my experience, is during the full moon. A fire full moon may feel completely different for you from an earth full moon.

Your moon sign could reveal your natural magical proclivities. Whatever positive and challenging traits the archetype encapsulates could be reflected in your own magic. If you are an air moon sign, you might be gifted at coming up with spells, chants, or poems. You might have ease communicating with spirit, guides, or ancestors. If you are a water moon, you may be particularly psychic in water, and in the role of being an empath or a vessel of creativity, beauty, and downloads. Your magical abilities might be heightened intuitive information and the ability to master the art of emotionalized visualization. If you know your moon sign, you can experiment with your unique and natural gifts.

If your moon is in Aries, you could possess the ability to make things happen really quickly; your intuitive sense is instinctual, not something to be analyzed. You may feel called to be a leader of your coven, to create a sharing circle or a new cult–cum–spiritual movement.

Those with the moon in Taurus could be skilled at energetic mastery and really gifted at the art of material manifestation. You may wish to create very symbolic, artistic altars, and wear, smell, and taste your magic.

If your moon sign is in Gemini, your magical gifts could be actualized through speaking, writing, and singing. Downloads and messages could come through when you free write or talk to yourself, or your guides, or the moon. Experimentation keeps you invested in a magical and spiritual practice.

If your moon sign is in Cancer, try utilizing your natural physical abilities in your spellcraft. One of your superpowers is your ability to feel emotions; when you learn to translate these into proper channels, you are a force to be reckoned with.

People with the moon in Leo have the ability to express or perform magic; acting, dancing, or channeling your desires into movement make these wishes court you just as much as you are courting them.

Those with the moon in Virgo fertilize their dreams with discernment and sensed details. When you see that being in service of yourself first is the most important work, your blessings will multiply.

If your moon sign is in Libra, you have an uncanny ability to collaborate with the elements, deities, and other symbolic items in your magical practice. You sweet-talk the herbs into even more potency. You meet the air, the sun, the sky so earnestly they have no choice but to do your bidding.

People with the moon in Scorpio have an amazing ability to regenerate quickly: to take the lessons of each lunation and spin that straw into gold. Your magic lies in the ability to express the unseen, the taboo, the subconscious and unconscious in healing or intriguing ways.

Folks with the moon in Sagittarius are especially equipped at the art of translating your thoughts into actions. You speak things into existence, and may need a variety of magical practices to match your ever-evolving state.

If your moon is in Capricorn, your magical ability could lie in the deep wisdom of your ancestral realm. Ancient customs and rituals could enhance your intuition; tune in to go deep. Your magic also shines in spaces of high visioning. Dream clearly of your mountaintop and you will do the work to journey there.

If your moon is in Aquarius, part of your magical gifts will be in creating your own personal rituals and spiritual practices. That innovation creates a spark that is a cosmic call to action. Trance work, meditation, and otherworld journeying all are practices to invest in.

People with their moon in Pisces possess an inherent ability to heal others—as doulas, nurses, artists, or by their presence alone. One of your magical powers is the ability to channel or communicate with otherworldly energies. You are gifted at visioning; this serves as an inspirational well for others to draw from.

In Vedic astrology, the moon, not the sun, is considered to be the most influential planet in an individual's chart. In this practice of astrology, the proximity of the moon to the earth is thought to especially affect us. Here the moon governs temperament, mood, instincts, intuition, emotional makeup, personality, emotional and psychological patterns, our motivations, and behavior. The moon also corresponds to our energy and our perceptions, our memories, fertility, and caretaking. It is our mental health, interests, instincts, and temperament. In Vedic astrology, a waxing to full moon is benefic, or positive, and a waning to dark moon is malefic, or negative.

In Vedic astrology, the moon is called Chandra, which in Sanskrit means "bright and shining." Similar to Western astrology, the moon in Vedic astrology correlates to themes of the mother and the feminine; beauty, comfort, nourishment, as well as general well-being and happiness.[5] The moon receives the light of the soul.

The sun is a projection, what we present to the world; it can become all the world thinks of us. The moon is our core inner self—who we really are, underneath all the layers and masks.

There are other concepts and philosophies around lunar astrology besides the ones mentioned. If this interests you, do research, take classes, book an astrology reading, and read books. Some resources on tropical lunar astrology are *Moon Wisdom* by Heather Roan Robbins and *Moon Phase Astrology* by Raven Kaldera as well as the work of Jan Spiller, Dane Rudhyar, and Demetra George.

The Moon as a Timekeeper

The moon can be utilized as one of its most ancient functions: that of a timekeeper. The Chinese, Hindu, and Jewish calendars are still lunar. Holidays, such as the lunar New Year, reflect the moon's influence.[6] The Kojoda is the calendar used by the Yoruba peoples of southwestern Nigeria and southern Benin, and the beginning of their year coincides with the harvest and the moon, in either May or June. Humankind's earliest relics are marks on wood or pieces of bone that correlate to the twenty-eight-day lunar cycle. Massive shrines were built to worship lunar and solar events; their remnants remain in sites around the globe such as Stonehenge, Woodhenge, and the Pyramid of the Moon. An archeological site in Guatemala found Mayan astronomical records dating to the ninth century A.D. that kept track of the moon's cycles.[7]

The lunar cycle can be used as a checking in, a way to keep track. Where you were, what you were doing, what was happening in last year's full moon. What has stayed the same, and what has grown. What needs to change. If you are feeling a certain kind of way, and you are not sure why, utilizing the moon as a remembrance tool can help.

Using the moon as a personal mythological timekeeper helps us write our own stories.

Think about larger cycles and patterns in your life. Do you have your own particular patterns or dates that your body keeps track of? Our body holds memories of all kinds. The body remembers trauma as well as triumph. Is there a running list of special-to-you anniversaries that it might be useful to have record of? Honoring our experiences somatically is useful. Knowing how our bodies hold certain memories and emotions, how to recognize this may help us release our attachments to them, and manage our nervous systems. (To find out more about trauma and the body, books that address this are *My Grandmother's Hands* by Resmaa Manakem and *The Body Keeps the Score* by Bessel van der Kolk.)

There's time, and then there is quality of time. Think about utilizing the moon around quality of time. Once you've tapped into your own energetic patterns, the moon works as a reminder to stay engaged with that most desired energetic alignment. This also helps guide future energetic movement; it is aspirational. The quality of our experience deepens as we sync with our energy into its natural rhythms.

Ancestral Work

Each culture around the planet has its own traditions and ways of working with the moon. The Talmud believes that the moon has a consciousness and contains a genius that transmits itself into willing practitioners.[8] Many cultures told stories of moon and sun as sister and brother, or as a married couple, gazing at one another or chasing each other in the faraway sky. Many cultures connected the moon to sustenance and food. In ancient Indonesia, a rice spirit lived inside of the moon. A Peruvian folktale interprets the moon as a man who helped bring plants to humans. He then married a human woman who gave birth to other cosmic bodies. There are countless other guardian moon deities across the globe who protected the fields, the earth, and all living creatures.

Each culture around the planet has its own folklore and stories, mythologies, and interpretations of the moon. Moon as home, moon as mother, moon as creator, moon as weaver of magic. Polynesia's moon is called Mahina, the home of Hina, the mother of Maui, who ran away to create art in the safe space of the moon. Odysseus was expected to arrive home at the new moon, an auspicious and holy time in ancient Greek culture. In traditional Chinese mythology, Chang'e, the goddess of immortality, lives on the moon. The Navajo and Ojibwa call the moon the "Ancient Spinstress." In ancient South and Central America, the Mayan lunar goddess was also a weaver.[9]

Other peoples equate the moon with animals: hares, buffalo, spiders, and cows are among the animals with a lunar connection around the globe. In numerous cultures—Inuit, Hindu, and that of ancient Greece—the moon was associated with dogs and wolves, some helpful, some fearsome.[10]

If you know your lineage, even if it is only the continent you came from, you can do research into folklores, myths, traditions, and rituals that your ancestors enacted. Whether beginner or experienced, research will only enhance your practice.

We can work with the moon for ancestral healing as well. All of us were given gifts by our ancestors. Many of us have also had trauma passed down. There may also be temperament challenges, like worry, anger, or paranoia, that your ancestors have passed on to you. We can work on healing these in this lifetime. Start by asking: What were my ancestors in need of healing?

You don't necessarily need to do family tree research or talk to your grandparents about this, but you can. Simply tuning in and listening, and writing down what you think, is a start. Write down what you know about yourself and how this connects to your family, with focus around some of the pain points and your inherent strengths. If you do happen to know your family's origin story, that can provide a place to begin. For example, my great-grandparents came to America incredibly poor and never learned English proficiently. Both sets also encouraged their children to assimilate. Some of those inheritances around this are healing scarcity issues, security issues, as well as feelings of alienation.

A well ancestor altar complements this process. "Well ancestors" are ancestors whom you had a good relationship with, or who were spiritually healthy.[11] There may be abusive or violent ancestors in your family tree that are not appropriate to connect with. If you have any photos of deceased ancestors who were special to you, put them on your altar. Have a conversation with them. Pray to them. Talk to them. Honor a quality that they gave you. If you know what plants, herbs, deities, or myths your ancestors used, you can incorporate that into your practice. Look up traditional recipes and make them. Leave some as offerings to your ancestors. Over time, you may develop a vibrant relationship with your well ancestors.

For some of us, it isn't appropriate to connect spiritually to any of the ancestors we know of. Maybe they were abusive, maybe the pain there is just too great. In that case, you can draw up boundaries with your ancestors. If you are the descendant of oppressors, healing work could include volunteering time or money to those who are oppressed, or connecting to where that oppression may still be inside of you, and clearing that. Educating yourself about the specific historical context of the time of your ancestors is useful and may provide information around some present issues.

For those of us unable to connect to our ancestors, create your own ancestral lineage. Maybe it is the artists, inventors, or activists who you admire that came before you and were of influence. It could be healers or witches or herbalists or teachers that deeply influenced you. Connect to ancestors who came from your specific identity: queer, Black, non-binary, Filipino, disabled, Cuban, Muslim, Korean, Jewish, Dutch, Buddhist. . . . Give gratitude for them. Call their energy into your lives. Carry on their lineage by living out their values. Continue their teachings by mentioning them, paying homage to them, and encouraging others to engage in their work.

There's the rich spiritual and traditional herstory of the moon to connect with as well. So many people have been working with the moon as their practice for so long, it feels like an added accumulation of energy to benefit from. Looking up at the moon each night and being reminded that my ancestors and everyone else's ancestors were looking up at the moon for thousands upon thousands of years is awe-inducing. This practice connects me to something greater than myself.

Working with the Moon Practically

Another way to work with the moon in a folk way is practically. Plan out your month loosely using the moon's phases as a practical guide. Your official beginning could be at the new moon; brainstorm tasks and what would be the best possible outcomes for you for each phase. Or, work with both the lunar phases and the Gregorian calendar. You can use the traditional agricultural themes of lunar phases to decide when to do certain tasks. For more info on this, make notes on each of the practical suggestions for each phase in upcoming chapters. Also, you can get the book *The Power of Timing* by Johanna Paungger and Thomas Poppe.

Once you've been tracking your energy, and are familiar with your unique rhythm, then you can plan even more effectively. If you know that the full moon wipes you out, then you can pad your schedule and take other precautions. If you know that you feel amazing during a waxing moon, then maybe that's when you schedule important dates. We can work with, not against, our own natural cycles to great effect.

Mimic the light of the moon with your behaviors. Weed when the moon is waning. Get waxed and have your hair cut when it is waning so it will take longer for the hair to grow back. Avoid surgeries around the full moon when humans are known to bleed out more. Redecorate, add to your space during a new moon or waxing moon. Plant seeds for your garden during a new moon, and harvest during a full moon when the water has been drawn to the surface of your plants. Rest and recharge during the dark moon, or utilize it for deep psychic exploration. Notice how you feel during eclipses, and proceed accordingly.

When you are tired, sleep. If you are sad, cry.

When you catch yourself feeling divine delight, let the joy sink into your cells.

The Moon and Consciousness Transformation

The moon helps us work above and below the line of our consciousness. The lunar cycle encapsulates the "circle of awareness." These concepts were created by, and figure prominently in, the work of Carl Jung and Joseph Campbell, and were brought to my attention first by Tara Brach.[12] What follows is my own interpretation of their ideas.

Our circle of awareness is all of our states of consciousness: our superconscious,

conscious, subconscious, and unconscious. It includes our ego, our intuition, and our shadow. There is not a hierarchy to these states; they exist and work together. Spending time tending to the various aspects of our own consciousness creates a healthier intimacy with our self. Working with the moon can help us form deeper relationships with all levels of our awareness.

You can ask yourself, where am I in my circle?
Above, below the line? Why?
What space is my ego/shadow/consciousness
    taking up?
Is my ego in my shadow, or somewhere else? Is my shadow in
    my consciousness, or somewhere else?

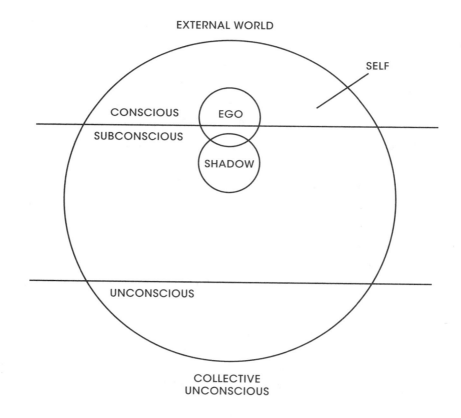

Above the line is our consciousness. Our awareness, our engagement with the present moment. To be in that state the majority of the time is rare. It is difficult to exist solely in the present moment—completely unencumbered by the past, or dragged into future projections. The present is where we can see, feel, and hear ourselves authentically. It is the energy of the new moon and the full moon combined. Our consciousness generally is associated with our actions, how we wish to be seen, and what we share so that others see us as we think we need to be seen. It is everything we experience. It is the awareness and the attention we bring to our energy. Consciousness is the self expressed and fulfilled.

When we are trying to create change in our lives, we must work with both the conscious and the subconscious self. The subconscious is 80 percent of the human brain. The subconscious controls so much of our behavior. Ever blurt something out rather rudely to a friend or sweetie? That's your subconscious. Ever tie your shoe, or drive, or somehow remember the address of your first home even though you haven't lived there in ages? That's your subconscious too. The subconscious is the storehouse. It is also the story maker. We program our subconscious with our consciousness through language, as well as different patterns, habits, emotions, and altered belief systems.

Proof that we are doing change work is the un-comfortableness. At first. Or for the next thirty-three times. Proof we are doing this is by sitting through the pain of an impulsive reaction, into a step toward vulnerability, thus creating different actions and different responses. Proof that we are reprogramming is a different outcome.

Our egos are some of the most psychic parts of ourselves. The ego can tell when we are about to end a certain way of staying small, or of self-sabotage, and will not go away gently. The experience of facing almost insurmountable internal resistance is a clear sign that you are in the process of rewiring and up-leveling. Stepping into more expansiveness often goes against your subconscious programming, and there will often be friction.

That below-the-line energy is the subconscious, our intuition, the depths, the dreams, and the unconscious. It corresponds to the full moon and waning moon. It is some of the most fertile energy we can work with—that which is underneath the surface. Consciousness is above-the-line energy—it's our behavior, our awareness. It is like the captain of the ship, and all the rowers are the subconscious. The sea that this is all taking place on is the unconscious.

When figuring out if we are operating above or below the line, a pause is required. A calm nervous system supports our inquiry; deep breaths are encouraged.

In the pause, we can collect information about:

1. Whether we are operating from an above- or below-the-line place. (Remember, neither is inherently bad or good; both give us information.)

2. Whether or not our above-the-line and below-the-line states are in alignment. Or, in other words, are the rowers taking the ship where the captain would like . . . is everyone in consensus? If not, what dialogues or shifts need to happen so that we are leading with our heart, our integrity, our intuition, and/or our authentic desires?

3. Is it time to focus on reprogramming our consciousness, our subconscious, or both? They have to be operating in a symbiotic manner; getting to the root of some of our harmful subconscious programming is the first step, then deciding what we want and creating actions in accordance with that happens next. Collaboration between the conscious and subconscious is key.

4. The time line that is influencing us the most currently. Are we being ruled by the patterns and stories of our past, what is currently true in the present, or by the unknown and possibilities of the future? Healing work, evolutionary work, and moon work will often require us to address more than one time line.

5. We are reacting, *or* we are responding. Are we behaving in accordance with our higher self, our soul, our heart? Part of evolution is remaining in your integrity, not simply reacting out of fear or attachment.

Collaborating with the cycle of the moon means attending to both our subconscious and our consciousness throughout our creation process. When we get both our subconscious and consciousness on the same page of our dreams and goals, they are more easily attained. You can do more internal, subconscious work during the waning moon, and focus on consciousness and external behavioral shifts when the moon is waxing. By flowing into different energetic patterns, actions, belief systems, sources of inner security, we create new imprints and time lines where we can flourish.

Nourishing Your Moon

Nourishing your inner moon fertilizes the soil of your soul. Your inner moon is a wide and expansive place that exists beyond language. It is a spectrum of the past, a source of ancestral wisdom, and a watery cave of healings and archaic hurts. This place is your ocean heart and your most exciting holographic visions. Your inner moon is a tiny, dark room of grief and tears, and a lava-soaked stadium where you are allowed to gleefully rage. This terrain is often ignored for fear that the pain surfaced will be too much to bear. It is a space that is available to you when you are ready to see how incredible you are. Nourishing your moon is acknowledging all of these spaces you hold and trying to give them what they need. This is how you reconcile the self; this is how you become your best parent, friend, and ally. This is how you walk the journey of self-trust: one small step at a time.

Our inner moon sometimes functions as a deep hunger that must be fed. It is what we yearn for. Our desires and dreams need attention and investment. Our inner child needs solace and acknowledgment. This is how we belong to ourselves.

Nourishing your moon is about developing a lunar practice that you deeply need. Keep this practice simple. Just show up for each moon. Drop expectations. Simply be prepared to meet and accept whatever comes up. What does your inner moon need from you? Maybe it is just one word. Think of ways to give yourself what your inner moon needs.

Create a self-tailored lunar ritual. Start at the full moon. Get comfortable, either outdoors or indoors. Bring your lunar journal. Sit under the moon. If you can't see the moon, that's okay. Invoke her energy by closing your eyes and breathing slowly and deeply for several minutes. Feel yourself being filled up by moon glow. Ask the moon: *What would you like for me to do? What would you like for me to recognize at this time? What am I ready for? What messages do you have for me, beautiful moon?*

You may wish to do this simple lunar ritual several times in a lunar cycle, or even in a week. As you begin to actively give yourself more of what you need, more love/ recognition/trust/safety/awakenings become available to you. As this grows inside, so does your experience of these qualities in various aspects of your life.

Tarot and the Moon

Using tarot cards is a great way to work with the moon. These modalities are natural and gorgeous complements to each other. Like the moon, tarot cards correspond to cycles of evolution. Like the moon, the tarot is a useful device for developing one's intuition. At the beginning of a lunar cycle, you can pull cards. Check in with yourself and ask yourself what you need to know. Ask the tarot to give you more information about the present lunar cycle. Even just one card will do: You can use that tarot card as an anchor for the rest of the lunation. You can also design a spread to answer the questions that you need perspective on.

You can also reflect on what the energies of a certain phase feel like, as reflected in a tarot card. At the end of each phase, go through your deck and choose a card that reflects the prevailing energies of that phase. Write down why, and what happened. At the end of a lunar phase, review your cards and your notes. Were there any patterns or surprises? Does looking back help you see ahead?

In the tarot, the energetic qualities of the moon are found predominately illustrated in two cards: the High Priestess card and the Moon card.

The High Priestess is the archetype of the subconscious, unbridled intuition, ancient wisdom, mysteries, rituals, and the void. When the High Priestess card comes up, it is an affirmation to dive into your own waters. An inquiry into your emotional imagination will culminate in answers. These answers you seek could come through in dreams, could come through in unexpected ways. The messages may not come through words—the High Priestess often speaks in symbols, visions, feelings, and our spidey sense. This information is collected through ritual, magic, underworld journeying, and meditation: by going within. In the traditional version of the archetype depicted by Pamela Colman Smith, the High Priestess has a crown of Hathor on her head, which corresponds to a womb, a receptive vessel to hold our intuition and magic, and to three of the moon's phases: new/waxing crescent, full, and waning crescent.

Sitting at the threshold between day and night, between the aboveground world and the underworld, she is a liminal figure—comfortable on the edges. She helps us believe that our realities are valid. Even the ones that are invisible.

The High Priestess is also a card about mining our experiences for lessons. The pomegranates in the background reference Persephone, reminding us that we need to swim down into our depths, touch base with our core woundings, and confront them in order to heal them. Nestled in these shadows are also our core superpowers, waiting to be brought up to the surface. The High Priestess wants us to kiss our wounds and reframe our shadows as our strengths. Our life becomes its own mythology.

The Moon card shows up when we are ready to surrender to mysteries. We don't have to see the side of her that is turned away from us in order to know it is there. We don't need scientific proof in order to feel her influence our internal tides. This is the practice of groundlessness as redemption. In the Moon card, we find ourselves in the sea of the nonsensical. The moon wants us to get wild, wants us to be our weirdest self. Tameness only gets one so far—our intuitive longings pull us the rest of the way home. Just because there are parts of ourselves that defy logic doesn't mean they aren't deserving of our attention and affection.

The Moon card also references different perspectives. What happens when we take a clear look with kindness instead of dismissal? When we don't let our fears control us, we shine the flashlight of the truth on the basement space of our subconscious. Previously unknown motivations make themselves available to us. We make amends with our memories.

This archetype references profound cycles that exist outside of the confines of civilization: healing from trauma; giving birth to others, ourselves, or major projects; certain life or spiritual apprenticeships. If you receive this card, you may be asked to identify the themes and patterns of a specific meaningful cycle in order to let its lessons and experience transform you.

The Moon card is about inner reflections and the magic that we hold within. When we are able to access these, we come into our own personal power. After we plumb the depths of our consciousness and decipher the potent messages there, we experience a unity loop. We evolve. This is transformation from the inside out.

Apart from tarot, there are many other modalities that a lunar practice supports. Meditation, Reiki, yoga, the Akashic records, astrology, and herbalism are some others you can pair with your lunar practice. Your intuition will tell you where to begin. Over time, you will create and develop a lunar practice that fits your unique needs. Play around and explore. There are constellations of resources waiting to be discovered.

The New Moon

The Seed and the Space

In astronomy, the new moon is the first phase of the lunar cycle. Technically, when the moon is new, it is exactly between the sun and the earth. The new moon marks the moment when the moon and the sun have approximately the same elliptical longitude. It is invisible to us, for it is completely in front of the sun. This period lasts for about three days, until the waxing crescent moon, when we can first glimpse her light. Astronomers, astrologers, and some witches acknowledge the new moon during the three days of "invisibility." This is the moon as blank slate, moon as void, moon as nothing. Nothingness is sacred because everything comes out of nothing. Nothingness is sacred because it is where we all return. Darkness is a gift; it is where germination takes place. A place where we can rest, renew, and move toward birthing or rebirth.

Many cultures, however, did not consider the moon as "new" until a sliver of light was seen in the sky. Ancient Jewish tradition had moon watchers who would usher in the beginning of the month by burning bonfires when the first glimmer of light was spotted in the sky. (The beginning of the "moonth" is still a minor Jewish holiday, called Rosh Chodesh.) Similar new moon timing mechanisms and observances were, and still are, utilized in Islamic tradition. Some witches observe the new moon as their dark moon: a time of rest and reconciliation. This means, at an exact new moon, we are still in a liminal, unknown space. The waxing crescent is the time when some folks cast new moon spells.

The way to decide when your new moon begins is to use your intuition. If you observe your internal lunar cycles and phases for a couple of months, and if you've noticed that on the "official" new moon you feel drained or like you've still got some clearing to do, then it makes sense for you to interpret that time as part of the dark moon. Either do magic related to the waning moon/dark moon at this time, such as uncrossing or clearing spells, or simply rest. When the new moon rises a day or two later, you can begin your personal and particular new moon observance. In my personal practice, I conduct new moon magic at this point. I'm excited when I can catch a glimpse of the moon's reflected glow, as it strikes a particular hope-tinged chord in my heart. As always, observe your intuition, and plan your rituals around your energy and your own personal practice. Experiment with beginning right when the moon is new or a few days after, to see what works best for you.

The new moon rises at sunrise and sets at sunset. The tides are higher at new moons. The increased gravity could intensify or enhance energy and emotions. From a magical perspective, the new moon, the full moon, and the dark moon are the more intensely felt or experienced phases in the cycle. They are the exclamation marks of a lunar cycle.

This time is an opportunity to reconcile situations from last month and forgive yourself and others. Foster intentions of hope, faith, and optimism in new processes and practices—or breathe new life into old processes and practices. Shake things up. Whistle a different tune. Plant your flag of courage in the sand and move onward. This is the beginning of the beginning. It is the first page of the heroine's journey; the first step, the door opening, the waking up. This is the energy that accompanies inklings and innuendos: what is unseen yet deeply felt and known.

The new moon can be the beginning of an enhanced consciousness and awareness, mindfulness, and focused attention. This is the moment when we decide to live life with more mindfulness, to step out of our comfort zone of habits, and to venture into the uncharted territory of Thinking Different Thoughts. It is where we build the prototypes for our reinvention.

IF THE NEW MOON IS HARD FOR YOU

Beginnings are hard. Transitions are challenging. New moons can be uncomfortable for those of us born under a full moon or waning moon. New moons can also be more challenging in the fall or wintertime—these seasons resonate more with the waning moon, with wrapping up and shedding. Adjust accordingly. Maybe your "new" beginning at a November or December new moon would be starting a project quietly, working behind the scenes, getting ready to take further flight at a later moment. The new moon comes with a lot of unknowns, a lot of spaciousness, and a lot of emptiness.

If the new moon is tough for you, gently explore that discomfort. The ability to move forward and onward is a helpful skill to have in one's toolkit. Being able to try new things, to experiment with taking risks, can be difficult for those of us with trauma. However, alongside trying new things comes play, comes pleasure, comes flow. These are ingredients for creating a healing practice for our trauma. Trusting our intuition to give us messages about what we need resourcing around aids us in recovery and reconnection with our core self.

The new moon is a harbinger of visionary ideas. This is the energy we must utilize if we are to liberate ourselves and others. This is the energy of the science fiction novel, the unlikely life-changing invention, the genius theory. New moon energy exists in every voyage to uncharted territories. The lands of make-believe, the realms of improvisation are found in this space. This energy lives in young children, filled with vitality and innocent curiosity. It is present in the willingness to try and try again. Being able to connect with hope is a requirement in these apocalyptic times. Belief is nonnegotiable, especially at the end of the world. Cultivating new beginnings and technologies is imperative.

WHEN YOU ARE IN A NEW MOON PHASE

When you are in a new moon phase, you feel a little messy. You feel like taking risks. You may be asking yourself *why not?* and proclaiming *heck yes!* And why shouldn't you? Life is for trying, for mixing it up, for exploring tastes and sensations and the entire spectrum of ways we can exist. You might feel invigorated by inspiration, or whatever else has convinced you to give it another go.

On the other hand, you may be teetering on the verge of overwhelm, surrounded by the hazy unknown. If situations and scenarios in the new moon provoke anxiety, this is the opportune time to rewire how you react. You won't find a solution for what troubles you by running through the same old loops that keep you frayed and ragged. Unless we do things differently, unless we enact new behaviors, we'll be trapped in an unconscious spiral, carrying on programming that most likely isn't even ours.

The new moon is a zero, usually invisible—it is a whisper of a whisper. The only way to hear its messages is to stay still. Past the noise of distractions, chatter, resistance. Tapped into the present moment, when we are neutral, when we've let down our defenses, when our assumptions have dissipated, we are in the generative void. This is an empty space of restoration. This is the space of enlightenment and answers. It is the space from where we can leap into faith. An empty vessel into which our most secret dreams flow.

The new moon is a place of pause. Maybe this time, you don't respond to the fuming, hateful email. Maybe this time, when your reaction is to be snappish or sharp, you soften, or hold your tongue. Good choices open different doors. These better choices, repeated, add up. Over time they turn into leveled-up outcomes. There is no better time than the new moon present to practice the pause.

A new moon is the opportune time to ask "What if?" It is most certainly not the time for imagination rejections. Do not deprive yourself in that manner. Let every winged dream in. Let every conceivable wish be a possibility. This can be the time to lay your foundation down in radically sustainable, radically rooted ways. This can be the moment you decide to announce: *Yes, I am ready to believe.*

THE NEW MOON IS A TIME TO SET INTENTIONS

This is a time to decide what your intentions will be for the next lunar cycle, season, or longer. Without a clear intention it is not possible to know what you want or where you are going. Your intention serves as both a beginning and your guide through a magical process.

Your intentions are the seeds you plant in your consciousness and subconscious. You nourish the seeds with your actions and your energy. As you believe in the possibilities of your intentions and adjust your vibrational patterns accordingly, transformation begins. As you apply effort to making your intentions show up, they will expand. So will your world.

When we set an intention, we affirm that what we would like is already done. It is already on its way to us. It will present itself to us in perfect time.

Without clear intentions, we are unlikely to achieve results. There is no metric or measuring stick. Intentions must include a way to chart our progress.

Before you set your intentions, start by free writing. Write for longer than you think you need to. Name all that you want to happen. Begin with where you would like to be and what you would like to feel. Experience what all your intended outcomes would feel like in your body. Bring up emotions, any scenarios, or vivid scenes that will occur as a result of following through on your intention.

After you've gotten it all out, take a short break. Stretch, drink water. Reread what you've written. What are the main patterns or words that keep repeating? These can serve as ingredients for affirmations and themes to meditate on. Out of your first free write, craft your intentions. Write them out simply and clearly. Frame them positively rather than negatively.

Once you've clarified your intention, answer the following questions:

1. How will I measure success? How will I know my intention has been achieved?
2. What will I do in service of this intention? What actions must I take?
3. What mindset do I need to cultivate? What behaviors and practices embody the mindset in action?
4. What daily practices must I adopt that I can rely upon when the going gets tough? What does my support system consist of?
5. What is the pure impulse present underneath this intention? (For example, if your intention is "write a book," the pure impulse might be "creative expression and experimentation.")

6. How could your pure impulse be brought into your life in other ways?
7. What might you need to change or leave behind? How will you move through the discomfort or pain of doing so?
8. What elements (fire/water/earth/air/spirit), or spirit/deities/sources, or other tools, will you utilize to support yourself in practical and magical ways?

After this reflection, you may wish to rewrite your intention one final time. Include more detail, make it more of an action plan, add any other information that gives you confidence.

Congratulations! You have now created an intention humanifesto. This is what you will use to create your spell. It is also a contract you are making between yourself and spirit. It outlines the qualities with which you most deeply wish to connect. These are the qualities you can begin working on conjuring at any time within yourself. Whatever you want you must give to yourself first.

Our intention must be for us and us alone. It cannot be motivated by what society tells us, or what everyone on the Internet appears to be doing. Our intentions generally arise in our intuition. Intention and intuition support each other.

You must stick to your intention. Sticking to an intention is the spot where so many of us stumble. We say we want something. *We really, really want it.* In a spell, we focus on receiving it. But our intention doesn't come to be. We get mad. We get sad. We blame ourselves. We blame magic. Trust gets eroded. We stop practicing. Why does this happen?

There is not complete belief in our intention.
Maybe we need to work on cultivating trust and confidence. It is one thing to say we would like something, but when we go deeper, we see there are no roots of belief to support the dream.

Our desires are too far outside our sphere of influence.
Everyone has a sphere of influence that consists of where they are (geographically and spiritually), what they know, who they are, who they know, and what they are doing. If you are casting spells for outcomes that are far outside the realm of your sphere of influence, it makes sense to focus instead on what lies within it. As a rule, cast spells just outside your comfort zone. If it fills you with tingly excitement and

a teensy bit of anxiety, but you know it *could* happen, then you are in the correct intentional corner.

There is no commitment to doing the work.
We want the thing without wanting to do the work to get the thing. We don't want to have to get up early, end certain relationships, or take other actions that support our intention. We believe our life is happening *to* us, not *for* us. Nothing will change if there is not a commitment to doing the work. Cultivating discipline will be covered more in the waxing period chapter.

We aren't acknowledging the results.
Sometimes, we are so focused on an exact outcome or a totally huge, final result that we aren't taking time to see what is actually transpiring. Maybe it is a lack of something, so we don't notice it—for example, maybe we cast a spell for protection, and ever since, no exes, catcallers, or online trolls have jumped in our inbox. Try to be as mindful as possible in the weeks following a spell. Sometimes the results are not what we had hoped for, but they are results. You cast a spell for a different job, and you lose a job. *For sure* you will be now getting a different job! Spells take time and humans can be impatient. Ask yourself how to use what is currently happening to your benefit.

Make Your Intentions Magical

When we make our intentions magical, we are asking to truly be transformed by the process. Our cells are ready to be shifted and imbued with refreshing energy. We wish to step into a deeper understanding of ourselves and our souls' work. There is an engagement with the process. Because we are connected to our intention magically— with magical practice, with a greater tether to source energy, with an openness to flow, a heightened wonder, with the awareness of synchronicity and empowered alignment—the work ripples out much further than we can quantify. This further facilitates transformation and healing beyond the container of the intention.

This is what occurs when there is connection to the *why* of the intention: the sensations and yearnings that accompany and lie underneath the intention.

A beautiful way to consciously and continuously direct your energy intentionally is to cultivate tiny anchors through your day. This is like "mindfulness" with a magical boost. This shifts your energy and keeps you aligned with your intention. It encourages a call and response with your intention. This practice poises you as an energetic ouroboros—the snake eating its own tail, plugging back into the core of your intention. Tiny anchors can be practices, rituals, or habits you create for yourself to do every day, to call all aspects of your consciousness to focus on and conjure your intention.

What are three tiny anchors you could tie to your intention? Choose areas where you need the most support. *What is your tiny anchor love language?* Pick some you feel excited about that will boost your intention and keep reminding you of it throughout your day.

THE NEW MOON IS THE TIME TO PLANT SEEDS

At the new moon, we clarify and commit to what we are ready to grow. What we focus on grows. Our intentions are the seeds. Our desires are the seeds. Our emotional yearnings are the seeds.

To plant a seed is to acknowledge what that seed will become. Imbued in the seed is totality. It is both the glimmer of the desire and the tangible form it will ultimately take. It is the signifier and the signified of our magical praxis.

The final form the seed will become has certain qualities: conceptually, energetically, and emotionally. At the new moon stage, at the preliminary phase of spell casting, it is imperative to embody these qualities in a visceral way. Think about what activities invoke those feelings, and find ways to do those regularly. Find people who are reminders of these qualities, and spend time with them. Figure out what qualities will support the growth of the seed, such as patience, pleasure, vulnerability, or experimentation, and embed them in our surroundings as much as possible. Act in totality.

There are other techniques to try at the new moon. Stop associating *only* the end goal with the particular feeling. (*When I get the thing, then I will be fixed/deserving/safe.*) Stop being conditional with love, praise, power, permission. (With yourself, and with others.) Drop the either/or, bad/good set-up. (It never ends well.) Try this in ritual, in meditation, in trance during the spell. After the spell has been cast, bring yourself back to this feeling in waking life. Watch your language and correct your communication accordingly.

A seed is alive, but in a dormant state. It needs to be planted, and watered, and placed in the dark in order to grow. Most seeds are made up of a seed coat, the embryo, and nutrients. The embryo is alive, and contains all the building blocks of the mature plant. This is our intention.

Be clear about the quality of energy, emotion, or somatic sensation that accompanies your intention. Does your intention require you to soften, to unclench your jaw, to get looser, and less judgmental? Watch yourself in your daily life; see how much of those qualities you can bring into your world. Does your intention need you to get a bit bolder, a bit more extroverted, a bit more communicative? Determine what qualities to embody. Think about what activities you are already doing that might get you in the frame of mind, or somatic sensation needed, and put that into your intention-setting toolkit.

The seed coat protects the embryo from harm. Your intention is to be protected. Hidden from the dream deflators of doubt, cruelty, and judgment. Keep your intentions safe. Do not share them. Allow them space to breathe, allow them time to get rooted. Keep them a secret between you and the moon.

In nature, each particular kind of seed has its own time line for how long it can remain viable—able to sprout, able to grow. In nature, each kind of seed has its own unique conditions for germination. Check in and get honest about time lines.

Leave room to broaden or alter your intention. Once you set out, the steps you take down one path may have to wind into another. Magic requires a bit of flexibility.

Be aware. Pay attention to what you see, what you read, who you meet, and any inspirations or impulses you have that are different, interesting, or that simply provide confirmation that something is shifting, and your intentions are supported. It is useful to write these down in a place you can revisit, such as your lunar journal.

Let the energy of the new moon charge all the seeds of your intention. Let it seep into your present and future selves. You are allowed to germinate in the cool, quiet black. You can burst gently open, little blooms of radiance, spilling forth with laughter, open arms carrying sparkling bouquets of blessings. You can tend to growth for the sake of growth, armed with flexible resilience, holding the torch of resolve. Let the awareness of possibility, the acceptance of all that is coming your way cascade through your crown, out through your lips, down your shoulders, throughout your body, and keep you safe through your seeding.

THE NEW MOON IS THE TIME
TO CULTIVATE THE SOIL

If you are *ready* to go, then the New Moon is *totally* the time to go for it. Follow your impulses and get to it. The majority of us need a bit more time to prepare for the life changes on the way, for the better habits we need to start. That's okay.

In addition to picking out the perfect seeds of vibration to plant, we must consider the soil in which we are planting our seeds. Create the conditions for optimal seed growth. Where will your dreams be taking root? Consider all aspects of the soil that is the groundwork of your intentions. Sometimes, it is the best use of a new moon to cultivate supportive soil. Seeds need the right environment to germinate. Dropping your seeds randomly in dirt, in any thoughtless way, in chaos and distraction and neglect will not allow them to grow into the lovely bouquets they were meant to be.

Your soil comprises where you are now and what you currently possess. Your internal and external resources. Your mindset and belief systems. The emotional state you must possess. Your habits, your actions. The hours you have in a day and how you utilize them. Consider all of these carefully. Identify what nutrients you lack, and work on infusing them into your baseline. Cultivate your resources, impulses, behaviors, and focus.

There are times to slow down in order to speed up. Going slower in the beginning and planning stages will save time in the end. However, over-planning is sometimes a procrastination device. Do not stay in the pre-pre-beginning zone forever. You will never be perfect. What a relief! Conditions around you will never be perfect. There is no perfect. There is only trying one's best, good, getting better, and over time becoming a master or expert. If perfectionism is the fear holding you back, you can examine that during shadow work in the waning moon. For now, take a little risk. Take one step forward, and one step after that.

Cultivating the soil properly means setting yourself up for success. There are endless items out of your control. Get serious and real about what you *can* control. The breath. Your focus. How you care for yourself. Spend time thinking of the best actions that serve as an extension of your intentions. Nurture those. Set yourself up for success because you are most definitely going to encounter resistance, obstacles, and other unforeseen challenges. Such drama is a definitive part of the heroine's journey.

While setting oneself up for success sounds basic and simple, it can be hard for many of us. There can be a cognitive dissonance between what we want, where we are, and what we need to support us. When we don't really take stock of where we are, when we don't really figure out how to set ourselves up for success, our intentions wither. It gets harder to try again. Our intentions fall into the intention-recycling bin, never to be considered again.

I am going to use my beloved dog Gigi as an example. Gigi the pit bull is approximately three years old and a rescue. She has three legs: a tri-pawed. She's gentle and funny and charming and outgoing. As a result of trauma she suffered before we adopted her, Gigi has pretty severe separation anxiety. Regardless of our efforts, when we leave the house, whether for an hour or for six, Gigi gets into the trash, the recycling, whatever is left out: she destroys shoes and other items, and just generally lets us know quite clearly that she is *not happy* to be alone.

We've realized that we need to "Gigi proof" the house when we leave. Lock things up, leave treats around for her, and generally make sure she is unable to cause harm. When we do this, nothing gets destroyed. While we aren't jazzed about this behavior, we are not angry at Gigi. Why should we be? She's innocent. A series of unfortunate events impacted her behavior.

This is, of course, the way you must treat yourself. Your inner Gigi is innocent—the lonely sweetheart who wants to destroy something when things are hard or set you off course is a result of conditioning. We've all been through a lot, and self-punishment is not necessary. Love is necessary. Being hard on yourself or judging yourself isn't going to help move you forward. Compassionate nurturing of your needs will.

If you haven't already, at the new moon time, get really practical about simple yet integral ways you need to set yourself up for success. If your intention is to write more, where is that scheduled regularly in your calendar? And how will you stick to it, no matter what? Do you need to join a writing group? Will you make writing time more alluring, surrounding yourself with endless mugs of green tea and snacks? Be very clear about what exactly needs to happen to bring the seeds of your intention through the soil.

The Space Is to Be Clean and Clear

The space in which you plant your seeds must be cleared of any distractions. Imagine yourself tilling the soil, tending the seed—what would hinder growth? Write it down.

You can work with any obstacles you identify during the waning moon or during your moon-mapping process. What tools would help you grow? Write those down.

It is okay if you only have three hours a week to till the soil of your dreams. Make that time the most focused, most aligned three hours possible. Bring in other sensations associated with your intentions—emotional and somatic—to other moments of your week. Connect all your activities through your intention. Make the way in which you do one thing the way in which you do all things. The feelings and mindset you are cultivating will infuse more areas of your life.

Cleaning and clearing is important energetically, practically, and magically. Cleaning our home is important, we all know this. Energetic hygiene is just as important. The new moon is a great time to make sure that our energy is neutral, and there is no unwanted energy cluttering up our energetic field.

On the day before the new moon, or on the actual new moon, do a cleaning ritual. Get rid of any items that no longer serve you. Clear the energy of your space. Put on your favorite record, move objects around in your space, organize at least a couple of shelves and drawers that need tidying. Generally, once we've cleaned, decluttered, and cleared, an energetic shift is felt. Whenever you need to re-center, cleanse, and clear: sweep, scrub, weed, mop, move.

Then, on the day after the new moon, you can do your intention setting and new moon ritual or spell work. In a cleared-out space, in a cleansed state of mind. Keep your energy clear by calling your energy back to yourself. Keep your energy clear by practicing mindfulness. Keep your energy clear by practicing energetic boundary work and protection. Keep your energy clear by reminding yourself of what your goals are. Again and again, come back to who you truly are.

THE NEW MOON IS A TIME TO USE YOUR IMAGINATION

Our imagination is one of our greatest gifts. It gives us innovation. Our imagination creates new legislation, envisions different forms of liberation, and creates restorative conversations. Imagination fosters improvisation, experimentation, and collaboration.

Imagination has brought us so many things: blue jeans, socialized health care, closed captioning, perms, biodynamic gardening, the printing press, home karaoke kits, seed bombs, airplanes, philosophies, and knitting blogs. Imagination has helped us escape death, delivered life, conjured haikus, and turned fool's gold into million-dollar empires. How would you like to use your vast imagination to create your own reality? How would you like to use your unique vision to remake the world? What do you have to offer that is completely original to you? We need your brilliant brain's art, your words, your gender-neutral fashion line, your solutions to the climate crisis, your ideas on organizing, your poetry, your databanks of resources—now more than ever. We need your belief in yourself. It reminds us to believe in ourselves too.

Connecting to our imagination connects us to our inner child. Think back to when you were young. What could you spend hours doing? Can you do that now, once a week or more? Allow your imagination to run free and express itself. One way to mend childhood hurt is to soothe our inner child with activities our younger self loved. This is a way of re-parenting. The new moon is a perfect time to begin a re-parenting process.

In her book *Emergent Strategy* and her podcast *How to Survive the End of the World*, adrienne maree brown talks about the concept of "imagination battles": an endless stream of ideologies and philosophies all vying for legitimacy.[1] Unfortunately, many of us are living in a reality created by oppressors' and abusers' imaginations. This is why we must prioritize our own, and the precious imaginations of others who are focused on building a better world. Collectively, it is time to prioritize certain imaginations: the imaginations of Black, Brown, Indigenous thinkers and leaders. It is time to cultivate more inclusive and compassionate imaginations. The imaginations of queer folks, feminists, trans folks, femmes, and women. All witches know that part of the great work is resisting psychic death. Resist the infections of harmful folks' imaginations in your mindset, spiritual life, and space.

The new moon is a good time to check in with exactly whose imagination you are living in. Is it your own, or someone else's? Is it your ancestor's or someone else's? What feeds your imagination? What thinkers, writers, lecturers, artists, musicians, poets, movies, and television shows are coming into your one precious imagination? At the new moon, if needed, reduce your sensory intake. Spend a day or two listening to nothing, reading nothing, watching nothing except what you absolutely must. Give yourself blank time. Ursula K. Le Guin used to schedule time to stare at the wall each writing day. Think about what you are craving to read about, craving to learn about, craving to listen to. Curate carefully. Name what you wish to be thinking about and engaged with. Choose nourishing and interesting imaginative fodder.

Visualization

Visualization is that age-old magical technique that every witch should be fluent in. There are thousands of books on this subject to read. A favorite is *Creative Visualization* by Shakti Gawain. I'm not going to get too deep into the how-to, as there are so many resources available.

Practicing visualization reawakens our generative subconscious. For those of us who suffer from PTSD and trauma, being able to practice visualization can help calm our nervous system down. If you are activated, and it is safe for you to do so, call to mind a place that symbolizes safety and calm while breathing deeply.

Visualization helps convince us that our intention can be attained. When practicing protection magic, we visualize symbols around us protecting us, such as shields, talismans, guardians, and rosebushes. Some witches imagine a bubble of protection, a diamond of protection, or even a protection suit they zip themselves into. This signals to our various levels of consciousness, energy field, and nervous system to act in accordance.

Practicing visualization aids us with our dreams and goals. There's a saying, in reference to representation in the media: "If we can see it, we can be it." In the very empirical "I'll believe it when I see it" overculture, it can be hard to summon belief from future dreams. Visualization can help with this. Witches are usually visionaries, creatives, and independent creatures, but even we can use extra support when we are undertaking something we've never tried before. Visualization is a very effective way to hypnotize the subconscious into believing dreams are reality.

If visualization is hard for you, or if you have aphantasia, there are other visualization-adjacent things you can try. Record yourself speaking about your dreams like they have already happened and listen to the playback while you rest. Spend time writing down your dreams in the present tense. Pretend you are writing a letter to a friend, describing the marvelous opportunity that just happened to you. Speak what you want to happen out loud, when you are alone.

At the new moon, going all the way up to the full moon, spend at least a few minutes visualizing yourself in the process of achieving your goal. Connect your imagination to your desires. Allow them to travel within your mind's eye. Let them unfurl into sensations that travel all over your body and into your heart. Deliver a fantasy to yourself that in time will become a reality.

THE NEW MOON IS A GREAT TIME TO CHANGE YOUR MIND

This is the time to examine your thoughts. At the new moon, track your thought patterns. Create more generative ones. For those of us reading this who deal with mental illness or are neuro-divergent, this might not be easy. People with OCD, who are depressed, have anxiety, or are unable to manage other cognitive issues cannot always "control their thoughts" easily. "Thoughts create your reality," a common New Age refrain, is not always true. Sometimes the reality of our chemistry and DNA directs our thoughts. And humans have a range of healthy, normal thoughts that are not always positive, anyway—from anger to rage, sorrow to grief, etc. A lot of so-called New Age truths have their roots in harmful dogmatic, capitalist, and white supremacist rhetoric that polices thoughts, emotions, and bodies.

Life is hard. It is frequently tragic right now, beauties. Of course your sensitive self is affected by all the chaos collectively and/or personally swirling around us. The world is totally fucked up right now—it has been, for thousands of years. If you are paying attention, you are sick, sad, disgusted. That said, therapeutic and psychiatric help can be a game changer. Don't deny yourself a better life by avoiding therapy, support groups, or counseling.

This is gentle encouragement to try to make your brain—your mind's home, the seat of your consciousness and subconscious—as kind, as soft, and as sweet, to and for yourself, as it can be. A non-allergenic featherbed, not a furnace. If your mind is a resourced place, you can help more people. If your mind is infused with positive momentum, your magic is much more potent. Your sphere of influence grows. Your positivity and your love grow too. Your strength and influence grow, and your patriarchy-smashing powers grow too!

If consciously changing your mind feels daunting, then focus on changing how you *relate* to your thoughts. When certain cruel thoughts take hold of your consciousness, must you believe them? What are the origins of these thoughts? What do you gain by attaching to thoughts of unworthiness or self-flagellation? What would happen if you choose kinder and gentler thoughts?

Consider your thoughts as a passing moment. Let them wash over you but not knock you down. Detach yourself from them with practice. Start by naming what you are feeling, such as "I am feeling confused" instead of "I am confused"; that switches from you identifying as an emotion, to identifying an emotion you are currently experiencing but will change. As soon as you catch yourself thinking something unhelpful, immediately change it to a helpful narrative. ("I can't do this" becomes "I need a break right now, I am actually doing really well in challenging circumstances.")

Decide to pick what record is playing in your mind. Use your breath to take you through to a calmer oasis. Taking slow, deep, and long breaths for several minutes will help. Focusing on a color, an image, or a soothing word helps as well. Meditating consistently absolutely helps.

Most likely, you would never talk to a friend or a stranger the way you speak to yourself at times. Treat yourself as you would a dear and treasured friend. Maybe you made a mistake; you are human. If you caused harm, then do your best to mend the harm and truly learn from it, and don't repeat the same mistake. Making mistakes, a lot of the time, simply means you are in process and actually trying, actually putting yourself out there.

Change your mindset, change your behaviors. Connect mindset with self-treatment and values with action. Is kindness one of your core values? Where is that showing up in how you talk to yourself? How are you expressing your core values with your thoughts, actions, and the energy you put out into the world?

Understanding Your Mindset

A mindset is a combination of our experiences, beliefs, values, attitudes, and thoughts. Mindsets are sometimes formed when we are very young—a reflection of what our family or caretakers believed and told us. They are further shaped when we go out into the world, and encounter successes and adversities. They are informed by culture and the collective; affected or created by trauma. Sometimes we subconsciously seek out experiences that will reinforce our existing mindset. Mindsets can dictate our behavior and affect life outcomes. Mindsets are malleable and can shift and evolve. Thank goddess! Figuring out what your mindset(s) around your dream needs to be, and how to transform it to support your goal is a potent form of new moon witchery.

At the new moon phase, do *not* look for confirmation of why your new beliefs or mindsets will not work. Do *not* obsess over how you need to get to your goals, or what steps you'll need to take. You don't need to have the thing yet. You need only to believe in your ability to attract and receive the thing. Give your dream some luxurious space.

Below are a few easy and effective ways to start changing your mindset or the way you relate to certain thoughts:

Gratitude lists and journaling. The reason gratitude practices are everywhere is because they work. Gratitude only proliferates. Gratitude literally transforms our somatic self. It rewires our brains. Many scientific studies have linked a gratitude-journaling practice with positive, long-term changes in the brain.

Consistently naming all of the things we are grateful for creates a baseline of abundance mindset, delivers us feelings of appreciation, and connects us to psychic possibilities of more goodness. Creativity begets more creativity. When we focus on all the love we have, we are affirming we can have more love. When we sing in the key of mauve and fuchsia sweetness, it attracts the butterflies that croon in that key too.

When we focus only on what we don't have, it drains our energy. The black hole of comparison and lack grows ever wider in our psyche. The dream seeds just planted cringe and wither.

Try listing all that you are appreciative of for at least one week, two to three times a day at the new moon. If you feel called to, include your dreams in your gratitude list. You may also want to leave an offering to certain items on your gratitude list. If you are grateful to the sparrows chirping outside your window, leave them birdseed. If you are grateful to a specific friend, cook them dinner. If a particular album got you through the day, tell your friends about it, or go to that artist's next concert. If you are grateful to the clouds, donate money to a clean air nonprofit.

Curiosity. Asking questions opens up exploration and possibility. When you catch yourself shutting down into resistance, pause. Question yourself. Keep going until you unearth a limiting belief. Ask it what it needs to be transformed. Reframe it and reword it into something supportive.

Asking questions opens the situation up for exploration and possibility. It also affords one space from the attachment of the judging or fixing mind. This in turn taps into our creativity. Paradoxically, when we resist or try to defend ourselves from negative thoughts, that resistance and defensiveness creates a tsunami of energy on which the thoughts can feed. We toggle between feeling the negative thoughts, and resisting the negative thoughts, which leaves us in a state of exhausted tension. Invoke childlike curiosity. Sit down with your negative thoughts and have a loving dialogue with them. Buddhists call this "inviting your demons to tea."

Positive thoughts. Take time, maybe three or five minutes a day at first, then longer, to focus on consciously thinking positive thoughts. At first, try doing this in neutral or pleasurable spaces specifically. Try it while burying your face in roses. Try it while in a eucalyptus-infused shower or bath. Try it while walking around a lake, through a park, at the beach. Work on memorizing those sensations during those moments of your life that are joyful. Then, begin extending those thoughts and sensations into neutral moments. Affirm yourself after you try something hard or risky. Give yourself a reward. Do not focus on the outcome, focus on the doing. Connect to any positive or neutral aspects you can. Breathe and believe into this state of mind.

Little Activities and Rituals to Try at New Moon Time

Give yourself swathes of blank time to do nothing. Move around the placement of your furniture. Experiment with your hairstyle or clothing. Research genres of music you've never heard of and listen to them for a week or a month. Read about a subject you know nothing about. Sign up for a class that interests you. If you always say *yes*, say *no thank you*. If you always say *no*, say *yes please*. Message the crush. If the first thing you reach for in the moment is your phone, place it out of reach. Ask questions if you don't understand someone, or a situation, clearly. Watch yourself when you jump to conclusions. Stop yourself before you swirl into a stalemate. Take one or two breaths the length of your favorite river and let yourself unwind. Decide to finally begin: the poetry project, the research on continuing education, the search for a therapist. Write, speak, listen, create: all in service of uncovering. Begin very slowly. Begin very small. Small things become big things.

New Moon Magic

New moon magic correlates perfectly with visions, dreams, and wishes. Seeding spells, growth spells, and attraction spells were made for this time. Sometimes, it is good to cast a spell to summon the solid baseline of your desire: creativity, discipline, openness—pick an energy that will help you begin your lunar journey with the right ingredients and support.

Spend time corralling your highest pie-in-the-sky hopes from the clouds. Bring them down to a place you can touch, understand, and hold. Daydreams, musings, and sketches all get your subconscious excited and on board with your desires.

Vision boards—art that expresses the overall feeling, emotions, or outcomes of your dreams—are excellent to create at the new moon. Writing poems, song lyrics, and collaging: these are all great magical activities for the new moon. Clearing spells like uncrossing spells, cleaning spells, and ritual work that facilitate release of the past all help to create a blank slate.

Spells that include hypnosis, affirmations, and guided meditations are especially appropriate now as these help reprogram the brain. Spells and activities that stimulate the imagination and the senses are excellent to try at this time: making playlists, buying divine-smelling fruit, and trying to use fascinating words in conversations all serve as a reminder that there are endless beginnings. This is a hallmark of this lovely lunar phase.

Creating Your New Moon Altar

A new moon altar could be the base of all the spells for the entire lunation. You may wish to leave it up for the duration of the entire lunar cycle. Start with a few items and then add to it every couple of days. Or, a new moon altar may be set up for your new moon spell only. Your new moon altar could be sparse and minimal, symbolic of a welcoming, clear space for your dreams to settle into. It could be a blank page, an open book, a hum of hope in the background.

Your new moon altar could be you, deciding to breathe deeply, alone in the dark, resting your hands over your heart. Your altar is the faith you affix to. It is the dreams you are remembering, the small steps you are taking in different directions, the way you imbue your gaze with the openness you are now ready to meet.

Magical Correspondences of the New Moon

Knowing what you will be casting spells for will guide the ingredients you will be using in your spell. For example, if you are creating a money spell, you would most likely use a green or gold candle, honey, basil, bay leaves or peppermint, cinnamon, maybe a lodestone, citrine, or a pyrite crystal, possibly actual bills, coins, and even a check made out in the amount of money you wish to bring in.

It is important to develop your personal set of correspondences depending on how you interpret each phase of the moon. It has to feel resonant and meaningful for you personally. For you, the new moon might be all tigereye and nettle, brown candles and smoky quartz, because grounding and strength is what is required of you at this time. For another magic maker, the new moon might be an homage to Mercury, complete with peacock feathers, mint, and celestite—they wish to revel in beauty, camp, and strange transmissions from the ether. Experiment and play! Below are a few suggestions:

Correspondences of the new moon: Seeds, eggs, feathers, magnets, lodestone, hematite, clear quartz, fluorite, moss agate, chrysocolla, kunzite, celestine, obsidian, aragonite, cinnabar, rhodochrosite; air, the direction east; the colors black, pink, peach, green; lemon verbena, peppermint, ginger, lemon, eucalyptus, catnip, chamomile; salt; the Aces in the Tarot, the Fool, the Magician, the Pages.

Deities: Artemis, Diana, Luna, Selene, Chang'e, Ishtar.

Archetypes: The life of Joan of Arc; the music and work and art of Prince; Alexandria Ocasio-Cortez, Agnes Martin, Octavia Butler, Ursula K. Le Guin, drag queens.

Animal guides: Ibis, kangaroos, dragonflies, colts, seahorses, butterflies, foxes.

NEW MOON SPELLS

Seed Magic Spell

 This is an early springtime to early summer spell. The best times to cast it would be between late February and before the summer solstice in June, if you are in the Northern Hemisphere. Adjust the spell as needed.

You will need:

- Seeds (or a small start of a plant)
- A pot (find or use a special container for your seeds)
- Soil
- Any other objects or talismans you'd like to put in the soil (think about what hope/intention/dream will be linked to these seeds—maybe you want to embed a small piece of citrine, for abundance, or a key, for finding solutions, in the soil)
- Gardening tools (spade, fertilizer)
- Paper
- Pen

Cast the spell:

Gather everything you'll need. Get quiet and focused. Call your energy back to you. Cast your circle and conduct any other practices in your spell work routine.

Write your intentions down on small, separate pieces of paper.

Take the seeds or baby plant and hold them/it in your hands. Imagine your

108

intentions infusing the life in your hands with positivity, electrical charge, and emotional fertilizer.

Bring these emotions and images in your mind as you begin to repot your baby start or plant your seeds. Put the pieces of paper in the soil, around the seeds, or roots of the plants.

Stay focused until the little life is inside your pot, watered, and you feel good. Acknowledge that what you want to start on or attract will grow with focus, care, and attention.

As time passes and you continue to tend to the life in the container, remind yourself to also tend to the new life of your intention. Know that as your plant grows, your magic does as well. Remember to engage with your plant and form an appreciative relationship. Work with it as a metaphor for your growth and change.

You can also walk through your neighborhood and throw intentionally charged seeds or plant them in a front or back yard, if available.

Attracting Spell

 The following spell is a simple attracting spell. It can be used anytime from the new moon to the full moon. You may wish to follow your written spell or petition with a caveat such as "this or better, for the greatest good of all," or another qualifier such as "no harm, only good, shall come as a result of this spell."

You will need:

- Two candles—one that represents you and one that represents what you are attracting (choose colors that correspond intuitively to yourself and what you wish to attract)
- Elements that correspond to attraction—lodestones, magnets, copper, silver, and/or specific crystals, herbs, or plants that correspond to what you are attracting
- A spell, petition, poem, or letter you've written to or about what you are consciously attracting
- Any other ingredient or symbol that pertains to what you are calling in, to place on your altar or to anoint yourself with (e.g., knots, or oils, or special incense)

Cast the spell:

Set up your altar and space: You will need enough space on your altar to put the candles far enough apart from each other, without disrupting the other ingredients you will be using.

Call in any guides/angels/helpers, if in your practice.

Within the container of the spell, charge and dress your candles. If they are in a votive, you may wish to embed crystals and herbs into your candles. You may wish to carve your candles with words or symbols, anoint them, and roll them in herbs. If nothing else, charge both the candle that represents you, and the candle that represents your desire, with your emotions and intentions.

Place the candles at opposite ends of your altar.

Light your candles.

Chant, recite, or sing your spell. Repeat at least three times. The last time you speak/recite/sing, move your candles about an inch closer together.

Spend time visualizing your desire moving closer to you. Feel it in your body.

Close your circle.

Snuff out your candles.

Repeat this spell for the next three days. On the third day, move the candles together so that they are touching. Burn them down together. If there is any wax left, or they are in votives, on the last day, tie them together with a string or a ribbon. Bury them or discard them together.

NEW MOON TAROT

This spread welcomes in the *new moon*. Arrange your altar with items that symbolize what you are calling in at this new moon. Light any cleansing herbs to clear the space, cast your circle, light candles, pull out your cards, take out your journal, and get comfortable.

Shuffle your cards, focusing on what you are ready to call into your life at this time. When you are ready, pull your cards and arrange them in front of you, in a pyramid shape, left to right, with cards 1–4 at the base, cards 5–7 in the middle, and card 8 at the top.

Card 1: What in my life is ready to be created during this cycle?

Card 2: How can I call this in effectively?

Card 3: How can this be expressed in a way that is evident to me, in a way I can see?

Card 4: How will this be expressed internally, in a way I can feel?

Card 5: Where must I focus my energy?

Card 6: What activities do I need to focus on more; what actions must I take?

Card 7: What must I let go of, to move forward more gracefully?

Card 8: What will a possible outcome be if I take these conscious steps?

Journal about your cards. What connects? What confuses? Make note. You may wish to meditate on your insights after journaling. What images jumped out at you? If there is a card you must embody more, how can you do so? Can you visualize yourself doing so under the new moon? Write an action plan or a schedule after processing your insights from the spread.

NEW MOON RITUALS

 Rituals can help us sink into the specific energy of each moon phase. Rituals can act as guides and support through transitions. Rituals can be created to offer ourselves what we need. Rituals can help us live more intentionally.

A New Moon Cleansing Bath

The only ingredients needed for this are a place to take a bath, a candle, and a salt scrub of your preference. If you don't have a bathtub, do this in your shower. The other ingredients are only suggestions. Add your own, based on your intuition!

You will need:

- A place to take a bath
- A scrubber/exfoliating sponge of some kind
- Salt/salt scrub blend
- Dried lavender or lavender oil
- Fresh or dried violets or violet oil
- Kunzite
- Clear quartz
- Blue kyanite
- At least one candle

As you run the water for your bath, ground and center yourself in your body. Envision what you want to invoke during this next cycle. Imagine it filling you up with colors, sensations, and images. Imagine the essence of your invocation integrating with the cells in your body. Place the herbs, salt, and crystals in the bath. Light your candle(s). Turn off the lights and slip into the bath.

Relax the body and mind. Call in hope by focusing on the word, or a calming color. Imagine tension, or the past, leaving your body. Begin scrubbing as much of your body as you can, from your toes to your neck. Once you've vigorously sloughed off the dead skin, take some deep breaths. Re-center. Spend as much time as you need evoking your desires and new story in your body.

Imagine the candlelight on the walls as the projector of your own new movie. Try to visualize your dreams and new behaviors coming through the flicker of the flame. Take as long as you need to create some of the scenes in the flame. Stay in the bath until you feel a shift in energy, spirit, body, flame, or all of the above.

Quickly rinse off under the shower. When you rise out of the bath, take this new energy with you into your waking life. Know that you are leaving resistance and unhelpful patterns behind you in the bath that were sucked down the drain.

Take your crystals out of the bath and place them by your bedside, on your altar, or carry them in your pockets as needed.

A New Moon Consciousness Check-in Ritual*

Start this ritual in your bed, or just before bedtime—give yourself at least one half hour, up to about one hour.

You will need:

- A piece of paper
- A pen

On a piece of paper, at the top, write down your intention. Draw a circle that takes up the rest of the space on the page. Draw a line in the middle of the circle horizontally. This circle represents you at this new moon. The top half of the circle represents your consciousness and your intention—your awareness, affirmations, and behavior around this intention. The bottom half of the circle represents your subconscious,

---

* Inspired by Joseph Campbell and Tara Brach

pre-consciousness, and your intuition—what motivates you, your core beliefs, and subconscious reactions.

Now, think about the specific consciousness your intention needs: your attention, affirmations, awareness, and behavior. Write down what emotions, tools, actions, thoughts, beliefs you must consciously focus on in the area above the line.

Think about what new subconscious beliefs and behaviors you'll need to reorient around your intentions. Write down these beliefs, emotions, and any other insights you'll need to prime your subconscious in the area underneath the line.

Pause and take a few deep breaths. Look at your circle. There might be a word or sentence that grabs your attention. Examine why. Make an affirmation around it.

You may wish to prime your dreamtime for more insights around that before you drift off to sleep. Ask your dreams to deliver useful information in the morning.

Leave your drawing out as a reminder for the first week after the new moon, or as long as you need to.

A New Moon Awareness Ritual

Once a day, go someplace you've never been and will most likely never go again (this can also take place in the mind and imagination). Move around for at least thirty minutes in this place you've never been.

Observe your surroundings as if you were a cosmic detective. Notice your noticing.

Practice thinking thoughts you rarely give yourself the opportunity to think—intriguing, beautiful, or loving ones. If a negative thought comes up, immediately change it to a positive or neutral one.

Try to take as long as you need to in the new space, in this new thought exercise.

Repeat this exercise for the three days directly following the new moon. Feel free to go other places. Try this exercise in your home, walking around your block, in your bed.

Record your insights in your journal.

JOURNALING PROMPTS FOR THE NEW MOON

Pick a few of these prompts to consider at the new moon:

What seeds am I planting at this new moon?

Why am I focusing on these seeds?

What is the quality of presence I must commit to, if these seeds are to grow?

What do my dreams feel like?

What are my intentions?

How can I remain curious about and engaged with my intention until the next new moon?

Where am I craving change?

Where am I afraid of change?

What must I clear away?

What are some very small habits or patterns I can change in my everyday thinking?

Who am I becoming?

What new beginnings am I ready to innovate?

The Waxing Moon

Doing the Work, Following Threads

The waxing moon is a period of approximately two weeks that begins just after the new moon and ends just before the full moon. After the reset of the new moon, our satellite begins to climb higher in the sky, little by little each day. As the moon ascends, her light shines brighter. This is half of the entire lunar cycle.

Growth, abundance, following threads, and taking action are all themes of this time period. This is the time to figure out *how* to do *what* you want to do. What are you building in your life? How is this reflected in your behavior, your surroundings? How can the vibrant energy of this time help you share more of yourself, more of your magic, encourage more of your most aligned actions? Bring that forth in your energetic vibration and spell work. Commit to being more in alignment through your everyday habits, thoughts, and behaviors.

In the circle of consciousness, the waxing moon is emblematic of instinct, mindfulness, and awareness—"above the line" consciousness. A deeper level of awareness creates prolonged focus. With prolonged focus comes altered attention. With altered attention comes acceptance and affirmation of choice. The waxing moon will support the positive actions we take in our conscious, waking life. This is the time to examine if and how our words back up our beliefs, if our actions accurately reflect our desires.

The waxing moon is the time of above-the-line consciousness transformation—a period in which we can work on changing our consciousness through will and actions taken. Our subconscious may still try to run the show, but it becomes easier to recognize and redirect. This is the work that occurs minute by minute, by utilizing self-awareness and mindfulness. Recommitment, that hard-won ability to dust ourselves off and try again, helps our progress.

This is also an opportunity to address connections between mind and behavior. Take steps toward consciously healing old wounds. What would a healing process actually consist of for you? Explore some modalities. Behavior-based therapies such as cognitive behavioral therapy, dialectical behavioral therapy, and embodiment practices such as somatics can help.

The waxing moon is the time of Venus: of sensuality and beauty, of enacting our desires physically, and through our various senses. Venus wants us to get serious about pleasure—biting into ripe green grapes dripping over the edges of handmade ceramic plates, wandering around museums and getting fashion inspiration from gold leaf paintings from hundreds of years ago, losing ourselves dancing in a crowd at midnight under hot pink neon lights. She wants us to get serious about how we adorn our life. This energy wants us to build our actions around our values. This time implores us to connect to love, to have awesome sex, to create in accordance with our heart, and to focus on self-care. Venus is about the fruits of our vulnerability. Our fierce devotion to love inspires the endurance of compassion. Venus is about self-respect, and with that self-respect comes boundaries. The waxing moon is a perfect opportunity to get some of both!

The waxing moon also corresponds to the archetype of Mars. Popularly known as the Roman god of war, Mars was originally a deity of Greek agriculture and gardens: the god of growth. As society became less agricultural and more warlike, understandings of Mars morphed to mirror this shift.[1] Now, Mars is generally associated with swift action, physical strength, and aggression. I prefer to interpret the energy of Mars as vitality, and externally focused, decisive action. Combining the different energies of Venus and Mars helps us make bold moves in service of love.

The growth energy will aid the risks you take. After the first quarter, the water rises in the oceans, in the earth, and in us water babies. Make the most of this time and channel your power into long-lasting results. Keep your momentum flowing by splitting those activities across items you can control and items that rely on others.

For example, if your goal is to be a freelance writer, your list would balance writing a certain amount daily alongside pitching your work. Imagine every intentional action as magical—you are pouring offerings of love and devotion into the chalices of your life.

The waxing period of the moon is considered to be favorable for announcing and sharing new work to an audience, and for showing others your evolution in a more public sphere. Introduce that new project to the world, share that selfie, launch that rebranded website, let others know what you want your next vocation to be. Give yourself a different title. Refresh your qualifications. Bring dreams into alignment through action.

PHASES OF THE WAXING MOON

The waxing moon period is comprised of three distinct phases: waxing, first quarter, and gibbous. The all-over feeling of the approximately two-week period of the waxing moon is one of accumulation, up-cycling, and growth, but particular days can feel quite distinct from each other as the lunar cycle progresses. Each sub-phase is characterized by its own set of themes. Some of these will resonate with your experience more than others, depending on where you are in your process and what season you are in—literally and metaphorically. Observe how you feel, day by day, through this entire phase. Your mood and energy may shift subtly or even drastically as the moon moves from "exactly new" to waxing gibbous.

Waxing Crescent Moon

The first few days after the new moon could be a period of regeneration. When the slimmest sliver of the waxing crescent appears in the sky, some people honor this as their new moon. You may be particularly receptive now, so be careful of what you are ingesting—physically and psychically. This time is one of moving forward, holding hands with hope. This is newborn energy: wobbly colt legs finding footing on solid ground. This is the time of the goddess Artemis, the hunter, the brave seeker. The arrow has been pulled back and launched. Where will our aim take us?

First Quarter Moon

About one week after the new moon/crescent moon is the half moon, or first quarter. This phase corresponds to balance. This is a perfect time for integration. If you've started your lunar practice on the new moon and been faithful to your moon map, this could be the point where you are noticing tangible shifts. There could be an adjustment in your mood. Perhaps you can feel your will and motivation expanding. If you have been focused on external results, then they might have become palpable. Invitations abound, opportunities flood into your phone, the check promised in the mail actually arrives. Synchronicities could be plentiful at this time. Pay attention to all the signs that point to a yes.

The first quarter moon is also the moment when we are at a crossroads. A time of tests. If you've started a new habit or practice at the new moon, you have experienced about one week of this experiment. This could be when you drop off or waver. Make the decision to stay the course. Courage, confidence, will, and rededication could all be themes to focus on. Spells, prayers, or affirmations around patience, devotion, and discipline are recommended.

Waxing Gibbous Moon

The waxing gibbous moon is bounty and beauty. Pyrite and citrine and lemon quartz opulence. This noticeably brighter sky mirror is an affirmation moon. It nods yes, absolutely, you can have what you want and you can get what you need. You will have to protect your energy. This will take vulnerability and boundaries and energetic refinement. It requires the terrifying process of opening and unfolding, without the cruel vise of grasping control. The waxing moon declares that abundance is our birthright because we are inherently abundant. Part of the work is detaching from anything or anyone who tries to tell you otherwise.

As the moon's belly blossoms, so might anxieties. Consciousness is on high blast! A pre–full moon wired loop might start brewing in your electrical system, keeping you up at night, making you second-guess your efforts. As you keep going, hurdles could appear in terms of rejections or delays. The only way through is through. Let the uncomfortable impulses enter your system, and ask them to leave. Switch up the way you've been relating to your reactions and break up the pattern. Call in more support if needed.

IF THE WAXING MOON IS HARD FOR YOU

If you were born during a waning moon or a dark moon, a waxing moon could be challenging for you. If you are a more conceptual thinker or spend a lot of time in your head, translating ideas into form could be a struggle. For the incessant dreamer, coming down to earth is a rough ride.

The waxing moon is a time of energetic and emotional accumulation. It amplifies all energy: impatience, irritability, or sorrow included. Find outlets to release or smooth any spikes that show up. The waning moon will serve as a respite; that may be your most productive time.

Waxing moon energy and activities can be challenging for introverts and highly sensitive folks. This is the time of the doers, the movers and shakers, the worker bees, the warriors, the armored knights trotting from the castle's drawbridge into the woods. It's a time of putting yourself out there. Raise your hand first. This is the time to go out and get it, to move forward fiercely, third eye on the prize. To reach for what you previously could not—or would not. That next version of yourself; the one that gives slightly less fucks, and needs slightly more hugs.

As stated, the waxing moon corresponds to abundance, love, health, the material world, beauty, and pleasure. She wants us to unapologetically dig into what we want, go after what we value and what makes our body feel the best it can. If some of these topics are triggering or objectionable for you—no judgment!—then this could be hard to relax into. An exploration of what feels beautiful to you alone is a worthwhile endeavor. We might be met with the harsh truth that we are not meeting our own needs regularly.

For the risk-averse and cautious, the waxing moon could feel challenging. When we take risks, when we try, when we put ourselves out there, there will be detractors. There will be critics and ill wishers and horrible reviews. This exposure can be brutal for sensitive folks, those that struggle with self-esteem, ADHD, and other mental health issues. Folks with a history of being bullied sometimes equate attention of any kind with abuse. Having a strong support system and the resolve to keep trying will help us stay on the path. Really enjoying the work and really understanding the greater vision that the work aspires to reach can help us keep moving past unconstructive criticism.

A waxing moon during autumn or winter could feel jarring; as the moon is blooming, the Northern Hemisphere is in rest mode. Remember to stay rooted in the season and spend extra time homing in on what your body needs. If what is coming up for you under the November night sky is painful, sit with it. Listen to it. Be with it until it floats away, up into the stars to form a constellation that mirrors the lessons you are learning.

When you are in a waxing moon phase, you are growing. Because we can be hard on ourselves, you may be paying more attention to what *isn't* working than all the hard work you *are* doing. The waxing moon is a wonderful time to unpack perfectionist tendencies.

You could be in a waning, dark, or new moon phase in life, so it may not make sense to focus on expansion. You might be grieving, depressed, or transforming in mysterious ways. If so, I suggest utilizing the waxing moon to focus squarely on your physical health—drink more water, add more time to an exercise habit, if your body allows. Transmute emotions through actions such as making art, boxing, banging a drum, singing, screaming, or crying.

If the waxing moon time or the concepts and themes presented around the waxing moon are difficult for you, I encourage you to examine this. What is stopping you from putting yourself out there? Maybe, at the waxing moon, you can write down all that you have accomplished. And yes, "getting out of bed" is most definitely an accomplishment! ("Staying in bed" is also one too!) Start by giving yourself a bit more credit. Make a list of accomplishments, of any sort, that you wish to achieve. Maybe you can start going after them one by one: moon by moon. With trying comes trust, with trust comes confidence, with confidence comes resilience, with resilience comes sovereignty.

WHEN YOU ARE IN A WAXING MOON PHASE

When you are in a waxing moon phase, the horizon widens. You've come so far because at last you've figured out what you want. You've come so far because here and now you are finally taking the steps. The inspirations and ideas glide in steadily. One thread leads to another, and then another; the tapestry takes shape as a gleaming web more intriguing than you could have ever imagined.

This is the time of training, of gaining muscle, of building healthy habits of all sorts. Of figuring out the balance between thoughts and habits, between goals and behaviors. When you are in a waxing moon period, you decide to go the distance. You keep going because quitting is not an option. You understand that the process requires you to sit down at the desk, day after day. Some days it is boring: a minute is an hour, an hour is thirty-seven weeks. Some days your bones are creakier, some days the inspirations or motivations don't show up, but because you know that unfocused time is lost time, you come back to focus.

We push the doors open with our will, with our repetition, with our consistency. We accept that for most of us, repetitive and hard work is our lot in life. Those of us who hold this reality are lucky. Because it is through doing the work—on the tarmac, in the trenches, in the cubicle, in the woods of our unconscious, sometimes with others and sometimes completely alone—that we learn who we are. It is through doing the work and building upon that work that we eventually get somewhere. And ultimately, that somewhere is close to our most realized, most whole self. This can only happen step by step, minute by minute.

The waxing moon is the time to stretch out into your life like a cat in the sun. The time to enthusiastically greet what is starting to steadily sprout, bursting out of the soil of your new moon intention. It is the time to focus your energy, grow through doing the work, follow the threads, and practice everyday magic.

THE WAXING MOON IS THE TIME TO FINE-TUNE YOUR ENERGY

As the light on the moon's face gathers, as we transition from intention to action, we must attend to our energy. We are all transmitters and receivers of vibrational frequencies. Energy moves, it is not static. Our vibration changes through awareness, via reprogramming and repatterning.

Obviously, we are affected by things we can't control—if we are chronically ill, if we are a new parent, if we suffer from insomnia, etc., our energy will be affected and that is no fault of our own. We do what we can to find our own unique energetic imprint, and shift our energy through awareness, rest, mindfulness, and intention. This starts with small, manageable actions. We can meditate, and focus our awareness on things that uplift or engage us. Whenever possible, we can choose to be in alignment with what we need to do and feel in the present moment. That might mean venting or punching a pillow. We might need to take a break, take a bath, or take a hike. Whatever helps restore and nourish our energy. Whatever allows us to access our own energetic mastery.

Like emotions or thoughts, "vibes" aren't good or bad, they just "are"—contracted, interesting, unhelpful, obsessive, joyful, etc. Our energy will form a habit or pattern that more often than not is reactionary or unconscious. When we can be mindful and transform our reactions into intentional responses that stay in alignment with our values, we approach mastery. We can alchemize our energy and shift it from one plane to another. That adjusts the frequency, the tuning, the dial turns the way we'd like. One way to do that is through making art. The work of Frida Kahlo is one example. She took her pain and made it into art. Truly, Kahlo made her entire life into art. Beyoncé's *Lemonade* is another example. She took her personal heartbreak and made an artistic masterpiece that rippled out into waves of meaning and healing far beyond her personal narrative.

Use the waxing time to check that your vibrations, energy, intentions, and magical work are in alignment with your ultimate creation. The energy we cultivate leads us to where we go, where we flow. This becomes a feedback loop where we receive more of what we are emanating. This enhances our day-to-day life in general.

THE WAXING MOON IS A TIME TO DO THE WORK

No number of expensive tools, no amount of the right-colored candles, lit on the right day, surrounded by the rarest, most expensive crystals will make your spell come to fruition if you don't do the work. There is a lot of fear, a lot of anxiety, and a lot of mixed messaging around the topic of work. When I talk about "work," I mean any activity, behavior, action, thought, or effort that helps you achieve a specific purpose or goal. Emotional development, mental development, and magical development all count as "work." (In Hermeticism, the Great Work is a reference to a culmination of the spiritual path: attaining enlightenment or transcendence.)

Work includes some of the following things: living, dying, creating art, being a parent, being a sibling, being a pet owner, healing your nervous system, learning a new technology, collecting a paycheck, solidifying healthy boundaries, gaining confidence, figuring out your life's purpose, dating, modeling vulnerability, ritual, maintaining a meditation practice, activism, drinking enough water, quitting, going to therapy, reading, committing to a very long project with no seeming end in sight, practicing healthy attachments, practicing healthy detachments, taking out the trash, listening, ending the relationship, mending the relationship, making new relationships, applying for grants, digging a garden, cleaning the toilet, becoming who you are, creating feminist futures, and never giving up.

The waxing moon is when to commit to all the work that surrounds your new moon dreams. Doing the work is the not-so-secret secret ingredient to your success. Doing the work is showing up for yourself. Showing up for yourself is one of the most profound gifts we can give ourselves. It is also really tough. In a world that has taught us to rely mostly on outside authorities and systems for permission, resources, and validation, choosing to do the work—to invest in ourselves, to become our best advocate—can feel unnatural or scary. Prioritizing ourselves and what we want can bring up a lot—especially if we were never taught to do it.

People want a shortcut, a proven method, and will ask:

"How did you get that thing?"
"Who did you know?"
"What did you do to make that happen?"

What they should be asking is:

"How long have you been doing this work?"
"What do you enjoy most about your work?"
"What has doing the work taught you?"
"What are the challenges you've faced in your work?"
"How has your work grown or changed over time?"

It is almost always about the work.

The work of summoning devotion, again and again. The work of seducing your inspiration. Of choosing to listen to your inner compass. The work of resistance and protest. The work of service. The work of your work.

At the waxing moon, define what the work is for you right now, especially linked to your new moon intentions. Connect your purpose to larger systems. Refine your goals so they resonate in the realm of deep meaning. Do the work to get back to yourself. Define or redefine success.

At the root of magic, of ritual, of life, is this practice. The true art of living, which is a practice of living for one's self and one's soul. Be clear about what you need to be, what help you must call in, and what your success will look like. Write it down, step by step, and stick to it.

The Work Looks Different for Everyone

Doing The Work is ultimately an investment in yourself. It is an investment in your future. In this way, it is also an investment in the collective.

Don't compare yourself to others. This process is for you and for you alone. It is easy to look around at what others are doing and think that your work has to resemble theirs. Comparison is a fool's errand. You can be inspired by others, yes. The friend that is just really good at living. That person on the Internet you think you know with the easy smile and effortless style. Capture that inspiration, let it flow into your bloodstream, magnetizing you to what you crave. Let your admiration act as fuel. Celebrate those who are doing their own work well.

If you start to take action and you aren't seeing results after one or two weeks, experiment. Try doing the work in a different way. Do it at a different time. Make it easier. Write the ending first. Use another medium. If you feel unsure of what next to do, that's okay. You can always ask yourself: If I knew that what I was doing could not fail, if I knew that the outcomes I dream of were on the way, what would I do in the meantime? Then do those things.

The work will look different for everyone. There is no other place to be but in your own life. Your job is to inhabit your own space fully and comfortably. Your job is to grow in the way you need to grow while remembering to enjoy the process.

Sometimes the Work Is Hard

Sometimes the work will be hard. Especially if we are trying something radically different and completely untested. Putting yourself out there in the face of repeated rejection is no small feat. The waxing moon is the time period between inception and culmination. Every creative knows this part is at times a foggy slog. If you are impatient, cast a patience spell. Remind yourself every morning why you are doing this.

If your desires are overly attached to a specific outcome—fame, fortune, not getting out of bed for less than ten thousand dollars a day—then you *may* wish to reassess your goals. There has to be some part of the actual process you enjoy, some part of the work that brings you joy—or comfort, or solace, or self-deliverance. The Bhagavad Gita teaches us: "You have the right to work, but for the work's sake only. You have no right to the fruits of work. Desire for the fruits of work must never be your motive in working. . . . Work done with anxiety about results is far inferior to work done without such anxiety, in the calm of self-surrender. . . . They who work selfishly for results are miserable."[2]

Though being uncomfortable can be part of doing the work, some ways to gut check if the work is the right work are: you find yourself daydreaming about it; it involves helping others somehow; it requires you to be in competition with absolutely no one other than yourself; it is connected to your intuition; you can't define how it will be worth it, but you feel like there is something glimmering around the bend that you must seek out; it feels so important it is scary; it brings you joy and contentment; it causes you to lose track of time.

Doing the work is an act of faith.

Sometimes the work is hard because we are raising the bar. We are asking great things of ourselves. We have decided to be around other people who are doing their authentic work well. To operate just outside of one's comfort zone is to witness a lot of growth. When we reach just beyond what we think we are capable of, the outcomes are generally astounding.

Sometimes the work is hard because we are choosing to relate to ourselves in more loving ways. Suspending blame, judgment, or punishment. The mind might short-circuit. The old script has been crossed out and erased. The beginning stages of the work of a self-love or recovery practice are raw and disorienting. There's no quick payoff. Remember to hang in there, to keep walking toward that gleaming horizon, step after step.

Sometimes the work is hard because ultimately it is a process of choosing oneself. It can be automatic for us to do things to get love, attention, or feel needed. It is easy to do things that uphold invisible contracts between your family constellation, certain prominent relationships, or certain ideas about what you think you *should* be doing related to a certain identity you hold. This is what many of us were taught: to put others, or basically anything else, before our spark, our joy, our self-investment. At the time of the waxing moon get into the practice of acknowledging that this work is a metaphor for inhabiting your life as fully as you dare.

Cultivating a positive obsession with the work helps. In her essay "Positive Obsession," Octavia Butler writes: "Positive obsession is about not being able to stop just because you're afraid and full of doubts . . . positive obsession [is] a way of aiming yourself, your life, at your chosen target. Decide what you want. Aim high. Go for it."[3]

What is your positive obsession? How will that sustain you through the rough patches? How does your positive obsession bring you closer to your truths?

Sometimes the Work Is Simple

The waxing moon is the time to infuse your new moon intention into your daily actions. This can be simple. If one of your new moon intentions was to slow down, then slow down. Walk more slowly. Do the dishes more slowly. Breathe more slowly.

Sometimes waxing moon work is really basic. Your job, at the waxing moon, is to just stick to your plan. If you miss a day, you just start back over at the beginning. That's it. That's all. Know what your plan is. Schedule it in your calendar, in your phone. Set alarms. Do the thing.

Part of your waxing moon homework must be to honestly examine your everyday habits and create more positive ones. Without judgment, write down all that you do in a day. Your morning routines, your daily habits: when you eat and where you go and what you watch and who you speak with and what your defenses are; how you deal with stress and what you think about before you go to bed. What habits are useful? Which habits must be replaced with more supportive ones?

Picking healthier and more aligned habits that support your intention and putting sustained focus on them is the next step to take after casting a spell. The more you spend your time and energy focusing on restorative and supportive habits, the less time you have to engage in destructive or unhelpful habits. This is a beautiful equation.

Your new habits could also be tiny magical prayers and offerings. Add small rituals into your day to make transitions smoother. Between tasks, perhaps you pause, call back your energy, reset your baseline energy. Say *please* and *thank you* frequently to the doors you walk through. Actions become more intentional by placing awareness and emphasis on the energy behind them.

THE WAXING MOON IS THE TIME TO FOLLOW THE THREADS

The waxing moon is the time where we are called to bring our dreams into form. Into something we can rub up against, quantify, or tangibly feel. Our own internal moon can be a resource. We can use the time of the waxing phase to notice what comes up for us—internally and externally—and find ways for our blocks to become our allies. The messages become a guide, offer us solutions, to help reframe our blocks and work with our fears.

There are spools of thread unfurling for us every day. They lead us from one point to another. These are internal and external. Internally, we connect to impulses that stem from our knowing. Our intuition acts as guidance that we can follow. This leads to external change.

For example, say one of your goals is to walk or exercise or move your body more. What are your blocks? Do you not have any time? Well, then that's your job: to make twenty minutes a day for yourself. Is the hardest part putting on leggings and shoes first thing in the morning? Sleep in your leggings and have your shoes and socks right by the door. It sounds really basic, but these are the kinds of basic things that stop us.

You can go deeper as well. Let's pretend your issue is procrastination. Follow the thread. Underneath the procrastination is perfectionism. Underneath the perfectionism is the feeling you'll never be good enough. So impossible standards are set, so that meeting them can never happen, which reinforces your belief you'll never be good enough, which reinforces the procrastination. And there you are, in an unspooled thread—feeling so separate from yourself, so far away from your goal. In actuality, you are so close to plugging back into self, if only you'd redirect the energy.

Noticing coupled with surrender equals acceptance. When we add a bit of compassion to this acceptance, we give ourselves space. Room to move. Acceptance is fertile ground to start from, because we are acknowledging what is—we are acknowledging reality. This is a freeing practice. Go underneath the first layer of resistance to connect to a place you can work with.

Another way to follow threads is through dialoging with mystery. Ask for help and expect to receive it. Ask for answers, for signs, for ease. Open up, stay in the believing place, and watch tendrils of new pathways and other threads of opportunity reach out to you. Step forward to meet these threads, follow them through the forest.

One way they will come is in the form of synchronicity. That is the simultaneous occurrence of events in a specific period of time that are somehow significantly related. Synchronicities can act as an affirmation, can offer us clues and answers and help us follow the threads on our path.

Synchronicities are one step beyond coincidence—they have an extra rare, magical, or fated feeling to them. Running into your neighbor at the corner store is a coincidence. A large number of coincidences—many of them uncanny or related to something specific brewing inside of you—in a short period of time equals synchronicity.

Decide to manufacture synchronicities. Make your life a synchronicity temple. Ask the universe to deliver you support or open doors in some way. Be available for them to come through in all areas of your life. One of their hallmarks is the feeling of flow. Keep them available by following through on what it is they require of you. Practice by creating smaller synchronicities in your life: train yourself to look for options, not limits.

Other ways I trust in synchronicities is if an out-of-the-ordinary occurrence or step forward is immediately met with ease or flow, or if timing- or scheduling-wise, an opportunity lines up. A friend invites in luck and opportunity by scheduling open times in her week, or even the month or year ahead. Those times are intentionally open for the unknowable blessings en route to her. When there is intentional space open for exciting opportunities to flow in, they will.

The waxing moon is a good time to notice what is already in your life that wishes to share insights with you. Look out for physical objects, talismans, or symbols that want to talk to you, or that indicate a message from the universe, or at the very least, from your subconscious. These can show up as physical symbols of psychic affirmations. My partner always sees hawks everywhere. They are his animal guide, his reminder to expand his view and perspective. A penny on the ground by my feet is a symbol that I'm on the path. The waxing moon could be a perfect time to create your bank of meaningful symbols, or be more aware of the ones you already have.

Try weaving different threads together. Are you interested in two or three different things? Maybe they aren't meant to be kept separate. Authentic collaboration facilitates an exponential deepening of power. Do you like gardening and poetry? Write poetry from the perspective of a peony. If one of the threads you are following is trust and the other is reigniting your creativity, form a monthly creativity group.

A centering practice that helps me stay aware of different threads and synchronicities is a morning practice of pulling tarot cards, meditating, and journaling. This can be added to your everyday lunar tracking. Tarot is an incredible reminder of magic, as it so often eerily mirrors exactly what is going on at some level of your psyche. If tarot isn't your thing, maybe it is journaling, drawing, singing, cooking, a movement or exercise practice, or meditation. Whatever connects you with *you*.

Following threads requires listening and trusting your intuition. It also requires taking action that might not appear logical on the surface. Leaving a "dream job" to go back to school. Breaking up with a nice partner whom everyone thought was the "one," but wasn't the right fit. These choices are painful in the moment, but end up being worth it. Equal parts patience and courage are required. This time may coincide with the strong message that you must make a difficult yet correct choice in order to move forward with the life you need to live. Remember that there is help available to you in the form of your community, your guides, and your intuition.

THE WAXING MOON IS THE TIME TO CONSIDER ABUNDANCE

Before the advent of electricity and industrialized farming, the waxing moon and its increasing light enabled farmers to be able to spend more time harvesting. Folks were able to work later, resulting in more productivity and in more abundance. Cultivating a mindset of abundance is some of the most important work we can do.

So much of what dominant culture prizes is based on numbers and material objects. Yet we can enjoy so much of our lives with much less than we think we need. A definition of wealth as only "money inherited or earned through doing jobs" is limited. Wealth, prosperity, abundance, and being resourced are all states of mind. Redefine what that looks like for you. Include time, inspiration, health, interesting experiences, a positive mindset, a calm and loving heart, community, connection, laughter, critical thinking, the cultivation of natural talents, a gentle breeze against your skin, authentic communication, deep listening, creativity, curiosity, altruism, snuggles, nature, and many other things that lie outside the scope of what money can buy. Spend time each week prioritizing qualities and activities that center your abundance.

If you have difficulty around the term *abundance*, or if it is hard for you to connect to a feeling of abundance, begin with all you have. Identify as many resources as you already possess. Your list could include:

- The languages you speak
- The skill sets you possess
- Your many talents
- The specific strong relationships you have to others
- What you've lived through and survived and learned from
- What brings you joy
- Interesting experiences and adventures you've had
- Your education (academic, trade, self-taught, or school of hard knocks)
- Skills and knowledge that have been passed down to you by your ancestors
- Certain practices you hold dear
- The food in your kitchen, the comfortable clothes in your closet, the roof over your head

Focus on all you have to connect to the energy of abundance.

The artist Jennifer Moon writes that the only true abundance is that which flows out for others to benefit from. True abundance is to be shared. Otherwise it is hoarding, which perpetuates scarcity.[4] Cultivating an abundance mindset is anti-capitalist. Capitalism wants us scared and complacent, perpetuating exploitation, competition, and transactional relationships. Capitalism wants us reliant and dependent on money as our most important or sole resource. Being in an abundance mindset allows us to authentically help others. Operating from a place of abundance means there are endless ways to participate in a life worth living.

When we are resonating with abundance, we let things go easily. Folks who can't authentically support us are free to go. Scenarios that don't work out, because it was not exactly what we needed, do not activate stress or self-blame. There will always be other opportunities better suited to our best interests. Grasping doesn't work, so we try not to do it. Enough is enough. *We* are enough.

For those of us who were told we were "too much," abundance work is vital. Intuitives, empaths, sensitive and creative folks, femmes, queer folks, peacocks, sissies, gender deviants, visionaries, women who know what they want, and others who have been marginalized and dismissed by the overculture as being "high maintenance," all benefit from an abundance embodiment practice. This allows us to feel comfortable in our uniqueness, ultimately raises our self-esteem, and supports our various creative expressions.

Utilize balancing actions to reconnect with a generative source. If you feel lonely, reach out to someone else who may be experiencing isolation. If you feel broke, name all that you have, and then give something away. If someone is cruel to you, be kinder to yourself, and then be kind to others. Actions like these remind us we have the ability to shape and change our world from a place of abundance.

During the waxing moon, use your resources to step resolutely into abundance around your goals. Resources could be a surplus of ingenuity, community, and emotional support. Right now, it could mean knowing where everything is on your desktop, in your room, and in your apartment. It could mean knowing where you stand with your most important relationships (including the one with yourself). It could mean getting clear on your core value systems: the mission statements that deliver you to wider vantage points. Abundance could mean having the privilege to live in accordance with these ideas every day.

Our culture generally equates abundance with *more*, when for many of us abundance is defined as *less*. Less distraction, less clutter, less complication, less obligation, less stress, fewer time sucks, fewer false friendships. Abundance could mean simplicity. Scaling back. Doing less so you can focus on what is most important.

To invoke abundance is to give ourselves more love and care. Affirming that we are worthwhile and have infinite value right now, exactly as we are, regardless of external circumstances, invokes abundance. Prioritizing joy, eroticism, calm, security, and sensuality in our day-to-day lives—in the little moments; in the hours you feel dismal or dragged down by the world—could be part of your waxing moon practice.

How much abundance we are ready to welcome, however, can be hampered by our "receiving capacity." If we get honest with ourselves, we could find that we do not believe that we deserve respectful treatment, intimacy, or a certain amount of money. If this is the case, work to widen your containers of receptivity. Practicing this during the waxing moon, around our new moon intentions, is useful when there is some sort of expansion we crave. This practice helps us reprogram and relaxes us into more abundance allowance.

 Sit quietly and close your eyes. Think about how much love you want to let into your life, or how much more money you'd like to make, or how much calmer you'd regularly like to be, etc. Think of a scenario, an emotion, or a number that correlates to that particular wish. Note what happens in your body or mind as soon as that scenario/emotion/number fully materializes in your consciousness. If some tightness or anxiety comes up, breathe. You might need to slowly ease into the scenario/emotion/number, bit by bit, until it vibrantly resonates and feels effortless to accept somatically. Connect your consciousness to that amount: affirm that your desire is already available and on its way. Practice saying: "I am currently in alignment with my capacity to receive _____."

Meditate on what it feels like to have enough. To give enough. To receive enough. To generate enough. To be enough. Then take that energy and apply it to your desires and actions.

WAXING MOON MAGIC IS IN THE EVERYDAY

The waxing moon is an opportune time for everyday, practical magic. Magical ceremonies do not have to be long and complicated in order to work. Our craft need not be sweepingly dramatic, overloaded with expensive hand-carved athames, silver chalices, and hard-to-source materials. Small spells repeated throughout the day are at the heart of some of the most effective magic. That said, in some magical communities there does exist a bit of a stigma against practical magic (magic based around a specific material outcome or other external outcome). That is because, traditionally, this type of magic (i.e., non-ceremonial magic) was practiced by working-class witches or folk magicians: people just trying to survive in a world where the odds were stacked against them. I'm a huge fan of working practical magic, every day, if needed, because I know firsthand that when you are broke or have limited resources, that getting resources or becoming financially stable is often the most pressing matter at hand. The practice of casting small spells and utilizing everyday magic is amazing for the short term and the long term. This practice raises and boosts our energy, keeps us focused and in our magical container, affirms our mindset, and keeps our actions aligned and flowing. The fact that it is cost-effective—we are working with what we already have—is appealing as well. Everyday magic materials include our voice, our thoughts, paper, pens, spell lists, water, clothes, tea lights, playlists, and other items we may encounter in our travels. A smooth pebble that lands at your feet in a walk by the park, a dandelion growing out of the sidewalk concrete: these are absolutely very magical materials.

During the countdown to the full moon, we can think about how we honor our intentions with our actions: from our morning routines, to the words we frequently use, to larger goals like changing careers, to activating the collective, to creating a body of work that will live on long past your brief and brilliant lifetime. Think about what small or not-so-small actions you can take. I call actions that are taken specifically to support one's magical intentions *symbolic actions*. These are actions that are charged specifically with the energy of your goal. This reminds you of the spell that is your life. Magic isn't outside of you, it originates within. At the waxing moon time, make a list of symbolic actions you will be doing, and be sure to do them every day.

Make magic every day. Greet the day with thanks before your feet hit the ground. Enchant your morning coffee or Earl Grey tea. As you spoon honey into it, bless it. Acknowledge all the sweetness and sustenance in your life.

Make magic every day. Imagine the water from the showerhead washing away anything unwanted. Draw a pentacle, draw an affirmative word on your steamy bathroom mirror. Stare at it until it pulsates or glows, an activated emblem of your will.

Make magic every day. Slip an item that symbolizes protection into your back pocket. Ground and protect your energy before you leave your home. Spend a minute moving your breath up and down your body, from your head to your feet. Promise to put your goals first, before giving away all your time to others' requests.

Words can be spells; use them wisely. Carefully craft your letters. Your language.

What you tell yourself on the daily. The messages that roll about in your mind, the missives that leave your mouth and enter the outside world. Your computer passwords, your email address, the lyrics you listen to, the texts you send: may they embody your intent for the present and the future. May they describe how you wish to be described by others. Set a one-word intention for your day and speak it out loud.

Practice loving yourself. Rest rose quartz against your closed eyelids. Find ways to enjoy simple pleasures more: rainbows of flickering light on your wall, the fleeting drama of a sunset. Affirm your power to change your surroundings, your choices, your journey, at any time. Give yourself what you need most: a dance party, a teacup full of strawberries, an afternoon in the park with a book.

At the end of the day, take time to uncord from any stress or turbulence that transpired. As you unwind, summon in peaceful dreamtime slumber. Dim the lights and light two candles, one for you and one for spirit. Thank your body, your ancestors, your angels, your supporters, for another day as you slip into bed.

Little Activities and Rituals to Try During a Waxing Moon Time

Force yourself to go out to one place you've never been before and have one conversation with one person you do not know. Consider the energy you bring to a space. Your bed is a space. The Internet is a space. At different times during the day, call your energy back to you. Start a savings account. Pick something you've really wanted to get into the habit of doing. Do it. Then repeat every day. If you've started some better habits at the new moon, add on more. Charm: your room, the water your drink, the encounters you have, yourself. Prioritize *being* more charming, especially to yourself. Add vitamins or herbal infusions to your daily routine. Focus on your health. Weave eroticism into moments big and small. Have more sex: with others or yourself. Consciously take an inventory of all you behold that is beautiful to you. Ask for a raise, or raise your rates. Say *no thank you* to offers that are not completely right. Reach out to one or more people you look up to and ask them out to dinner. Start work an hour earlier or stay an hour later: putting the focus on what you love. Bring more of your actions into alignment with what you value.

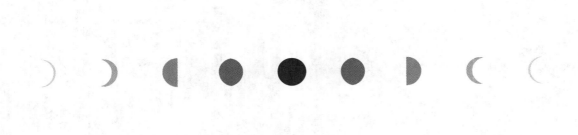

Waxing Moon Magic

Abundance, expansion, and external outcomes are the focus of waxing moon magic. Protection spells, love spells, money spells, fertility spells, beauty spells, creativity spells, abundance workings, health spells, acknowledgment, fame, promotion, and recognition spells are all supported at a waxing moon. Blockbuster spells are perfect here. Victory, success, and overcoming-obstacles spells are all great to do during the waxing moon. This is the time to cast spells for getting things done. And this, of course, is the time to get the things done.

Sex magic, sympathetic magic, creative magic such as making art, charms, talismans are especially supported here. Repetitive spell work—where you repeat the same spell over a period of time, or do a spell that takes place over a period of days—is especially supported by the growing energy of the waxing moon.

CREATING YOUR WAXING MOON ALTAR

A waxing moon altar could be up for a few days or the full two weeks until the full moon. It could be up until the next waxing moon—though I've never done that, I've known others who practice differently than myself who leave their altars up for one entire lunation.

A waxing moon altar could have important symbolic objects on it that correspond to your waxing moon actions and focus. Your altar could be an interpretation of your waxing moon energy. It could also serve as a reminder of what you are working on. Create visual representations of where you wish to grow. Personally, I like to keep my waxing moon altar overflowing with symbolic objects, offerings, and asks.

Your waxing moon altar could be a ceramic pot you paint in a meaningful pattern and put next to your workspace. Your waxing moon altar could be you, saying what you want to do, then doing it, no matter how many butterfly nerves are fluttering in your belly. Always remember—your altar is you, and that can change! Your altar is the devotion you keep and the wonder you conspire to create. It is the work you put out into the world. It is how you treat yourself and how you decorate your own precious vessel.

Magical Correspondences of the Waxing Moon

Following are some suggested waxing moon correspondences. It is important to develop your personal set of correspondences depending on your own interpretations. Leave what does not resonate and add your own.

Pyrite, citrine, brown tigereye, blue tigereye, carnelian, pink moonstone, honey calcite, lemon quartz, malachite, green opal, jaspers—such as Picasso jasper and crocodile jasper—just opened flower buds, horns and hooves, pink, red, green, yellow, orange, brown, nettle, bee pollen, rosemary, yarrow, ginger, rhodiola root, ashwagandha, bamboo, earth/the direction north, pebbles, bark, honey, any blooming flowers that are almost ripe, the Empress, the Lovers, the Knights in the tarot, and any personal special objects you wish to work with or charge under the growing light of the moon.

Goddesses that correspond to the waxing moon: Venus, Zirna, Hathor, Bridgid, Yemanja.

Archetypes that correspond to the waxing moon: the work and lives of Frida Kahlo, Beyoncé, Mary Oliver, Kate Bornstein, Marie Laveau, Kerry James Marshall, Ana Mendieta.

Animal guides that correspond to the waxing moon: leopards, horses, mountain goats, bunnies, ants, bees.

Simple Money Magic Humanifestation Spell

You will need:

- A white pen and a red pen
- A green or gold candle that is not in a votive (you will need to carve the candle)
- An athame, pin, nail, or other sharp utensil
- Money—especially money that correlates to the amount you'd like to be making: for example, eight dollar bills for eighty thousand dollars, etc. (coins will work as well)
- Crystals that connote abundance and prosperity to you such as pyrite, malachite, crocodile jasper
- Herbs that connote prosperity such as basil, frankincense, bay leaves, cinnamon

Spell set-up:

Set your altar up so your spell ingredients surround your candle.

Think about what you want to create or call in more of. Get specific and pick one thing. If this is a dollar amount, be specific. Pro tip: It is better to wish for an amount that you want to make for an entire year (or a stable income for the next few years total) rather than to do stopgap spells for money (such as "I need to make rent"), because then, every few months, you might find yourself having to do another "make rent" spell. Also, being open to money coming in through all possible healthy ways that are for the good of all is a tactic to try. Similarly, wishing for vibrant long-term health or helpful health practitioners for the next few years makes more sense then casting a spell to end a flu. Be careful with spell phrasing; be specific.

Write down your desire and add "this or better."

Casting the spell:

Cast your circle, and initiate any specific actions that you usually do to ground your spell and raise your power.

Carve and dress your candle with your intended desire. There are three suggested ways to do so: 1) make it very simple, with the dollar amount, or one or two words that express the desire; 2) get creative and carve a symbol of that desire; or 3) make your own sigil.

Light the candle.

Chant your spell, or read aloud your desire, three times. Then put the paper into the flame.

Put the money into your hands to charge with your energetic intent.

Visualize your intended outcome, or summon the energy or feelings your intended outcome would have in your body, as you hold the coins. Draw the symbol, word, or sigils that you made on your candle on the money, if they are bills.

Burn the candle for at least three days when you are home. (Never leave a burning candle unattended.)

After the candle has burned down, dismantle your altar. Spend or give away the money that you used in your spell in a way that is meaningful to you. Commit to doing any and all work required of you to expand and receive more prosperity.

Energy Spell

This is a spell to help boost your energy and support momentum and motivations around desired actions.

Suggested tools:

- Paper
- Red pen
- Red string
- Candle (preferably red, yellow, orange)
- Bay leaf
- Crystals that symbolize energy and movement, such as carnelian, citrine, bloodstone, silver, copper, fluorite, or clear quartz
- You may also want to pick out a soundtrack for your spell, to also listen to later, full of pick-me-ups and invigorating jams.

Before you begin, think about what you've truly been wanting to do, and what you've been putting off. This is a spell to jump-start those impulses and bring them out into the world. This is a spell as much for courage and energy activation as it is for anything else.

Cleanse: Either take a shower, wash your face and hands, light your dried plant matter bundle and pass it up and down your body and energy field, or take a salt bath.

Set up your altar by placing your chosen spell ingredients in a placement that symbolizes the support, energy, or motivation you need. For example, maybe you need discipline and consistency: you may wish to place your items in a square shape on your altar. Maybe you need more freedom: you might put them in a playful pattern with space around each ingredient. Do what feels good.

Cast your circle.

Light your candle and focus on the flame. Hold your hands around the light, and imagine the light from the candle going into your hands and moving all around your energetic field. Connect to the feeling of the flickering flame and bring this energy into your heart, into your third eye, into your hands, and all around your body.

Write down what it is that you will be moving forward on. Put the bay leaf on your paper and fold the paper around it.

Place one of your crystals on the bay leaf.

Wrap the string around it all while chanting or singing your wishes.

Move your body around in some way to move the energy around. Cheer, stomp, or dance—whatever gets your blood pumping.

Affirm that you will begin taking the next steps forward in the physical realm during this waxing moon period, if not sooner. Know that this or something better will be making its way to you once you start moving forward.

Place the talisman you just made (the paper, crystal, bay leaf) next to your candle. If you have other items on your altar, place them around the talisman to charge them. When your candle burns down, take the talisman off your altar and carry it around with you to remind you of what you need to do.

Waxing Moon Tarot Pull: Staying Centered

This is a simple choose-your-own-adventure five-card pull to keep you centered in your work and movement during the waxing moon.

Card 1: Go through your deck and pick a card that corresponds to what you are working on at this time. This card must mirror the finished state of the goal and how you want to feel as you do the work.

Relax your body and take some deep breaths. Focus on your desire as you shuffle the tarot deck. Every person has their own shuffling ritual: you may wish to shuffle between each card pull, or shuffle and then pull the cards in succession.

You will be creating a square with the other four cards; moving clockwise:

Begin by placing card 2 at the top left of the original card: this is the next step or action to take in service of your goals.

Place card 3 to the top right of the original card: this is a block, shadow, or challenge that is coming up or will come up as you move forward.

Place card 4 to the bottom right of the original card: this is how you can address or work with this challenge. (Take specific note of this; if this is a challenge that is a theme in your life, and if this rings true! Taking action could also help break other long-held patterns.)

Place card 5 to the bottom left of the original card: this is what will transform or heal for you after doing the work.

You can choose a tarot card from this spread to engage with as a patron archetype, to keep you focused and moving forward. Keep it as a screensaver on your phone, draw it, write down what advice it would give you.

Waxing Moon Charms

From around the waxing crescent to the first quarter is an excellent time to create a magical charm. A charm is a magical spell or object that is infused with luck or intention. Across the globe humans have utilized these symbols: the Venus of Willendorf, thought by some to be a fertility amulet; the Eye of Horus, or all-seeing eye, an Egyptian amulet for protection, power, and health; the Hamsa, a Jewish symbol of luck, good fortune, health, and protection. You may wish to make a charm out of items from your particular culture's symbology or herstory.

Charms act as tangible, portable reminders of our current intention. Make a charm or talisman for protection: you might sew a dark-colored pouch and fill it with black tourmaline, yarrow, and rosemary, a small shield, and a handwritten poem about safety. A love charm could utilize rose petals or rosewater, rose quartz, violets, and a love letter you've written to yourself.

Some witches cast a circle, ground, and charge their charm with the elements: pass it through a candle flame, to charge it with fire, breathe on it to charge with air, sprinkle water on it, or salt for earth (or touch it to your pentacle, if you have one). You can visualize your intentions with the charm in your hands, and then ground it to the earth. You can put the charm on your altar until a lit candle burns down, then wear it or put it in your pocket as you go about your day. You can utilize the charm indefinitely, or until you feel as though it's done its job, then make an offering of it as thanks.

If you are not a super-crafty witch, there are easier ways to make charms than creating your own. Simply buy or use an item that symbolizes what you need: maybe it is a horseshoe for luck or a shield for protection. Hold the item in your hands and focus. Sing a song to the item or chant a spell. Picture your desired energy flowing out of your hands and into the item, infusing it and circling it with your magic. Put the item in a space where you can see it, where it reminds you of its purpose.

A Neutralizing Waxing Moon "Bless It" Meditation

This can be done seated or lying down, as long as you are in a comfortable position. After you've gotten comfortable with this exercise, you might want to do this while walking or standing.

Take a few measured breaths in and out. Slow your breath and balance it so that your inhalation takes as much time as your exhalation. When you inhale, fill your lungs with air as much as possible, pushing your belly out. When you exhale, exhale all the way down to the bottom of your breath.

Now, imagine your exhalation expelling unwanted energy into the earth, releasing it so that it goes down into the layers of the earth—deep into the center's molten core—becoming transmuted into a different, helpful form. Perhaps this energy is in the form of a color. Perhaps this energy can be described, has a tangible, sticky, or tarry quality. Perhaps you have to consciously detach from this energy in order to let it go. After a few rounds of release, do an energy check-in. Do you feel different? More spacious? Does more need to be released? Stay in nervous system regulation mode for as long as you need to.

When you feel ready, re-center by bringing your awareness back to your body in this present moment. On your inhalation, imagine the life-giving, resourceful energy of the earth coming up and rejuvenating you through the soles of your feet, grounding and supporting you, giving your cells sustenance. Let this energy go all the way into your body, your lungs, into the crown of your head. The energy cascades through your arms and hands.

With your inhalation, bless a helpful situation. "Bless this apartment," "Bless my cat," "Bless my health," "Bless this breath," etc. Say it out loud if you can.

With your exhalation, bless a stressor. "Bless this bill," "Bless this layoff," "Bless this fear," etc.

With your inhalation, respond to the stressors with a solution or affirmation. "Bless my resourcefulness," "Bless my ability to ask for help," "Bless my savings," etc.

Do this for as long as it takes for you to get out all the blessings on your current situation. Take a few more breaths. Maybe you want to make a few loud sighs or yells, shake your body out, or release in another way to close the exercise.

Journaling Prompts for the Waxing Moon

Pick some of these prompts to consider and write about at the waxing moon.

How am I translating my new moon intentions into waxing moon actions?

What is my work at this time?

What do I have resistance around? Why?

How can I work with or through this resistance?

What threads are coming up for me?

How do I follow those threads?

What synchronicities are occurring right now? What do they symbolize?

Do I need to manufacture some synchronicities? How will I do so?

How would I describe my energy?

Where do I need to get my energy in alignment?

How will I do that?

Where do I need to level-up?

What does abundance look like for me?

How can I operate from a place of abundance more?

How can I take up more space in my own life?

The Full Moon

The Alchemy of Consciousness

A full moon occurs when the earth is located directly between the sun and the moon. At a full moon, the elliptical longitudes of the sun and moon are 180 degrees apart. This is the only time of the lunar cycle that these two celestial bodies are completely opposite each other. Due to the positions of the moon and earth, we can see all of the reflected light of the sun on the moon's surface, making her our collective lantern, our glowing crystal ball in the sky.

The full moon rises in the east at sunset, and sets at sunrise in the west. Depending on the weather, we can see her above our heads all night long. If our lunar cycle observance began at the new moon, then the full moon is the third of the primary moon phases. It is the halfway mark of an entire lunar cycle. This time marks a potent point on our moon map. We recognize what we now know, what we've learned, and name everywhere we have traversed since the new moon. The full moon lights our path to the embodiment of all we are becoming.

Before electricity, nighttime was a dark and treacherous place. Evening was synonymous with danger and the unknown. The moon was a light bulb in the sky before streetlights existed. Full moons made connection easier. Your lover could look into your sparkling eyes and adore you. Traditionally, the full moon was a time for witches to gather. Sabbats, the religious and spiritual gatherings of witchcraft, were scheduled around full moons. The word *sabbat* comes from the Hebrew *shabbat*, which means "cessation" or "rest." In Judaism, Shabbat is a weekly holy day observed from sundown to sundown at the end of every week. As Judaism follows a lunar calendar, many of its major holidays coincide with the full moon. Many Indigenous and pagan traditions also mark their rituals and holidays with this lunar phase. Folks could gather, could feast and commune safely, could get home safely. This time became an auspicious one. The cauldron—a means to nourish, a container of magical concoctions, a site of alchemy—is a metaphor for the full moon.

Full moons also made it possible for people to stay up later to do agricultural work like harvesting. Traditionally, herbalists made medicine at this time. During the full moon, people knew they would be fed, knew their loved ones would be taken care of. It is still a time when farmers sow seeds. Depending on the time of year, this is also when gardeners divide cuttings and propagate more plants, as the water in the soil is closer to the surface.

The tides are highest at this time. The water inside of us is heightened, making its way to *our* surface. Folklore has it that we bleed more during a full moon. During a full moon, our water, our emotions are moved around, brought up; we are forced to reckon with them. This can be unsettling. Emotions are powerful—they control elections, cause people to sail across oceans, lead civil rights movements, write operas, and create new life. When we don't know which way our waves will crash, or how to ride our waves, we experience emotional uncertainty and instability, which leads to fear.

The heightened emotions we may experience during this phase led to a belief in being "moonstruck" during the full moon—overcome with emotion and lust, overtaken by heated reactions that the full moon supposedly triggers. But the moon does not create anything that isn't already there. She is only underscoring that which needs an outlet. Her reflection is simply showing us the aspects of ourselves that need attention and tending to.

When we are in touch with our emotions, our needs become known. When we can work *with* our emotions, when we can emotionalize our thoughts, and when we program our emotions to help us heal, evolve, and move toward our desires, we become profound vehicles of alchemy.

The full moon is the stuff of legend: human beings morph into werewolves, witches cackle around cauldrons, and people turn into lunatics. The lunatic stigma could have origins in the Church wanting to turn people away from lunar worship: one of the names of a Roman moon goddess was Luna. Her followers were condemned by the Church as "mad."[1]

A lot of the fear around the full moon can be attributed to old-fashioned misogyny. The full moon has long been associated with the feminine, with feminine sexuality, with menstrual blood, with the untamed, the uncontrollable, the wild. The feminine has long been associated with the internal and all that resides in the realm of the emotional, the intuitive, the intangible.

The full moon is where our subconscious and consciousness meet. Our desires and fears commingle. It is a site of alchemy. It is an opportunity. The "everything all at once" feeling that the full moon heightens for us is not a gift to be wasted. We receive revelations and illuminations. We are shown *what* we must next process *in* our own particular process. The more we experience it as a gateway into our body, as a decoder of emotions, as a rope leading us down into the tunnels of our subconscious, the more we can access its powers as a guide. Our transformation becomes tangible under the portal of the full moon.

FULL MOON TIMING

The moon is technically in her "full" phase for a few seconds. To the human eye, the full moon appears "full" for about four days. That's because it takes about four days for the moon to move from 95 percent illuminated to full to 95 percent illuminated on the other—waning—side.[2]

The moon is in one astrological sign, on average, for about two days. If you are working with the astrology of the full moon to harness the particular energy of "a full moon in Aries," then you have about two days to create your ritual and cast your spell. A good rule of thumb is to observe the full moon within three days of its occurrence. If you are very sensitive to full moon psychic downloads or heightened messages, it might make sense to cast your spell or create your ritual a day or two after the full moon, once you've received more guidance. The way to decide when and how to work with *your* full moon is a similar process to figuring out the nuances of your new moon experience. Check in with how you feel physically, energetically, emotionally, and intuitively. This is your practice, and you get to create it in a way that resonates personally.

Full moon timing is one thing; full moon feelings are another. The Full Moon Feels may start coming up as early as a week before the actual full moon. Fitful sleep, insomnia, feeling wired, anxious, or overwhelmingly emotional are all effects of an almost full or full moon.

The full moon, along with the new moon and dark moon, is one of the moon phases that has an all caps lock, exclamation mark of intensity around them. The full moon reminds us that everything eventually comes back around again. If we can, we deal; we are here, now. If we are too overwhelmed, too harried, too distracted to look up at her and receive her messages, we have another opportunity the next night, or at the next full moon. If we pay attention, are mindful, we become more available to ourselves and those around us.

WHEN A FULL MOON IS HARD FOR YOU

The full moon phase is downright uncomfortable for so many. It is challenging to be exposed: all the squirmy secrets and your seeming worst parts projected on the big screen of your life. The full moon can reopen very private wounds. This can feel like shining a cruel flashlight on the exact place you wish to keep hidden. If this happens, try to sit with whatever emotions come up. Be with the hurt, give it some space. Give the inner child, or your shadow, the support and validation it needs.

Under the intensity of a full moon, we can no longer ignore the tension between what we need and what we want. Or what we have and what we actually need. These contrasts can feel unbearable. Ambivalence can be a friend, actually, because in between the worlds of heart and logic, dreams and action, present and future are vital spaces to explore. Time spent blending those lines instead of compartmentalizing them can transform patterns.

The full moon might also be a rough time for you if it is challenging for you to name and ask for your needs and desires to be met. Vulnerability is not for the faint of heart. This time of downloads and messages can also be rough for sensitive folks who do not practice energetic clearing regularly or could use some stronger boundaries.

Then there are the physiological effects. For many folks, the full moon is a time of little to no sleep. If the glaring full moon is keeping you up at night, work with what is coming through. Journal the downloads you receive in the middle of the night.

Pay attention to what familiar patterns lie underneath the wired inner chatter. If you know that you generally do not get a lot of quality sleep around this time, proceed accordingly. Do not overschedule. Preplan meals, chores, hard decisions, hard conversations. Be your own best friend.

The full moon falls directly in the middle of the lunar cycle. Middles are hard. The spark of the unknown and fresh experiences keep us engaged at the beginning of something. Everyone loves a sexy new moon! Once we get going, though, issues arise. Problems pop up that need to be solved. There are more reasons to quit than to keep going. At the full moon, we've been through the waxing moon phase. There's been mountain climbing and tears and sweat. We might be a bit bruised or banged up; we might have encountered the embarrassment of things not panning out the way we had thought. Maybe we've quit and are dealing with the shame around that. Or, we *have* put in all the work: lived through the late nights, survived the difficult conversations, put in the spiritual and physical effort, and by the time the full moon comes, we are totally wiped out.

There can also be a pressure to perform ritual or spell work under a full moon, as if it were the only chance available to spark big magic. It is not. The point of a successful spell is to be present, to be able to shift energy, to transform, and to even have some fun. If you are unable to do those things, that is your reality. Don't beat yourself up. Maybe an overwhelmed full moon means a movie in bed, or pulling a couple of tarot cards and journaling. Maybe you give yourself ten minutes to stand outside, gaze at the moon, and allow gratitude to shine down on your beautiful body. Working with the cycle holistically means making magic through the entire spiral of it—not only on a new or full moon. As we collaborate with the energy of the moon through each phase, we are connected to the whole cycle, full moon included.

WHEN YOU ARE IN A FULL MOON PHASE

When you are in a full moon phase, you are all the way turned up. You are overflowing at the edges of self, and it feels so, so good. There you are, precious earth angel, feeling alive, feeling inspired, feeling invigorated. Feeling yourself. You are held by the cosmos as you navigate through the rapids on a river called destiny.

Practice gratitude by way of enjoyment and celebration. On any other day, you might want to change one or two things, but for now the present moment is impervious to criticism. The fact that these magical moments do not come along every day makes the experience of it all the more humbling. Pace yourself through the firework parade of your moment, however—if you aren't careful, you could tip over into burnout.

When you are in a full moon phase you are nourished by connection with others. You gather, you listen, you want to hold space. The threads you've followed now weave into the magic of the collective.

When you are in a full moon phase you anchor down deep, reconnect with sheer will, and get to the finish line. Reach for what you previously could not. You grab the vine and soar to the other side of the chasm; give that last push up the switchback and get to the top of the metaphorical mountain.

When you are in a full moon phase, answers are everywhere because you have fully paid attention to the wisdom within. You've jumped off the dock and swum too far out to go back. Intuition and faith steadily carry you to another shore.

THE FULL MOON IS AN "EVERYTHING ALL AT ONCE" ENERGY TO BE USED HOWEVER YOU'D LIKE

The future is not promised. Every human has a unique list of wished-for "one days." One day I'll go on a hot-air balloon ride. One day I'll get over my fear of being onstage. One day I'll get certified in CPR, stop being late to yoga/therapy/movies, explore my sexual fantasies, meditate every morning, apologize to that friend I fucked over, commit to eating breakfast every morning, write that important teacher a thank-you letter, and actually get eight hours of sleep on weeknights. One day one day one day one day!

At a certain point, our "one days" need to become "todays."

What our lives look like is in part due to what we've done in the past. And much of what the future looks like will be directly influenced by what we do today. What full moon spells will you cast by doing what you've needed to do for ages? *How can "one day," in some way, begin today?*

The full moon shows us the one days. What we are ready to examine, what we are ready to embody, why we are ready to release. What has been forgotten that is now ripe for remembering. Let the full moon help you see and accept the entire spectrum of yourself. The full moon phase is an especially potent time to consider larger life themes and patterns that relate to both our subconscious and consciousness.

The full moon can show us what we must address in order to turn the corner in one or more areas of our lives. This reflection often illuminates those places where we are most vulnerable, most afraid to attempt transformation, as well as our deepest desires and potential. That dreamed-of life you keep yourself from going for, over and over again, because if you try and don't get it, you are sure you would be heartbroken beyond repair? That is exactly where you must go. There is no wrong way, there is no right way to decide to truly meet ourselves. When we operate from an empowered place, we know we can hold ourselves through hurt and shame. Our energy shifts as we remind ourselves that we are the magic, we are the spells.

In terms of traditional magic and spell work, we know that the full moon is the most potent time for casting spells for *anything* one feels drawn to: manifestation, guidance, protection, energy raising, abundance, fertility, closure, peace, harmony, support, creativity, psychic messages, and so much more. Those who know clearly what they want are most poised to benefit from this.

Some full moons demand more introspection. Sometimes we can just sit, awakening to the pause between our inhale and exhale. Sometimes the victory is remembering the pause is always there waiting for us, a way to expand time and space. Sometimes all we may be capable of is just getting through the day and leaving it at that. Bed is the celebration. The fact that it is over is the celebration. That can be enough.

Remember that the stars and the moon don't know how they shine, but they gleam and enchant just the same. Remember that you shine too. Give yourself a wink in the mirror. Let yourself crack open into a smile that lights up your entire beautiful face. Then do whatever you must under the potent energy of the full moon.

The full moon is the brightest permission slip in the night sky.

It reassures us that the answer is yes.

Yes it is okay to cry.

Yes it is okay to quit.

Yes it is okay to say no. Or yes.

Yes it is okay to love yourself.

Yes you are beautiful.

Yes it is okay to unfollow/ignore/block that person.

Yes you are allowed to stick up for yourself.

Yes it is okay to walk along your own path.
Yes it is okay to Go For It.
Yes it is okay and safe for you to trust yourself.
Yes.

THE FULL MOON IS A TIME TO HARVEST

Harvest is both a verb and a noun. The harvest refers to mature crops that are ready to be gathered. Harvesting is being in a state of discernment and labor. Harvesting is the culmination of all our efforts sowing, growing, and nurturing. From the new moon seeding and tilling and the waxing moon tending comes the full moon fruits bursting against our lips.

On farms, harvesting is the most labor-intensive activity of the growing season. Harvest season requires the most human power and the most resources. Your harvest season might last longer than you think and take a bit more energy than you're prepared for. If you've been giving it your all during the length of the waxing moon, your energy is already compromised by the time the moon is full. You may need to adjust accordingly.

The harvest itself isn't always a longed-for *thing*. It can be an important lesson learned. It can be an experience gained. Internal harvests are absolutely as meaningful as external ones.

In our culture there is a very real pressure to grind, to hustle, to push so hard that many of our daily lives teeter on the edge of unsustainability. Growth is as much about being rooted securely as it is reaching out. The soil needs to stay fertile, needs to be able to support life for long periods of time. We want our success to be intertwined with others' strong roots. We want the collective canopy to remain vibrant and strong. Part of a sustainable process includes the acceptance that our success is ultimately woven in with the success of the whole. We need one another. This is the shift from a "me" to a "we" state of being.

What would it mean to harvest healthily? Not pushing ourselves to the brink of exhaustion. Taking care of ourselves as if we were our most precious resource. Acknowledging that our energy is infinitely more valuable than gold. Expressing gratitude for the resources, for the ancestors, for the lessons that got us here. Not taking just because we can. Valuing human lives and the earth over profits. Thinking of others—maybe even folks we will never meet—and how we can help them. These are the kinds of harvests that will feed us the longest.

Ask yourself: What am I harvesting? How and why? What are my long-term plans and goals for my work? Am I in survival mode? Why? How can I switch to thriving?

Be Strategic About What You Are Harvesting

This part of the cycle demands strategy. Work smarter, not harder. The pace of our harvest must be measured by the amount of self-care we administer along the way. If you tend to think of yourself last, only after almost every drop of energy you have has been given away, then this harvest time could be an opportunity to give a cornucopia of care back to yourself. If your pattern is to quit just before you've reached the finish line, then figure out how to circumvent your tendency to give up right before the fruit ripens. Develop your strategy to do more with less.

It might be that at the full moon, or when you are in a full moon phase of your life, part of your harvesting strategy is to let the blessings you've been cultivating come to you. Take your foot off the gas. Coast for a while. Share older work that didn't get enough attention the first time around. There's a reason you've learned certain lessons. Use and share that wisdom.

Effective harvesting is also about taking the path of least resistance. Not trying to make those who won't budge, bend. Imagine that being in a long hotel hallway lined with eighty-two doors, and I tell you that behind just one of those doors is an amazing party that a loved one has planned in your honor. All your favorite people are there, your favorite food is being served, your favorite music is playing with a dance floor right next to the hot tub. All you have to do is open the right door. Would you stop at the first door you see and then, when it won't unlock, try to bang it open all night? No way. You'd knock on every door until you found the one that was just for you. Life can be like that exercise. We have to find the door that will open easily for us, not force the ones that will never swing ajar. This isn't about giving up on a dream. It is actually about trying a variety of different ways to actualize your dream. Don't let one not-so-great outcome determine the next phase of your life. Don't force a situation that isn't working after you've given it an honest and healthy effort. Go where you are wanted. Go where the love is.

Look around you to see what in your life is ready to be harvested. What is blooming? Everything has its own cycles, its own timing. Just because something isn't coming up right now doesn't mean it won't at a later date. Patience means experimenting with different methods, mindsets, and vibrations. Focus on what is here now. Focus on what you can try doing differently.

Embodiment as Harvest

Embodiment is where we get down and dirty with our actual, factual, overwhelmingly exciting desires. Embodiment is harvest magic. The harvest is a time of receiving plenitude. So it would make sense that the full moon is the time to double down on embodiment, which directly relates to our abundance—to fill in the space between what we long for and what we actually believe we deserve. Consciously practice receiving. Behave as if you live in abundance, not scarcity.

Start simple, if need be. One of the students in my Moonbeaming class set an intention around an office get-together she was planning: "I want my holiday work party to be a fun celebration." This is a very clear statement and intention. The words *fun* and *celebration* define some of the sensations to embody. In your own harvest work, be clear with your intentions. Identify the feelings inherent to the intention, connect to them, and embody them in your actions.

It can be hard to become a bridge between states of longing and embodiment. It can be tricky to go from the promise of an expectation to the hours of sitting with the reality of what it will take to fulfill our actual needs. It isn't a lie when folks say that sometimes, the hardest part is getting out of your own way.

Embodiment takes time and practice. The only ingredients you need are a body, your consciousness, and your desire. After practice comes progress. Once there is progress, we practice presence. After presence has been established, then we root. The present moment becomes our grounding technique. There is no lost time. Our fuck-ups are no longer reasons to hate ourselves or quit. A fear-based mindset is diminished, so missteps aren't daggers puncturing our dreams anymore. In practicing embodiment, our current harvest becomes easy to gather.

Harvesting and Release

Many astrologers and magic workers consider "release" to be one of the dominant themes of the full moon, and suggest "releasing" any strong emotions you may experience at this time—usually by shunting them aside. From my perspective this is a waste of the energy of the full moon and stems from people's fears around emotions.

Many people's first reaction to being flooded with emotions is to get rid of them, which often means bypassing and ignoring them. The problem is, when we stuff our emotions down without properly processing them, they aren't actually released at all, just stifled.

True releasing includes doing the emotional work of processing that the full moon sometimes asks us to do. Don't discard your emotions by way of rejection, feel them. Listen to them, sit with them, and channel them into something greater than you. At the very least, you name the emotion, acknowledge the source, give yourself compassion, then move the unwanted energy out of your body in some fashion.

If you are going to work on release at the full moon, be clear about how you will think differently, what you will do differently, and actually commit to changing yourself so that what you are releasing goes easily and will not return. Ask yourself: Am I using release as a stand-in to avoid dealing with really challenging feelings? Where must I take accountability? Does this situation just need me to look at it and address it head-on, not ignore it? How can I take this energy and channel it into something greater?

Rotten Harvests Happen

Sometimes the harvest shows up as a lesson of what we really, really don't want. Outcomes can be used as lessons; these are all information we use for the future. Sometimes the greatest lesson we can give to ourselves is the knowledge that fundamentally, we are resilient—we can withstand almost any kind of weather.

Often, all failure means is that you tried.

Success is usually found on the other side of many failures. Don't let one or two rotten harvests in a row make you feel like you are the one who is rotten. In nature, there is disease and illness. In nature, not all seeds grow. Try to shift your perspective and hold the energy of compassion through the setbacks.

So-called failures are necessary in order to experience success. Learning what not to do is invaluable for future endeavors. Sometimes, knowledge does happen to be gained the hard way. At the time of a failure or setback, we can't see the future, and so the snag becomes all-encompassing. In time, what is learned will offer us new insights, opportunities, and relationships.

If you are having a less-than-stellar full moon time, be gentle on yourself. Take some deep breaths through it. Notice what is coming up for you. Are there some patterns that are being illuminated here that echo an ongoing larger issue? Is this about how you treat yourself over perceived failures? Take note of where you can make different choices. This moment will pass eventually. Turn off your phone, close your eyes, and place your hands over your heart. If you can, go outside, and let the moon listen to you as you cry. She can hold your sorrow. She can be present for your grief. In her 4.53 billion years of existence, she has witnessed many tears.

The next beginning is around the corner. But for now we rest. We gather ourselves within the forgiveness of a long sigh. Later we assess. What can I learn from this situation? What did I do well? Where can I do better? Who am I now?

With all endings come the glimmers of different beginnings.

THE FULL MOON IS A TIME TO CONNECT TO OUR INTUITION

To work with the moon is to work with our intuition: our inner knowing. The processes of lunar work reveal varied aspects of the self as we move through the moon's phases, which broadens the scope of our intuition. Our senses, our inner wisdom, our impulses, our creativity, our emotions, our actions are all under this umbrella. Our intuition is the most direct gateway to intimacy with the self.

When the moon is full, this gate is open widest. A full moon is an incredibly rich time to experiment with any and all focused activities that consciously expand our intuition. Traditionally, there are held to be seven types of psychic abilities: clairvoyance (clear seeing), clairaudience (clear hearing), clairempathy (clear emotional feeling), clairsentience (clear physical feeling), clairtangency (clear touch), clairsalience (clear smelling), and clairgustance (clear tasting). Each one of these is a channel for intuition. Though almost no one is able to strongly access all of these abilities, each of us have clear access to at least one—and we can practice tuning in to our intuition through strengthening our natural gifts. Try not to overcomplicate accessing your intuition. Your intuition is a part of you no matter what—even if you have anxiety, or if you do not feel confident accessing any of the previously mentioned abilities.

Simply notice what you notice. Pay attention to what you are most drawn to. If it is art and visuals, you could have a stronger connection to clairvoyance. Clairvoyance is not just being able to visualize and see things in your third eye; it is also the ability to receive messages and interpretations through visuals—i.e., the way tarot readers, film critics, and art historians do. Every "clair" functions in this same way. If you are particularly sensitive to music, or are a musician, then you might be clairaudient. This "clair" isn't just hearing voices internally. It could also be that when you talk, freestyle sing, or just start chanting in a flow state, that you access this arena of psychic ability. You may be particularly sensitive to song lyrics; hearing the right chorus at the right time helps you to answer a current quandary. The only way to develop your intuition is to experiment and play with practices that you are drawn to—you don't need to explain why you like nature walks, tarot, or meditation. Start with what you are most interested in and drawn toward. Swim in the most familiar ponds of your nature.

Channeling is another related intuitive ability and activity that connects directly to the full moon. This is a process of connection to something greater than ourselves. We allow information, emotions, archetypes, or spirit to flow through us. We become both the vessel and the gifts it holds. We are both medium and messenger.

Being both receiver and transmitter requires concentration. This involves a close listen before imparting information. In taking the information we've received and moving it along, we stay in our flow state. Be open to playing around with channeling. Ask yourself, or spirit source, your angels, your guides, or the moon questions and allow energies to flow through you to answer them.

Once in a while, I meet someone who is nervous about channeling. They are worried that cruel spirits or entities will come through them. Or they worry that they will lose control. I believe a lot of such fears stem from both religious dogma and also from social stigmas around psychic abilities as a result of misleading media representations. When we set clear intentions and instructions to receive loving, helping, kind guidance only, then that is what will come through. Grounding and putting up energetic boundaries before channeling is always a good idea.

There exists a misconception that if you are very in touch with your intuition, then everything becomes much easier. That isn't necessarily the case. Often, trusting your intuition and following its guidance means making inconvenient, even difficult changes. Moves, breakups, and career loss may accompany heeding your intuition. Following your intuition can be painful at times. It is heeding the call of the soul and spirit. This is not always convenient!

Intuition teaches us to detach from the unhealthy parts of our ego. That which keeps us separate or unavailable to transcendence. While the information we receive is sometimes not what we had hoped, if collaborated with, it will foster growth.

Our intuition helps us to help ourselves, and also the collective. In my experience, intuitive hits and downloads tend to carry potent truths not only for us personally, but for others as well. One sign that a message or download contains greater collective wisdom is when you receive it with no ego or resistance involved.

Some Ways to Access Moon Messages

There are many ways to access spirit and self. Divination tools include coffee grounds, tea leaves, pendulums, tarot or oracle cards, bibliomancy, runes, and much more.

Scrying, or the art of second sight, is the act of gazing into a reflective abstract object in order to receive information by way of images and insights. Objects that have been used for scrying include crystals, mirrors that have been painted black, and even a bowl or glass of water with droplets of black ink added to it. Think of it as a psychic Rorschach test.

When the full moon has risen, gaze into a bowl of water. If possible, position it so you see the reflection of the full moon in the water. Gaze into the reflection of the moon. Stay watching for many moments. Let any and all answers or impressions float across your subconscious without edits.

You can also try filling up a black bowl with water and gazing into it in the dark. What do you see in the water, in the darkness? Noting patterns or types of symbology that frequently occur in your divination helps you to connect to your own intuition.

Use the full moon as your scrying device. Magic makers throughout the ages have done this. Look so long at her that she looks back at you. Stare so deeply that you begin to see yourself. Describe what you see.

Free writing also connects us to our intuition. Sit down, put pen to page, and start writing whatever is on your mind. If you are interested in gaining messages from your subconscious, start with that intention. Do not edit, do not pause. Just keep writing, even if what you are writing is gobbledygook. Keep writing until what is coming out has some sort of message, content, or form. Keep writing until something of interest shows up for you, something clicks, or you've gained an insight or two.

Start slow. Sit by your window, or outside somewhere safe. Get quiet and gaze at the moon. Ask her a question and then answer it. Think about all the ways the messages ring true. Act upon one or more of the truths. Allow the lunar-fueled intuition to ripple into the artistic expression that is your life.

THE FULL MOON IS A TIME TO CREATE OUR OWN MYTHOLOGIES

The full moon has been a rabbit, a buffalo, a tortoise, a frog, a toad, a man, a woman. The moon has been the sun's lover, the sun's sister, and the great goddess in the sky. Full moon deities have been ambassadors of peace, harbingers of destruction, creators of the entire universe. Every culture has lunar deities, every people has their own moon mythologies.

Myths give our lives meaning. Myths are a translation of our collective subconscious and its yearnings. Myths act, at times, as metaphorical guidebooks on how to live our lives. Myths also serve as a mirror of their cultures—including those cultures' problematic ideologies. There are many cultural myths that need revising or destroying altogether. There are present-day myths we need to recognize as lies and leave behind. Doing so will grant us the space to explore what we really think. To name who we really are.

There is power in sharing our stories. We discover and rediscover ourselves through this expression. There is power and liberation in sharing parts of ourselves we were told were wrong, were weird, were too wild for this world. When we tell stories about these parts, the repressed is expressed. Our subconscious self, our exiled parts are reassured that they are safe to come out, safe to play, safe to exist. This is one way to integrate the shadow. This is one way to heal.

The full moon is an opportune time to reflect on what myths you've subconsciously taken in about yourself that aren't actually true. The myths you've told yourself that have stopped you from being brave enough to live your life the way you really want. Think about your own relationship to these beliefs. Think about what personal stories you are ready to revise and rewrite.

Write in the past tense, and write in the future tense. The past tense helps us to turn the page. "I used to be scared of public speaking, but I'm excited to be using my voice now." Be aware that when we are beginning to rewrite our stories, it is likely that imposter syndrome will try to start subletting space in our psyche. Pay attention to those doubtful voices, but do not let them take the wheel. Prove to yourself who you truly are with your actions and your energy. This can also be an important part of your moon-mapping process. We tell our own story in the way we wish to be remembered. We write and speak ourselves into existence.

At the full moon, think carefully about all of the ways you wish to share your story. You may wish to share your story with others in a moon circle, or in a memoir. Your story may work best in mentorship: in helping someone younger than you who might need your advice or guidance through your counsel.

We need every remembering. Every last one. We need to encourage the telling of other people's stories—particularly those who have been historically marginalized and oppressed. We need to ask our loved ones about their lives. We need to listen compassionately, we need to buy books and zines about people's stories, we need to feel safe to share. We need to lift up and signal boost one another as much as possible.

A lot of our ancestors were not able to tell their own stories. There are only remnants of some of their legacies, in ruins and fragments, in artwork not destroyed by the ravages of time and violence. In some cases there are only tiny clues in old books of what the dominant culture was afraid of, wanted to ignore, and wanted to bury. There tend to be more accounts of the ways that humans tried to destroy one another, tried to make certain beliefs and traditions disappear altogether. It is part of our responsibility to both research forgotten ways and also to create new ways. The creation of new tales sends love letters into the future. The witch adage reminds us: "What is remembered, lives!" We remember, and our stories live on.

Little Activities and Rituals to Try During a Full Moon Time

 Plan a full moon circle with friends. A craft night, a movie night, a spell night, a potluck. Share yourself with someone you love. Share yourself as you have never shared before. Delve into a part of yourself, your skill sets, your talents, your intuition, your interests that you haven't practiced. Think about where you need to close some loops, wrap it up, close the circle. Ponder where and how time functions as a spiral in your life. Cast a spell you've never tried. Choose how and where you are bending time. Pick an activity that moves energy: walking, breath work, cleaning, screaming. Spend an hour listening to whale sonar or drinking in the music of the ocean waves. Accept you may never fully heal, and also hold space for the possibility that you can, and will. Massage your body and tell yourself you are always deserving of care, and will. Draw down the moon. Rub some essential oil in your hands, hold them like a bowl, and breathe in deeply. Say *please* and *thank you.* Give people a chance to tell you *yes.*

Full Moon Magic

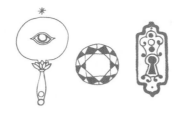

The full moon amplifies our emotions and affects our bodies. She makes us want to have sex, dance, scream, revel, and be truly wicked. It is only natural for us to take our desires, our yearnings, our talents, and our connections, and use it all to make all kinds of full moon magic.

Sex, procreation, and creation of all kinds are associated with the full moon. Pregnant bellies, menstruation, and the realm of growing life and birthing have been the domain of the full moon for millennia.

The iconic image of the witch riding on her broomstick is always against the backdrop of a full moon. This indelible visual is made up of one part masturbation and one part psychedelic herbs. It is told that women would apply hallucinogenic herbs—to induce flying—via their mucus membranes. Hundreds of years ago, women would "take flight" by rubbing these herbs into their genitals, and would blast into a world that was much brighter, much freer than their waking life. No doubt that vision of a woman on a broom flying high and happy has endured through the irreverent magic and metaphors it references.

Coming Together Is Full Moon Magic

The full moon traditionally is the time for people to gather. It is a cosmic coming together; the sun, the moon, and the earth are all in alignment. Why wouldn't we wish to mirror this by coming together with others? Coming together with others affirms we are not alone. Full moon circles can support connection and facilitate beautiful group magical workings as well. Get together with the same few friends consistently over periods of time. The sweet witnesses of time and friends are the cheerleaders to your progress.

Circles have an element of sharing and of listening. Being able to relax, to show up, honestly and vulnerably, with intention are the best ingredients. Many people wish to feel more spiritually connected; they just need an invitation. If you have the capacity to host, then do so. Ask your friends what they would want; co-create together.

If you already have a coven, then you are already meeting every month, and/or at the Wheel of the Year Sabbaths, or during the solstices and equinoxes. Even if you are a solitary practitioner, rituals with others are important from time to time. Sharing your desires in a group creates more momentum and amplification. Being lovingly witnessed is important for a witch. If you strongly identify as a solo practitioner, once in a while, under a full moon, gather with at least one other person to share and honor your growth and dreams.

Intention turns a casual hangout into a ritual. A potluck is just a get-together. But if the potluck has everyone cooking meaningful recipes, and you come together to share and talk about what your biggest wishes are in a circle, and then partake in a meditation that everyone co-creates, that is a ritual.

Out of all the phases of the moon, the full moon most supports spells for the collective. Witches have used spell work as activism for ages. The group of British witches who made ceremonial magic to keep the United Kingdom safe during World War II is the stuff of legend. The anonymous activist group W.I.T.C.H. (Women's International Terrorist Conspiracy from Hell) that was started in the United States in the late 1960s has seen a resurgence in various cities during this current political movement. It makes perfect sense that so many witches are activists, and so it makes sense that their magic would also engage in activism as well.

Spells worked for the collective without any action-based accompaniment, of course, have about the same weight as "thoughts and prayers" after yet another horrific school shooting. Always combine magical workings with actions. Get together after a working and create a petition. Write letters to your representatives and senators, or volunteer for a political campaign. When doing spell work for the elements, or for animals, or for the planet, do a practical action in accordance. For example, if you are casting a spell for clean water, give money away to an organization that supports clean water for folks in need, such as in Flint, Michigan.

No less than one full moon a year, I cast a spell to protect and honor the full moon. I take the time to thank her. You can do this practice for the earth, an animal, an element, or a deity you worship. Pairing up your spell work with consistent actions will make your protection magic even more sacred, even more powerful.

If you are claiming to be a witch, and you aren't trying to use magic to make the world a better place, what are you doing? Witches historically have been healers, helpers, counselors, herbalists, health care providers, and activists. Witches are inherently political. Part of the great work is creating care, safety, and equity for.

Practice Kitchen Witchery

Kitchen witchery naturally pairs with the full moon. We are the most nourished when we can provide for ourselves, feed others, and can completely accept gifts from others.

The moon and food go hand in hand. Many traditional group spell workings are not complete without some form of feast. The full moon can be a time of considering our consumption and putting focus and follow-through on what makes our bodies feel best. Not what toxic diet culture tells us, not what works for others. By paying attention to what kinds of food make us feel better, we can continue to take care of ourselves.

Kitchen witches generally work with the magic and energy of the season, the home, and what the home contains. This includes the kitchen and hearth, but kitchen witches also tend to be crafty. They make flower arrangements, create beautiful gardens, and make works of art for their walls and others'. Kitchen witches utilize their magic while cooking or preparing foods. They integrate certain ingredients of their symbology into their cooking. Kitchen magic can be utilized every day. Knowing correspondences are helpful, or create your own. Cinnamon and honey for love. Red peppers for passion. Rosemary for protection. Violets for forgiveness.

Creating flower and vibrational essences under the full moon is a traditional activity to do as well. You can make your own to use as an extended spell to aid you in your manifestation work. For more information on how to create essences, consult an herbalist's book such as *The Gift of Healing Herbs* by Robin Rose Bennett.

You can also leave food out as an offering. If you practice deity worship, identify as Buddhist or Hindu, or wish to honor your ancestors, then leaving out a plate of offerings for your god/goddess/goddexx/orisha/spirit of worship is a common practice. Partake in a full moon feast for yourself and loved ones. Maybe there is a theme to the feast: seasonal, magical, or metaphorical. Themes could be cooking the food of one's ancestry, comfort food, what is growing seasonally and locally, the astrological sign of the moon, or create a meal that expresses feelings you wish to embody, sensations you wish to share. Express yourself through food.

Or, simply let the moon *feed you*. In the 1800s, witches in the Shetland Isles would lie all night in the moonlight to gain powers. An Indian Muslim tradition was to "drink the moon": pour water in a silver bowl, hold it in the light of the full moon, then drink it, supposedly to cure nerve disorders. Women in Brittany also "drank the moon" to help them conceive.[1] Go outside and open up. Open your hands, heart, mind. Open your energetic field under the open face of the full moon. Let her moonbeams wash over you, let her infuse you with healing, love, and power. Drink her in with every cell of your body. Let her teach you how to fully receive.

Creating Your Full Moon Altar

A full moon altar could be up for almost a week, from about three days before the full moon to three days after the full moon. Or you could set your altar up for your full moon spell only. If the full moon is feeling particularly vibrant, electric, or potent for you, leave your altar up until the next full moon. You could leave your full moon altar up for a season, if it feels particularly resonant or you are practicing seasonal resolutions.

Many witches make their full moon magic outside. If possible, go to a safe space nearby, or into your backyard, and create an altar out of the ground, the rustling of the trees, the crickets' songs, the offerings of your open palms, stretched out under the spacious expanse of the crisp air.

A full moon altar could be an interpretation of how you feel the full moon energy is landing with you, right here, right now. It could be a meditation you create, an invented labyrinth you walk around in the folds of your mind. Your full moon altar could be layers of sonar you sing along to, as you slowly trace the wavelengths of your heart over a turquoise-water-colored piece of paper. Your full moon altar could be a dinner party for all your precious beloveds, holding space for everyone's stories, everyone's joy, everyone being everything perfect over fizzy water and blueberry crumble.

Always remember: your altar is you. Always remember—your life is your altar. You adorn it with your intentions, your thoughts, the quality of your breath, and how you need to be held. How you treat yourself, express yourself, and carry yourself is the magic!

Magical Correspondences of the Full Moon

Knowing what you will be casting spells for will guide what ingredients you gather. A spell for forgiveness looks and feels a lot different than a spell for fame, and so the ingredients you'll use will be very different for each.

It is important to develop your personal set of correspondences depending on how you interpret each phase of the moon and how you feel. The full moon might be all apple pies and red wine, pink candles, sex toys, and bedroom dancing, because self-love, romancing the self, and making love is what is required for you at this time. For another magic maker, the full moon ritual looks like a crying session in a hot bath. At the bare minimum, every witch could charge or cleanse the crystals or objects they are interested in working with for their current goals underneath the moon.

Below are some examples of full moon correspondences to spark your inspiration. Tune in to your intuition and create your own. These could also be specific colors, or animals, or words that come up for you around the full moon that have meanings for you.

Water—from your faucet, or from the ocean, or water that has been charged by the energy of the moon, aka moon water; body fluids (blood, spit, tears); moonstone (all kinds), sunstone, silver, copper, selenite, lapis lazuli, Herkimer diamond, clear quartz, celestite, jaspers of all kinds; seaweed, sea glass, seashells, sea foam, coral, pearls, ocean wind, energy from a waterfall; mirrors, cauldrons, bowls, circles, spirals, salt, holograms, terrariums, a full cup, projections of light or visions; a long and hearty belly laugh; a container filled with your favorite things; the direction west; any shade of blue, white, black, gray, silver; lotus (all parts, from the root to the flower), rosemary, mugwort, motherwort, nettles, blooming roses, sunflowers, apples, the Moon Card, the Sun card, the World Card, and the Queens in the tarot.

Goddesses/deities: Ch'ang-O (or Chang'e), Tsukuyomi, Kuan Yin, Mawu, Oshun, Hathor, Venus, Aphrodite.

Archetypes: the work and lives of Solange, Frank Ocean, Collette, Venus of Willendorf, Tara Brach, Octavia Butler, Remedios Varo.

Animal guides that correspond to the full moon: whales, dolphins, kangaroos, seahorses, crabs, lobsters, turtles, scarabs, blue herons, lionesses, platypodes, wolves, spiders, moths—especially luna moths.

FULL MOON SPELLS

Full Moon Spell Work

Throughout this chapter, we've discussed all the types of spells that a full moon supports. Collective spells, group spells, kitchen witchery, abundance and expansion spells, protection spells, ancestral spells, lunar deity spells, offerings, long-term sustainability spells, uncrossing spells for intuitive and psychic enhancement, alchemy spells, love spells, sex spells, health spells, rewriting spells, release spells, and pattern-breaking spells are all supported at this time! Magically, one cannot go wrong at a full moon. If moon mapping, conduct a spell or ritual that supports your current goals, or one that serves as a celebration and affirmation of all the work you have done.

Full Moon Expansion Spell

You can work this spell anytime between the waxing gibbous moon phase and the full moon. It is suggested you start this spell a couple of days before the full moon, in order to end it on the evening of the official full moon.

Before working your spell, set up your space/altar accordingly with your objects/elements.

Suggested tools: Tarot or oracle deck

Four candles, in your favorite colors or color combination, that represent what you are calling in and what you want to transpire in the next six months or sooner

Suggested crystals: garnet, cinnabar, pyrite, honey calcite, celestite, ametrine

Suggested oils/scents: sesame, frankincense, ylang ylang, geranium, pepper or peppercorns

Plants/herbs: plants, flowers, or herbs that represent expansiveness and pleasure to you

Elements on your altar that represent water, earth, air, or fire

Get clear on what four aspects you are ready to expand out into or embody more. They could correspond to the four elements (fire, earth, water, air) or be completely different and represent what you need to cultivate more of in your life. Be very clear about what they are, and be committed to carrying them out and working on them energetically, spiritually, and physically/behavior-wise. On small pieces of paper, write down what they are. Later you will place these under your candles.

Choose a tarot card from the deck that most represents you, your desires, at your highest level at this time. Place that in the middle. Decorate and place any other powerful and meaningful elements around on the altar. Dress your candles appropriately, if that is in your practice. Place your candles closely around your tarot card. Tuck your written correspondences under each one. As you light them in a clockwise fashion, you may wish to say your incantation or read your petitions.

After the candles are lit and burning, spend time visualizing and imagining yourself transmuting and transforming your desired energy into form. Experience embodying all the feelings that come along with this. Imagine yourself doing the work, energetically and physically, to amplify the desires you are calling in at this time.

Over the next three days, spend intentional time at your altar. Every day, move the candles a few inches away from the tarot card representing you. Light them and again imagine your expansion. Imagine your desires, your feelings, and your actions reaching a greater audience, fulfilling more and more of your potential, inviting in opportunities that have no end.

On the last night, as your candles burn down, imagine sending out your specific light into the universe for it to be reflected back more brightly. You may wish to burn your wishes to charge them, or tape them on your mirror, or put them in your wallet for a time to keep your attention.

In the days and weeks following your spell, do the work you've promised yourself in order to continue the expansion process.

18-MINUTE ABUNDANCE RITUAL

Eighteen is a sacred number in Judaism; it corresponds to *chai,* or "life." It is a good omen for a long life well lived.

This spell's title is a bit misleading, as the set-up part is longer than eighteen minutes, and you can sit at your altar for much longer than that time. But for people new to spell crafting, focused visualization, or meditation, eighteen minutes is a good start.

You will need:

- Things that define abundance to you
- 1–4 candles in your favorite colors
- 2 pieces of paper
- 1 pen

Set up your abundance altar.

Add anything that symbolizes abundance. Apples, jewelry, lipstick, plane tickets, lingerie, plants, etc. Don't hold back and don't edit. Include anything that is particular to what you wish to call in. Checks with your name and amounts on it, an acceptance letter addressed to you from a school you want to attend, fruits and veggies that symbolize good health are all examples of items that represent continued abundance.

Get out your pieces of paper.

On the top of one page write: "Things I am grateful for." Number it 1–18. Then write down one thing next to each number. Keep it in the present tense.

Express future gratitude.

On the other piece of paper, write: "Things I am grateful for that are on their way to me." Then write down all the things you are grateful for that will be coming to you—dreams and desires and bounty. Stay in the present tense. Do not edit yourself! Set a timer on your phone for 18 minutes.

Light your candles.

Spend time reading your present gratitude list until you are completely blissed out. Let it sink in how lucky and blessed you are.

Do the same for your future list. Let all the future energy seep into your consciousness and subconscious. Allow it all into your cells. Allow it all to become believable, until it becomes energetically integrated and feels very real.

Do this over and over again, as much as you like or need to, until the timer goes off. You may wish to spend more time in this happy, abundant state, watching your candles glow, seeing and feeling all that you have, so excited for all the blessings making their way into your life.

FULL MOON MIRROR MAGIC SPELL

This is a spell to align with true self and true self love.

You will need:

tarot cards, a mirror (on the smaller side, such as a hand mirror), paper, pen, any and all candles, crystals, other pieces for your altar that you will use that symbolize love, and compassion.

Before this spell, make sure to take a relaxing shower or bath, dress up in an adored outfit, wear a favorite scent, and do any other grooming that makes you feel your best.

It is preferable to do this ritual in darkness, only in candlelight. Turn all technology off. Let the full moon and candles light up the room.

Put the mirror at the center of your altar.

After you've cast your circle and settled into your spell space, pick up your mirror. Look deeply into your own eyes and connect to yourself with love.

While holding the mirror up, conjure up your inner child. Imagine a younger version of yourself looking back. What do they want you to know at this time? What do they need from you?

Pull a tarot card. Write down any messages.

Pick up the mirror again and connect to your present self with love. What is your present self wanting to embody? What is ready to come forth presently?

Pull a card. Write down any messages.

Pick up the mirror again and connect to your higher self, or future self. What messages are from the future? What gifts are waiting for you? What messages does the universe have for you?

Pull a card. Write down any messages.

Spend time meditating and receiving any messages that wish to come through. Arrange the cards you've pulled in a manner that makes sense. Do any other spell work or energy work that you feel called to do. Close your circle. After the spell is cast, start working with the messages you received.

Suggested affirmation: "My outer actions align with my inner self. I am recognized for all I am and for all I share and show."

FULL MOON TAROT PULL

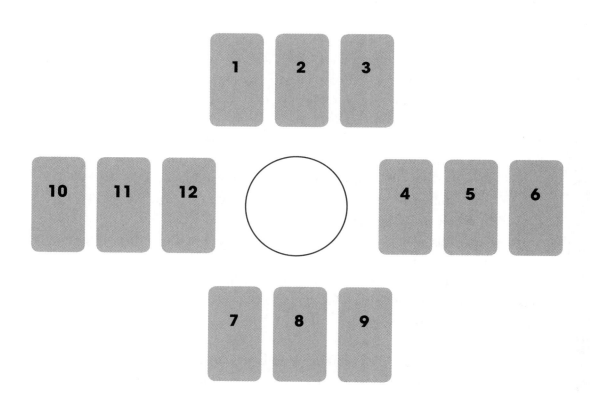

 This spread can be done as a divination tool, as well as an overview for the lunar cycle ahead. You will need a tarot deck, your journal, a writing utensil, and at least one hour.

Get cozy and relaxed. Take a few deep breaths, or meditate beforehand, if that is your practice. Shuffle once, or either between each pull or each card.

1. Pull three cards for today's full moon.

   Card 1: What does my soul need at this time?

   Card 2: How can I belong to myself, and support this need?

   Card 3: What does spirit/source/the universe want me to recognize at this time?

2. Pull three cards for the waning period.

   Card 4: What may be a hard lesson that comes up during this time?

   Card 5: Where will the solution lie?

   Card 6: What must I release in order to welcome change during this time?

3. Pull three cards for the new moon period.

   Card 7: What messages must I be open to receiving at this time?

   Card 8: What bounty can I begin to call in?

   Card 9: What seeds must I plant?

4. Pull three cards for the waxing moon period.

   Card 10: Where/what is the work of this time?

   Card 11: What are some practical steps to take?

   Card 12: What is optimal for me to explore/express at this time?

MOON MYTHOLOGIES
AS SPELL WORK

Do some research and see what lunar deities (if any) your ancestors worked with. Are there any elements of the stories, traditions, or the deity you resonate with in your own life or in your current process?

Write your own myth. Your very own full moon mythology. It could be a myth about this time period, a myth of your life, a story about your desires, or your fears, or your lineage.

Thinking about what myths or traditions are coming up, find a way to incorporate them into your spell. Maybe you make a cake as an offering to your ancestors, maybe you use an herb, or a word, or a phrase that speaks to you. If you are totally making your own myth, you really are making a choose-your-own-adventure spell! Become the themes you are writing about. Try to translate your own mythology into colors, movements, and specific ritual. Become the essence or elements of the most important pieces of transformation you are currently summoning.

FULL MOON SUBCONSCIOUS/ CONSCIOUSNESS EXERCISE

For this exercise, you will need at least four sheets of paper and a writing utensil. Give yourself about an hour to go through the prompts.

On each one of four pages, draw a big circle. This symbolizes you, and your desires at this full moon.

Page 1. Considering your desire: everything all at once.

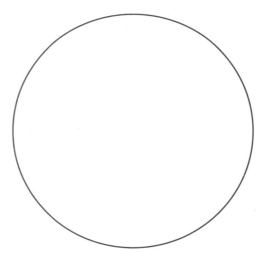

In this circle space, write down all of the thoughts, plans, dreams, themes, key words about your desire—everything all at once! You might need more space, or to journal, as well. Follow the threads of your thought process. Do not edit yourself.

Page 2. Considering your desire: fears, resistance, and where they live.

Now, examine some of the fears or resistance that there is around your desire. Do they live in your subconscious or conscious mind? Do they live in your body? If so, where? Why? Do they live as a result of your personal history, trauma, or what someone once told you? Are they a result of our society, the dominant culture we live in? Really unpack and get to the bottom of your fears or blocks.

Page 3. Considering your desire: attraction, alignment, and purpose.

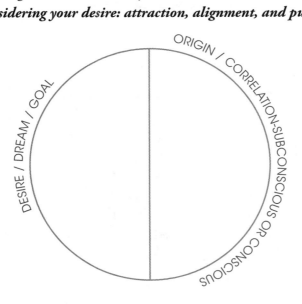

Now focus on all of the wonderful correlations around your desire. What would it look like to be living it? What are some key words or themes around this? And where is the origin of these beliefs: conscious, subconscious, history, the dominant culture, etc.? Do the same thing as you did for your fear-related beliefs, but really sink into why you want to feel the way you do, and what this tells you about yourself and who you are.

Page 4. Embodiment: everything all at once.

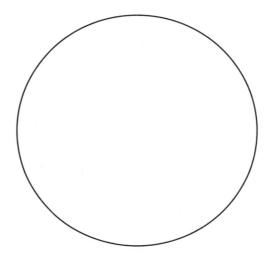

After reviewing your resistance and your desires, now it is time to get nonlinear! Below, write down the *most* potent key words around both your fears *and* your excitement. Put them in the same space. They can live there together. Sit with them, read them. This is what you will be doing the work around, and this may or may not also reflect other patterns in your life. Know that they can exist in the same space—it doesn't have to be either/or. You don't have to be perfect in one area to move forward, to love yourself and claim your desire. Reflect on where you are ready to work with this insight, and in what capacity. Let it sink in, let yourself accept all of *you*.

*After reviewing the state of your desire, you may use this information to cast a specific spell, set specific goals, or take specific actions.

JOURNALING PROMPTS FOR THE FULL MOON

Pick a few of these prompts that inspire you to journal at the full moon:

What is the present moment bringing up for me?

What needs my attention?

How will I honor myself?

How can I fully embody my needs?

What are my emotions telling me?

What is my intuition telling me?

How am I honoring my intuition?

If I zoom out on the patterns of my life, what is a recurring emotional or behavioral pattern that keeps coming up?

How can I change this—what is one shift I can make today, in order to change this?

What healing could that bring myself and/or my ancestors?

What healing could that bring to myself and to the future collective?

What is culminating?

How can I celebrate and enjoy myself more?

What is my magical superpower?

What does alchemy look like for me right now?

Who is my community? How do I connect to them?

What is my personal full moon mythology?

How can I honor and thank the moon?

The Waning Moon

The Gateway into the Unknown

The waning moon period begins right after the full moon and ends the day before the new moon. Raise your left hand and make it into a "C." The waning moon will nestle in the left portion of your left hand. Our heart is on our left side. In ancient times, our left side was thought to be the more receptive and intuitive side. Over the course of about two weeks, as the moon orbits closer to the sun, the light hitting the face of the moon declines, and the sky becomes darker. The retreating moon makes way for the stars to dance on the inky evening stage.

At the waning moon is where we reap the rewards of the entire lunation. If you've been doing work during the new, waxing, and full moons, then now might be a chance to coast, rest, and integrate. If you have control issues, or tend to not know when to stop pushing, then this part of the lunar phase can help you relinquish tendencies around forcing, or being attached to the endless hustle, which hinder growth and evolution.

The waning moon signals it is time to clear the fields. Before we plant new seeds, we must weed and till and rest the soil. Before we move into new phases, we must tend to *our* soil: our foundations, our roots. Just as we need to let fields lie fallow, we must allow ourselves to rest, to make and take space in different areas of our lives, at different times in our lives. Practice allowing and receiving.

If during the waxing moon you made a few big shifts in your behavior, then the waning moon is the period where you continue to stay the course, and begin to notice the benefits of your earlier decisions.

Despite the fact that the waning moon period takes up half the lunar cycle, popular culture, astrology sites, and social media rarely mention, let alone celebrate, this time period. Within "love and light" communities there is often bias against anything darker, shadowy, or quieter. Examining our shadows and our shame isn't going viral anytime soon, even though this culture desperately needs to address these processes collectively. We all need to offer our pain attention in order to heal. The waning moon is the optimal time to address the difficult aspects of our lives.

As covered in the full moon chapter, the full moon can bring everything to the surface. Now, at the waning moon, we process this information head on. If we do not examine all of the parts of ourselves, especially the seemingly unspeakable ones, we cannot be whole.

As the moon orbits counterclockwise around the earth, she heads toward Venus, the planet of love and values. If called to, we can move toward greater love and self-regard. In the myth of Inanna, the waning moon is when Inanna, the ancient Sumerian goddess, begins her descent into the underworld. This is a time of shedding that precludes transformation: when all that is false fades away, intimacy is gained with our core self.

When the moon is on the wane, sap flows down to the roots of plants and trees. Root vegetables are to be planted at the time of the third quarter. During the fourth quarter, after the last quarter moon, is the optimal time to weed and to turn the soil and the compost heap. This information can also be used to tend to our metaphoric gardens.

The waning moon phase is synonymous with interiority. Interior work is crucial for our development. Even though what we are working on can't be easily seen by others or performed for social media, that doesn't mean it isn't worth investing time and energy in. Interior work is also incredibly active—it takes a lot of energy and a lot of discipline and focus! Give yourself credit as you also allow space for rest, decompression, and integration.

PHASES OF THE WANING MOON

Within the entire waning moon period are four distinct phases. Each phase is characterized by its own set of themes. Some of these will correlate with your experience more than others.

The Waning Gibbous Moon

The waning moon phase begins with the waning gibbous, which mirrors the waxing gibbous. This is any time from just after the full moon, to just before the first quarter moon. During the waning gibbous phase the moon goes from approximately 99 percent to 51 percent illuminated.[1] As the moon wanes, it rises later and later each night. The waning gibbous rises at about 9 p.m. and sets at 9 a.m. This period usually lasts about one week. You can look at what came up for you during the waxing moon to try to gain more insight into this phase—sometimes all we need to gain clarity is a flip of our vision.

The astrologer Dane Rudhyar calls this time the "disseminating moon."[2] Disseminating is synonymous with spreading something freely. The information you have, your unique wisdom, and who you've become is to be shared with the world. This is a time for you to stand in your power and share your voice.

The time period just after the full moon is the time of the second harvest, a time of receiving useful messages—*if* we are paying attention. Calm your nervous system and try to make sense of the more surreal experiences you've just passed through.

The Last Quarter Moon

The last quarter moon occurs during that fleeting day or so when the moon is 50 percent illuminated. As with the first quarter moon, during the last quarter moon the tides are at their lowest, potentially evoking a feeling of calm or equilibrium. Because it is a pivot point, the last quarter moon phase may also provoke tension within: we may feel torn between the old and the new. Past hurts and resentments may need attention. There may be things we need to release—we might be faced with making a big decision.

The last quarter moon is nature's alarm clock, a reminder that the moon will turn new sooner than we think. It marks the halfway point of the waning moon period, and so it is a final call to do any associated activities we feel called to do. Pull out the weeds that have grown in between the cracks of your life. Clear out guilt, sorrow, or perhaps your inbox. Slough off the dead skin of perfectionism. Make time to have hard conversations in order to clear the air or communicate needed good-byes. The last quarter moon is the time to reflect on what you are ready to sacrifice in service to gaining something better.

The Waning Crescent

The waning crescent is also sometimes called the "balsamic" moon. (The etymology of *balsamic* is "healing" and "soothing"—*balm*.) After the lull of the last quarter, the tides build again. You may experience feelings of surrender and a sense of recuperation. Whatever has come up throughout the lunar cycle that has not been reckoned with may swirl around you. This is a good moment to examine our egoic impulses and dissolve any false safety nets.

This time also correlates with low energy: emptiness and exhaustion may wind through your body. Allow yourself to rest and pay attention to what your inner voice has to tell you as you do so. Clean and declutter. Engage in intuitive enhancing practices like meditation or tarot. Do the work of preparation: wrap up, review, reconcile. Look back in order to move forward.

The Dark Moon

The dark moon occurs during the three days leading up to the new moon. Because the energy and traditions of the dark moon are complex and because many practitioners, including myself, honor this period as its own separate phase, I address it separately in the chapter that follows. The dark moon marks the end of the waning moon period and the entire lunation.

IF THE WANING MOON IS HARD FOR YOU

If the waning moon time is hard for you, dear one, you are not alone. Many of us were not equipped with the tools required to examine and deal with our hurts, shadows, and limiting beliefs. Many of us were taught to see our powerful intuition as something to be ashamed of and hidden away. Part of your waning moon practice could be healing your relationship with your intuition. Connecting to that quiet inner voice.

The stillness of this time period can be challenging for those of us who are impatient. When we don't see immediate results, we may be tempted to quit. Part of your waning moon work could be patience cultivation. Humans love to know when something challenging or painful will end. When we don't know, we tend to resist, panic, or numb out in some way. What are some ways that you could show up for this moment without tearing yourself apart?

A waning moon can be hard for those born during the waxing moon or the new moon. For morning people, too, or for folks who feel more comfortable in action-oriented roles, this time of mystery and stillness, this space that encourages non-doing, is quite uncomfortable. If that resonates with you, sweet one, try to understand that not doing anything *is* doing something. Pausing is an action. Resting is one too.

Your waning moon mood might not match the conventional descriptions of this period. If you were born during a waning moon or a dark moon, you might feel energetically at home in this phase: full of glow, flow, and heart homecomings. During the seasons of spring and summer, this time may resonate more with rest and play. During the seasons of fall and winter, you might feel called to more therapy or shadow work. This could be the most productive time of the entire lunar cycle for you; I've created classes and written multiple chapters of books during the waning moon. Over time, you will be able to notice your own personal patterns and figure out what the benefits of this phase are for you.

The waning moon marks an end. And endings are hard. Even endings that aren't negative can feel sad. Humans generally fear any kind of loss. But our sadness around loss is also part of what makes us sensitive, empathetic, alive. Endings are the gateways to the unknown. Give yourself space to process endings of all kinds.

Becoming well versed in the art of letting go makes us available for the gifts of the present moment. Clearing out all types of clutter—emotional, psychic, and literal—helps us set a wide new moon stage. Rest and relaxation helps us integrate. Addressing our energetic leaks saves us precious time. The waning moon can support us with all of this and more.

WHEN YOU ARE IN A WANING MOON PHASE

When you are in a waning moon phase, you have crossed the threshold of questioning and are seated in the realm of your own wisdom. There is a calm confidence that comes with the knowledge you possess. The doubt has stopped thrashing about in your nervous system. Your intuition has become your anchor.

When you are in a waning moon phase, one or more areas of your life are ready to be revised. Something needs to change. Even if you don't exactly know where you are headed next, you know you cannot stay where you are. And so, you pull out the scrolls of memory and reread them. Your regrets point the way toward what you now know must be finished. You will need time. You will need distance. You will need space. Let yourself have all three components of this slow holy trinity.

When you are in a waning moon phase, harmful parts of your ego dissolve as you break up with your own bullshit. If you've done the processes of the previous lunar phases, by the waning moon, you've gained a fundamental acceptance. You're cool with how powerful you are. You get it. You get that it might be of you, and it might help you, but it isn't *for* just you. You've got your marching orders and you are proceeding confidently. Playing small doesn't work anymore. It isn't a part of your paradigm.

Following are some ways to think about and to work with the waning moon. Check in with your moon map and figure out what suggested activities correspond with your process. Remember to always follow the desires and energy that were started at the new moon, the threads that appeared during the waxing moon, that you just experienced and downloaded at the full moon. This helps turn the wheel in a focused fashion.

THE WANING MOON IS THE
TIME OF THE SECOND HARVEST

The second harvest takes place over the first few days of a waning moon, during the waning gibbous phase. The day or two after a full moon can still be a good time to cast a harvesting spell. At this time, the moon still appears to be full. The energetic imprint of the few days after the full moon can function like a full moon without all the spikiness.

Conjure up what you need to feel satiated. Determine what you need and ask for it. Begin to close the loops on your particular process. In almost any creative process or large undertaking, harvests are staggered. This is the time of bottling, of fermenting, of drying out herbs, of mining the dug-up dirt for gold. At this time, look around your life and make note of what is emerging, and what is still up for harvesting. Reap what ripe opportunities that still can be found.

The second harvest has legs. This last pass can really deliver us somewhere. We can utilize our growth to decide where to focus and why. There is an emphasis here on what we are focusing on growing long-term. We zoom out on our process in order to zoom in on what is most important. Quick fixes won't work anymore. It is time to set up systems in our lives that empower us to respond rather than react. Doing so fosters security and stability; the roots of our abundant self is what will anchor us to resilience.

At this time, we recognize the importance of our sovereignty. Our considerations are long term, we understand that cycles take time—and making that time golden is an investment with endless returns. Roots planted in the right soil have no choice but to infinitely grow. When we recognize what we actually need to flourish, we can no longer go back to anything less.

Naming and claiming what is most meaningful to us is the potential of this type of harvest. As we gather, as we organize, as we archive, we ponder the most far-ranging inquiries. Who are we doing all of this for? Why? What are the healing themes of our lives? What do we want to be remembered by? What do we want to accomplish, experience, or learn by the time we leave this planet? What do we want our legacy to be?

THE WANING MOON IS A
TIME OF CLEARING AND RELEASING

After the harvest the fields are clear. Weeding becomes much easier. Take time to consider the garden of your life. An overcrowded garden has no room for different plants. Roots can't grow if they haven't got any breathing room. Our roots might need a transplant! We might start making lists of what big bold moves we need to make next. We might start doing more moon mapping for the next cycle now, with all the wisdom we have acquired.

This is the time to get rid of stuff. Go through your spare room, your bottom drawer, your cabinets. If you are tracking your own rhythms, you may also notice you naturally get the inclination to purge around this time. What do you need to do in order to feel like you are preparing to embark on a fresh start?

This is also the time to Let Go Of A Bad Habit. Replace what you are letting go of with a healthy substitution. Think about what is going to help guide you and offer you positive reinforcement. This could be actions, but it could also be thoughts. Actively choose thoughts that feel better and, over time, these will become your core beliefs.

Discipline building work continues at the waning moon. Doing hard things that will eventually make things easier is a perfect use of this phase. Often, once we sit down to do the thing, it takes less time than we thought, and wasn't even as horrid as we assumed it would be. You may wish to make a "life to-do list" of items that tend to eat away at you and take up precious energetic space. Put them in one long document. Pick at least one or two annoying tasks at each waning moon to check off your list. Little by little, this makes more space in your brain and life.

Sometimes, when clearing out our emotional baggage, when decluttering various parts of our life, we are absolutely brutal on ourselves. Waves of self-judgment swell up. Doubt threatens to stop all proceedings. Notice your feelings and reframe. This will help move through them. The feelings that have come up are information. The information is a lesson. You aren't stuck; you are just figuring it out. You aren't broken; you are just more aware.

Emotional Weeding Is Important

Some of the most powerful magic we can enact during this phase of the moon is emotional weeding. Often, on the flip side of a desire are emotional attachments: to fears that we are unworthy of the desire, to beliefs that what we desire is inaccessible to us. Those of us in trauma recovery, or those of us who have been abused, are especially primed to view our fears as a type of survival mechanism; a way to keep us safe. Part of our work in recovery, and in therapy, can also be seeing where our fear-based responses hold us back from fulfilling our desires. Showing up for our desires can help dissipate some of our fears.

Emotional weeding is the process of naming your harmful emotional patterns and defense mechanisms in order to transform them. It means getting to the root of your resistance, or harmful self-fulfilling prophecy. Take an honest inventory of your subconscious patterns. Understand why you are doing what you are doing. Figure out what you need to put in place to feel healthier and supported, what you need to trust in yourself and your ability to effectively meet your own needs.

Focus on the root of the pattern. Keep asking yourself *why, how,* and *what* until something breaks through. Once you've named your root and know the source of it, then you can transform it holistically. For example, your desire might be deeper intimacy in close relationships. The root might be a fear around expressing needs; the protection mechanism could show up in a number of ways. If the desire requires you to be more vulnerable, examine where to practice that in your everyday life. Communication is a perfect place to start. Maybe previously, in an argument, you would hide your vulnerability by shifting the focus to your loved one, and becoming defensive: *You aren't listening! You never listen!* Maybe previously, you would hide your vulnerability in relationships by swallowing any anger or disappointment around something important, letting the moment pass, then downplaying your needs later in resentment: *It isn't a big deal. My needs aren't important. I'll just let this blow over.* Practice speaking from a place of vulnerability: *I'm feeling like you aren't listening. That hurts my feelings. I'm not sure we are understanding each other. I love you and I want us on the same page. Can we slow down here, together?* This is one example of emotional weeding. Pull out the old ways and plant new seeds of action and communication.

You can also do a ritual or ceremony to tug the root out from your emotional body. Before your ceremony, get in touch with the part of your body that resonates the most with the belief or emotional response you are looking to release. That is where you will focus your breath, your energy, your awareness. You can give that part of your system love and acceptance, and let the root know that you are now letting go of it. Feel it leave your body, your psyche, as it floats out of your energy and into the stratosphere to be transformed into something better.

When we weed the garden beds in the backyard, or clear out a drawer in our home, we usually aren't attaching intense emotions to these activities. But often an emotional weeding process is accompanied by shame. This narrows our access to relief; we are trapped in old stories. The weeds are too tangled up with those heavy stones of the past to be cleared away. If this happens, notice that your shame or judgment is just one story, but it is not who you are. This can help unhook you. Humor and kindness can help redirect your suffering into a gracious humanity. Make a song up about your story, befriend your story as you would an innocent child. Guide it into security by asking your story what it needs, or assuring it can rest now.

Try to release with compassion and a side of hope. I'm sure you can think of an instance when you let go of a relationship, a job, or a habit that no longer served you. This might have been really painful for a long time. Perhaps part of you thought you wouldn't be able to make it through. Eventually, something different and healthier emerged. It always does.

If we are doing the work, something ultimately more aligned will always come in. But first we need to clear, and understand that what we will encounter next is the in-between space. It is difficult for many to be okay hanging out in the in-between zone. Humans are creatures of habit, who frequently take the not-so-great known over the total unknown. If this has been a challenge for you, look at what blocks you have around being in the unknown. How much of your "known" is actually not promised? The truth is, reality could change at any time. The unknown will be discussed more in the dark moon chapter.

Releasing Is Repairing

It can be difficult to release pain and suffering when it has gone on for so long. Some of our wounds run so deep they feel almost etched into our bones. Sometimes when we are suffering or dealing with loss, we become so identified with these sorrows that we can see nothing else. Do not become so attached to your pain that your pain is all you become.

Remaining static is not natural. Everything in nature changes, including us. Nature is the birds migrating high above our heads. Nature is the dangling caterpillar preparing to dissolve and digest itself to become a butterfly. What is unnatural is believing that change can't happen, that it must be painful, or that if your world suddenly changes around you that it's your fault.

Releasing and letting go allow for new beginnings. At first, not doing the same things you've been doing for years can be terrifying. During the waning moon time, kick one of those comfortable yet constrictive cloaks you have been using as a disappearing device to the curb. See how it feels to experiment with different forms of self-expression and identification.

Part of the process of letting go includes understanding why you've been holding on to the thought or the behavior, and focusing on getting those needs met in healthier ways. Part of the art of letting go is understanding the sacrifices you'll have to make, which often turns up as that emotional cord you'll have to cut. Walking away might mean having to deal with the aftermath of profoundly altering lifelong, or lifetimes-long, relational patterns. Decisions might have to be made that will not look conventional or be rewarded immediately. Eventually, this bravery will lead to spiritual and emotional fulfillment.

When you let go of your need to people-please, fewer people will like you. But you will like yourself more, and the relationships that you cultivate from truth will be more authentic.

When you let go of your need to fantasize or project or procrastinate, life may feel harsh or boring. But when we come from a place of radical acceptance—when we acknowledge what is actually here, or who is actually showing up, or what we are actually doing—clarity solidifies. Discernment helps us make more empowered decisions, instead of staying trapped in the foggy realm of delusion. Instead of waiting for others to change, instead of saying "someday," we change ourselves in the present moment.

Letting go can look like no longer expecting an apology that will never come. It could look like apologizing to yourself.

Letting go could look like forgiveness meditations: rose quartz over your heart, telling yourself you are sorry for self-betrayal, that you are committed to now leading with love.

Letting go is the untangling of emotions. It is emotional recalibration. Letting go is the changing of behavior. It is removing obstacles to your many potential futures. Letting go includes awareness, acceptance, space, time, giveness, compassion, practice, patience, and the belief in other possibilities.

The waning moon is a time to figure out what habit or pattern is stopping you—or making it much harder—from moving toward your desires. The waning moon is a time to figure out what your art of letting go looks like, and what your release process must consist of.

Handing something over to the goddess, or to your higher power, is release work.

Sitting with an urge or impulse until it passes is release work.

Crying is releasing too.

To release is to repair. Release what stops you from coming back to yourself. Begin again. Endings are beginnings are endings are beginnings.

Some ways to practice letting go:

Respond from a space of growth: of where your best self would like to be, not how your current self is reacting. Practice this over and over. Give away something you love to someone else. Know you will never see it again. Give something you've labored over creatively to the world. Expect nothing in return. Feel good when people say nice things or feel sad when people say bad things, but always remember that almost none of it has anything to do with you. Repeat as often as needed. Do the next loving thing you need to do.

Consider Your Consumption

The waning moon is an excellent time to examine yourself critically as a consumer—a consumer of the material, but also an energetic consumer—a consumer of thoughts, a consumer of spirit, as well. Think about the books you are reading, the apps you peruse, the music you listen to, and the people you let influence you—in person, on the Internet, and in the media. The voices you pay attention to—those in your head or in outside dialogues. Be particular about whom you let into your space. Be conscious about what you let into your brain. Be clear about what is allowed to access your energy field.

Question if what you let into your energetic field is an accurate reflection of who you wish to become and what your values are. If during this process you need to distance yourself from others who judge you, who criticize you, or who are unsupportive of the positive and healthy activities you are embarking on, do so.

This phase also supports detoxes of all kinds. Maybe you need to delete an app from your phone for these waning moon weeks—or longer. It could be an opportunity to get back to total basics in your life. Focus on eating the best foods for you, doing the most supportive activities for you, surrounding yourself with the best people, and taking care of your body, mind, and spirit properly. These are baseline practices that help our energy but that we often neglect as life gets hectic. Our magical impact is much higher when we are fed properly, when we sleep properly, and when what our body and mind are ingesting is intentional. Go back to those basics for the entirety of the waning moon period and notice the rewards.

THE WANING MOON IS THE TIME FOR RADICAL REST

The waning moon is the time to practice radical rest. This is the act of rest without multitasking. Rest without caveats. Rest without beating ourselves up. Letting our bodies and minds simply rest. Our earth rests for about five months a year.[3] In colder climates, animals go into hibernation. Periods of rest are completely natural. We all need to rest more. We all need to slow down. To try to do one thing, and only one thing, at a time. Count our breaths per minute, and slow down our nervous system.

Capitalism wants us to be addicted to getting our validation in the form of productivity. What we are doing, who we know, how much we are making, what we own. Supposedly we aren't worthwhile unless we've got a lot of those, unless we are the busiest. But we will never feel like we are enough, because someone else will always have more, and be busier. This is how the system is set up. We aren't worthwhile unless the to-do list has been checked off, the form has been sent back, every minute in our lives has been accounted for in our resumes. If this feels exhausting, that is because it is. It is supposed to exhaust us. Prioritizing rest and normalizing guilt-free rest subverts this system.[4]

The idea of forsaking productivity can be hard to comprehend. But there is a huge difference in produce from natural, organic, untreated soil that has been allowed to rest and soil that is depleted, been treated with artificial fertilizers, and over-farmed.

Our yields will be juicier and more impactful when we rest. The quality of what we give to others is enhanced if we rest. Burnout and fatigue are very real. They take a long time to recover from. Taking the rest we need helps us treat ourselves like the priceless treasures we are.

When we practice radical rest and mindfulness, we can complete our tasks with calmness, one at a time. Often, when we are moving quickly, we contract. Think about the state of your body on a daily basis. Are you tense? Running around, rushed? Jaw clenched? True rest and relaxation helps us soften. Our lungs get the air they need. Our brain receives more oxygen and we can make better decisions.

Rest and time spent with relaxing activities are also important because they stimulate the muse. I receive the majority of my creative messages when I am meditating, practicing breath work, running, walking, or in the shower. If I didn't do any of these activities regularly, I would not have a business! Every single creative process includes time away, time spent letting solutions flow in through the ether. After we practice yoga, we rest in savasana. To rest is to integrate.

Rest bolsters our intuition. In the quiet, we come back to ourselves. Rest provides a clear space for intuition to come through. A place to pray, collect downloads, and receive. In rest mode, we are out of the "fight/flight/freeze/fawn" response of the parasympathetic nervous system. Our brain produces alpha state waves. When our brains enter alpha, our creativity is enhanced. So is our suggestibility. If we wish to retrain our thought forms as effectively as possible, we have to rest!

Most of us can't radically rest or do nothing for a whole two weeks out of the month. Scale back in different ways. At least once a season in your lunar practice, try doing the bare minimum you need to do for one to two weeks during the waning moon phase. (Do what you must to pay the bills or keep yourself/family/friends fed and clean, etc.) Spend the rest of the time getting more rest, going to bed earlier, or doing nothing more often. Integrate restorative practices such as reading a book, self-massage, restorative yoga, knitting, listening to music, or being with loved ones without phones.

If you are disabled, chronically ill, or are in a body that requires you to rest frequently, this is a gentle reminder to take all the rest that you need, always, with no guilt, with no shame. You are not the problem, sweet one. The productivity-obsessed, ableist, rest-shaming, sick-shaming culture is.

Many of us were taught that our worth is to be measured in what we could do for other people. This can sometimes be a stand-in for vulnerability and intimacy. Giving becomes a shielding device. It can feel really foreign, or even scary, to stop thinking of everyone else, start putting our own needs first, or ask for what we need. If we are to develop true intimacy with one another and have balanced relationships, our needs have to be expressed and met as well. Many of us feel guilty at the thought of quitting all the emotional caretaking we do. Guilt will come up as we stop compulsively giving. Sit with that guilt and allow it to pass. Use the time of the waning moon to try to give all exhausting emotional labor a rest.

Taking Breaks and Knowing When to Quit

Another way to utilize the theme of rest is to step away from something that has been preoccupying us without end. Artists take a break from their art so they can come back to it with fresh eyes. Lovers take breaks to sort out if they wish to continue the relationship, or move on for good.

Right after a spell is cast and completed, witches often will immediately leave their altar and shift their attention elsewhere. Taking a break from energetic activation allows it to enter the universe. The intentions of your spell can now move around freely; the stardust weaves its way out, up, and around. This also signals to the universe that you are trusting its help. We can't go it alone. To give it over to the goddess is to trust that something even better than we could have imagined is on its way.

Sometimes we confuse exhaustion or burnout with a need to quit. Do we really need to burn the whole project we've been working on for so long all the way down to the ground? Maybe we just need to walk away from it for a while.

Sometimes, we mistake our own impatience with failure, or confuse silence with negative feedback. Don't quit when in reality, things need to take their time.

However, there are times when the only answer is to quit. The relationship, the job, or the project has long passed its expiration date. Figuring out when to simply take a rest and when to actually quit can be part of the work of the waning moon. Some guidance for knowing when to quit are, if:

- You've been trying for a long, long time and you honestly feel as though you've exhausted all possibilities, and the situation is truly not serving you on some very fundamental levels.

- Deep down, you know you will not regret quitting. You will not always wonder ... what if?
- Contemplating the idea of quitting gives your body an immediate relief.
- You've been talking about quitting the thing or leaving the relationship for a long time: months or years.
- Loved ones in your life repeatedly point out that the thing is making you frustrated, that you frequently complain about that same thing, or the thing is causing a strain on your relationship.
- Something gorgeously compelling is calling you to follow it. An enticing candlelit party on the other side of the lake. An exciting new prospect crooking its finger at you, beckoning you to go for it. Quitting one thing would give you space for another.
- If what you are quitting is harming you, sucking you energetically dry, or abusing you. In that case, quit. Immediately. Or as soon as you can.

Whatever we've put our time and energy into was not lost. While you might not be able to immediately see the benefits of quitting a particular situation, with hindsight, connections might surprise you. A skill you've learned might be useful for future projects. A person you met in a situation, or as a result of a partnership gone awry, might end up becoming a future ally. Quitting can offer us incredible lessons. Don't forgo making a decision that will be painful in the short term for more joy and relief in the long term.

THE WANING MOON IS THE TIME TO DO PROTECTION MAGIC

Protection magic is some of the most important magic a witch can master. Protection magic keeps us safe, grounded, and balanced. When we are protected it is easier to stay focused, productive, and in alignment.

It is a good idea to work protection magic consistently—before anything happens to you. Doing protection magic spells every season, or more frequently if you are in a public role, in a service-provider role, or if you are regularly in contact with many people is worth your time. Try clearing your space at the end of a long day for multiple days in a row and see how you feel. The better our energetic hygiene practices are, the less defensive or offensive protection magic we will need to do.

Usually staying out of harm's way is the most effective form of protection magic. Not getting involved in needless drama, not saying cruel things intended to provoke. When a conflict arises, not going nuclear—not even thinking of respectful conflict as a bad thing, necessarily. Think of what is best for all parties involved. Focus on meeting mutual needs and creating solutions. If a person abuses you or is unsafe in other ways, detach yourself from them. Never feel guilty for keeping yourself safe and respected. Never feel bad for advocating for yourself and upholding your boundaries. If more folks behaved in this manner, less protection magic would be needed.

Of course, a lot of times scary situations arise not as a result of anything you are doing. In a culture where abuse is completely normalized, marginalized folks often bear the brunt of this toxicity. Many of us need to protect ourselves from the spectrum of violence that is enacted on us—interpersonally, institutionally, as well as from the government and the state.

The following suggestions for protective work are not just specific to the waning moon time. The waning moon is an opportune time to focus on clearing and protection, as what gets cleared away stays away longer. If you weave small protection magical practices into your life, just once or twice a day, over time you will notice a difference. Following are a few small daily acts you can try. All take no more than a few minutes. (There are also protection spells in the next chapter.)

Touching Base with Your Core Energy

It is important to tune in to what your core energy feels like. The more you tap into yourself, the less space there is for any other energy to tap into you. The more you can check in with your core energy, the easier it is to figure out when your energy feels off.

Close your eyes and take some deep breaths, slow and steady. Loosen your jaw and soften your eyes and as much of your body as you can. On your inhale, bring your breath all the way to the top of your crown, and exhale it out of the base of your spine. Imagine all the energy that is not helpful to you leaving your energy field as you exhale, easily and gently. Call back all your energy into your body. It returns from wherever it was tied up: the phone, work, last week, etc. Imagine all the energy in your body being yours and yours alone. You may wish to imagine a calming color, say a calming word, or say your name out loud. After sitting and breathing like this for a while, you will most likely feel calm, clear, and in the present moment. That is your core energy. Touching base with yourself like this once a day will help to center you and will let go of any outside energy you may be holding on to unconsciously.

Grounding

Getting grounded is an important practice. When we are grounded our energy is less likely to fly out of our body. Our inner wisdom is easier to access. A simple but effective grounding practice is to take your shoes off and stand on the earth. If you have a yard, go barefoot there. If you live by a park, go there. Imagine the energy of the earth moving up into your feet. (This is also sometimes called "earthing.") If you can't go outside, you can imagine a golden cord of energy flowing out of the base of your spine, or through your legs and feet, and connecting to the earth's core. Feel yourself connected to gravity, and completely supported by the earth. Doing this for even a minute or two a day can be restorative. If you have the time and the access, lie belly down on the earth while breathing slowly for some time, releasing any unwanted energy or thoughts. After you feel lighter, let the earth fill you up with its vibrant green and brown energy. Allow the ground to completely hold and support you. (If you have CPTSD or nervous system deregulation, take time to invest more somatic practices to soothe your nervous system.)

Creating Energetic Protection

Before you begin your day, get in the habit of creating a strong energetic shield (many witches call this "shielding"). Imagine your aura as a shell of shielded energy, all around your body. No harmful energy can get in. There are no leaks or holes. You may wish to infuse it with a color chosen intuitively. You may wish to imagine it being an actual shield, or a bubble, or a rosebush. Some witches imagine a symbol, like a pentacle, as being a protector that they place in front of them at all times, that they charge with positive protective energy. You may use any other symbol that makes you feel safe.

You can also draw pentacles all over your body as part of your protection meditation. You can work with symbols of protection, such as cactus, shungite, tourmaline, kyanite, roses, and rosemary. Meditate on what correspondences feel protective to you and create your own ingredients.

Boundaries

No amount of protection magic can help you if your boundaries are nonexistent or flimsy. The waning moon is an excellent time to examine our boundaries and see where they need more maintenance.

Good, consistent boundaries make you feel at home and protected almost anywhere. Boundaries are reasonable preferences that help you feel seen, respected, and cared for. Boundaries can include the physical, the material, the mental, the emotional, the sexual, and the spiritual. Oftentimes, boundaries are referred to as something only to utilize with other people, but the best place to start is with yourself.

Appropriate boundaries, when considered and worked on, provide us with even more alignment and momentum. You and only you get to define what you need to give yourself. This could include space, habits, treatment, affirmations, process, mindset, and more. Some ways to tell that it is time for a boundary check-in and recalibration is if you feel overwhelmed, resentful, angry or irritable for little or no reason at all, jealous, or exhausted. These could all point to needing different boundaries with your time, your thoughts, your habits, your emotions, and other behaviors. Name them and claim them without justification. As you develop more self-love and self-care, your relationship to yourself is not the only one that will transform. So too will the other relationships in your life.

Human relationships are complex and challenging. Conflict is normal and natural in any kind of close intimate friendship, love relationship, family dynamic, or work relationship. With any long-term relationship comes a lot of forgiveness, a lot of patience, a lot of dialogue, and a lot of listening. If you've given it your best efforts, however—if you've been patient, if you've tried—and nothing has worked, your boundaries and self-respect require you to walk away. For every person who treats you with disrespect there are many others who will treat you with the love you deserve.

THE WANING MOON IS THE
TIME TO DO SHADOW WORK

The waning moon is a supported time for shadow work. The quietude of this time allows for introspection. Dive deep into your subconscious, your fears, your limiting beliefs. Air them out. Pull them out of your psyche and toss them into the fire. What are you letting go of? What truths are still staring you down in the middle of the night?

The concept of the "shadow," as popularized by Carl Jung, are the aspects of the personality and the self that we reject. The parts we have pain around or were made to feel inferior about. It is the part of yourself that you have not fully integrated into your consciousness. All of us were taught at some point that we needed to stifle aspects of our personality, aspects of our desires, or aspects of our gifts. Sometimes it is our very glow that society turns into the shadow, and we end up internalizing this. Part of your waning moon work could be resurrecting all aspects of your identity, your gifts, and your genius, and spending time celebrating and nurturing them. This acts as a potent soul integration.

Part of spiritual growth is acknowledging, examining, and loving all of your shadow self—viewing these rejected components as teachers and resonant reflectors, going beyond the pain into awareness of their origin. Some of these parts are your deep desires and dreams. Some are basic ego traits that we all grapple with: jealousy, insecurity, control, or arrogance. There is also shame, blame, self-hatred, and guilt. Mindfulness will help you parse out whether you are being consumed by your shadow side. Procrastination, avoidance, projections, passive-aggressiveness, possessiveness, lying, anger outbursts, and extreme defensiveness are all indicators that parts of your shadowy subconscious are running the show.

Is it any wonder we wish to step around this work? Humans are sensitive. Our bodies process emotional pain as physical pain. These aspects hold truths about who you are, what your life path themes are about, and how your soul needs to evolve in this lifetime.

Exposing our vulnerable parts in safe settings is a powerful tool. Our shadow holds all of our fears, all of our ego's motivations, all of our own limiting beliefs—and in this way, it is a veritable Pandora's box of insights and lessons to our own behaviors. The emotions of our shadow side give us creative fuel. What are the unique gifts that only you possess, which feel scary and exciting to show the world? What would happen, ultimately, if you began sharing them? Would this open up new worlds, different experiences?

Shadow work is ongoing. It is a lifelong process of discovering, uncovering, loving, integrating, and transforming. Be aware of the shadow, but do not identify as it. See it truly for what it is—a part of you that can help you step into more freedom. The understanding and inclusion of your shadows will help you learn to love yourself unconditionally.

It is dangerous to ignore the shadow. The consequences of this are all around us, in our current reality. We live in a shadow culture. Abuse and violence are normalized. The climate crisis is ignored by the masses. Addiction is rampant. Death is feared. Dominant culture does not yet know how to process shame or pain in a way that transforms it. There are no true accountability processes collectively around all of the harm that has been done to Black people and Indigenous people in the United States. Until we develop processes to deal with our collective shadow, it will continue to cause harm.

It is frequent in popular New Age culture, where many practitioners will conveniently "love and light" everything away. Spiritual bypassing is the name of the game—ignoring structural inequities, the history of colonization and how it still affects the collective, as well as other various oppressive systems in the form of denial; gaslighting and deeming anyone who speaks of the human condition and oppressive systems as "not high vibe." This impetus to deny and victim blame is always a sign of someone who has not integrated their shadow. It is a clear sign of someone caught in huge projections, unable to deal, trapped in their own delusions created by an imbalanced ego. This is the six-figure white money coach who never discusses their own privilege, never mentions the word *capitalism*, nor discusses the structural inequities that affect the financial lives of historically marginalized folks. There is the male New Age leader who victim blames and gaslights the women coming forward as part of the #MeToo movement.[5] These examples and many others serve as a blueprint of exactly how not to let our unchecked shadow blot out our compassion and our awareness for others' suffering and experiences.

There are many ways to explore shadow magic in your practice. Shadow magic is focusing on working with the shadow aspects of self, first and foremost. The majority of our attention is put on the examination and acceptance of our shadow aspects: dialoguing with the subconscious, trance, underworld journeying, hypnotism, and embracing and moving through our inner demons are all aspects of shadow magic. Datura and obsidian. Burying ashes, breaking glass, and cracking eggs. Black mirrors and gray moonstone. Hecate and Medusa and Inanna and Kali and Ishtar and Sedna and Pele and Isis and Morrigan and the High Priestess and Lilith and Baba Yaga—and every innocent human who has ever been vilified or misunderstood, every person who has ever protected themself or stood up under threat or tried to protect others.

Working Through Blocks and Limiting Beliefs

Limiting beliefs create resistance to our desire. Limiting beliefs can become a self-fulfilling prophecy. Our past and our subconscious are sources of our programming. If we are programmed to run on a baseline of lack, then lack is what we will feel comfortable with, and lack is what we will encounter. If we train ourselves to see and be and encounter abundance, we will steadily begin to resonate with abundance.

When you are moon mapping, take note of the limiting beliefs that come up as part of the desire or goal. If you cannot access your limiting beliefs, then just look at your desire. Your fear around the desire is the shadow of it. For example, having one's work publicly recognized as a desire could have a shadow side of being ignored, which could be tied to past instances of neglect. Dig a little deeper, and there could be some fear around being seen. Invest in greater inquiry, and you will start to figure out where that fear originated, and all the ways that it got triggered throughout your life, in family, friends, work, school, or the community.

Generally, if you undergo this kind of inquiry, you will then come up with the core limiting belief associated with that fear your subconscious has identified with. *Being seen means I will be punished. If I am to be safe, I must stay invisible.*

The waning moon is the time to meet the resistance. Go to the block first. Write down everything you are scared about around the desire. Think about what limiting beliefs they are connected to. Immediately make space for those beliefs to share with you, give them love and compassion, and then reframe them. Remember that this could happen every time you set a goal. Almost every time you expand, there will be the impulse to contract, to sabotage, or to doubt. Push through to the other side of your new self.

Facing and naming our limiting beliefs and our blocks is imperative to the creation and humanifestation process. There is literally no way we can go after our desires and create long-lasting contentment without working through these pain points. If we've done our moon mapping, the blocks around our desires have been located. We know what they are, and how they show up. The waning moon is a great time to take steps around moving through those blocks and fears.

Whatever creates fear and resistance in your psyche and in your world may never completely go away. Even after years of therapy, doing the work, and enormous successes, folks still come up against internal doubt and resistance. The suggestion here is to deal with your blocks by changing your relationship to them.

If you usually find yourself ignoring them, stop. Go to therapy to work on those beliefs. Pay attention to them when they pop up and act as a gatekeeper. Notice the voices and what they say. When they do show up, what are correlations? Over time, you may be able to predetermine what situations are going to cause a part of your shadow to flare up. You'll have your tools ready to go, to help you through.

Get to know your inner child, the one that doesn't feel safe around change—even the fantastic kinds. The one that doesn't feel safe around being recognized, the one that doesn't feel safe being vulnerable or sticking up for her needs, or creating healthy boundaries. Get to know her and figure out how to offer her unconditional love and support, in order to move forward.

Get to know your inner saboteur. It is probably annoyingly sneaky. This little snake oil salesman makes up stories when you are getting closer to what you want. It makes up stories about not being good enough to receive those things. Figure out a way to dialogue with this saboteur, and let it go. Give it a name, tell it to climb into the back seat of the vehicle of your life as you continue to drive on.

You may need to really love on these different shadow parts. They could need a lot of affirmation that you are safe, that it is okay to change. Assure these different parts of self. Look for proof of the opposite. There are endless examples in your life that you are loved, you are worthwhile. There are endless examples of things working out. Choose to connect to those.

Another way to process the block is through considering the magical idea of sacrifice. In magic and in self-development, sacrifice is not a bad thing. (The etymology of *sacrifice* is "holy.") What are you leaving behind so that you can transform into something greater? Staying small must be sacrificed so that others can see your work more and can benefit from your gifts. Making sacrifices is not bad, when what we are sacrificing is holding us back from reaching our potential!

Get clear on what you will sacrifice; send that identity or behavior appreciation. Step forward in love; you may wish to do this formally with a ritual or spell. You could hold a sacrificial transformation ceremony. Thank and honor the old. Name, celebrate, and inhabit your new identity.

Spend time examining how you utilize and work with your emotions. Examine where and how your "fixing mind" rushes in to make sense of your emotions, or when the "fixing mind" tries to spin those into harmful stories. If uncomfortable emotions come up for you, don't push them aside. This creates resistance. Tell the "fixing mind" to rest, and invite the "allowing mind" to the forefront. The fixing mind and the allowing mind cannot exist simultaneously.

The "allowing mind" invites our subconscious into the conversation. It is curious about what messages come up, even if they seem irrational. The allowing mind is an observer. It can give you a lot of information about your current core subconscious beliefs.

You can ask yourself: What limiting beliefs are coming up for me now? Where can they give me more information about my needs? How do they give me information about my subconscious narratives? How can I reframe those narratives in my mind? How will I redirect unhelpful emotional loops into supportive affirmations?

Little Activities and Rituals to Try During a Waning Moon Time

Cultivate patience. Send out that first draft or that final draft. Bless what is leaving your life. Bless what you already see or feel that is coming in. Honor and trust your intuition. For each day of the waning moon, go through and organize and declutter: one drawer, one cupboard, one closet, one box, one corner of your home. Let go of any or all toxic expectations. Lie on your floor for ten minutes every day, with rose quartz, tourmaline, or another supportive stone on your heart, tummy, or reproductive organs. Breathe and release any stress your body is carrying. Before you go to sleep, ask your future self to have a solution ready for you in the morning for a problem you have. Write down all your current "shoulds." Read them aloud. Burn them. Go through your phone and delete all the numbers you don't need anymore. Practice ease. Invite in radical rest. Throw out anything in your space that you no longer need or that no longer pleases you. Stop doing things you don't like for people who don't treat you well.

Waning Moon Magic

Waning moon magic covers a wide range. It is not all hexes and banishing spells! (Though banishing spells and hexes, if in your practice, are most supported at this time, as well as in the dark moon period.) As covered earlier, the most supported types of spells are those that facilitate release and letting go of things.

Casting spells for removing problems, eliminating trouble and hurdles and obstacles, neutralizing adversaries, and reducing harm is most effective when the moon is on the wane. The waning moon and dark moon are optimal times for breaking curses, breaking attachments, and breaking alliances to harmful behavior. Uncrossing spells do well during this time.

If you have been moon mapping, this is the time where you may wish to release attachments to your fears around your desires. The waning moon might also be the time to do some subconscious reprogramming work around the belief systems that have been underscoring fears, doubts, or ways you resist moving forward. You can combine self-inventory with ritual or magic. Take action around clearing all that stands in the way of actualization—whether self-imposed or external.

This is also the time to focus on banishing spells. Banishing spells can be used to get rid of any energy you no longer want in your energy field. Burying spells, burning spells, and freezing spells work well at this time. (Some of these types of spells are detailed below, and there is more information in the dark moon magic chapter.)

During the full moon through the entirety of the waning moon is a time when we are especially open to our intuition, psychic abilities, and dreams. Start dialogues with your intuition. Experiment with different ways of accessing your intuition. (Reread the section on intuition at the full moon if you need more ideas.) Maybe one lunar cycle you try trance work, during another you could focus on communing with plants.

For many, this is the time of heightened productivity, deepened creativity, and getting a ton done. The waning moon might feel closer to a traditional waxing moon phase for you. This could be the time to shine, begin new projects, and take some risks. If you feel fantastic, make that list and check it all off. If you know this, use this time in accordance with your personal energetic patterns.

Your Waning Moon Altar

You could leave your waning moon altar up for the duration of the entire moon phase. Or, you could construct it around your spell, if you are doing one, and take it down afterward—specifically because waning moon spells tend to include burning and burying. Releasing unwanted energy is a focus at this time, so your altar could be a place to go to process grief or sorrow. Your waning moon altar could have photos of you from the past, or your ancestors. Your waning moon altar could be a place to record what you are letting go of, before saying some final good-byes.

We can imagine the activities we undertake at this time as our altar as well: Post-it notes of plans all around us, plotting out that rough first draft. It is having the hard phone call, making that appointment, taking care of business in a determined fashion. Your altar could be sweeping and scrubbing.

Your altar is also you reaping the benefits of doing the work of the new, waxing, and full moon phases. A time to practice receiving, a time to trust, a time to rest. It is your inner voice coming in clear and loud. It is the insights you receive as you make the time to sit each night in quiet candlelight.

Magical Correspondences of the Waning Moon

It is important to develop your personal set of correspondences depending on how you personally interpret each phase of the moon. Below are some suggestions that might resonate with you. Feel free to leave what does not resonate and add your own.

Roots, such as ginger, turmeric, potatoes, dandelion root, burdock and lotus roots; datura; bones; the colors brown, black, red, white; salt of all kinds; rosemary, agrimony, pepper; snakeskin, insect carcass; ruby in fuchsite, mugwort, motherwort, fossils, petrified wood, redwood trees; spiders, webs; smoky quartz, yarrow, black tourmaline, amethyst, chrysalis; the Hermit, the Hanged One, the Devil, and the 7's in the Minor Arcana tarot cards; and any special objects you wish to work with or charge under the growing light of the moon.

Deities that correspond to the waning moon: Hecate, the High Priestess, Persephone, Baba Yaga, Lilith.

Archetypes that correspond: the work, art, and lives of Mark Rothko, Sylvia Plath, Robert Johnson, Nick Cave; crones, and elders of all kinds.

Animal guides that correspond: snakes, snails, spiders, owls, bats, jaguars, moles, cicadas.

A PROTECTION SPELL

This is a spell to aid with protection from self-destructive thought patterns or behaviors, or protection from the energy of destructive people.

You will need:

A white or black candle, one that burns for at least one day, dressed with your preferred banishing/protection herbs and/or oil

Rosemary, salt (feel free to research and add your favorite protection plants, like yarrow or oregano)

A bowl

Any crystals that resonate with you around protection and loving clarity, such as jet, rose quartz, tourmaline, obsidian, and clear quartz

Paper, pen, scissors

Before the spell:

Clarify what you need help with banishing. This could be internal, such as procrastination, doubt, or manufactured distractions. It could be external, like emotionally manipulative people or coworkers who steal your work. Take responsibility for any underlying subconscious allowances of this pattern. (For example, underneath "procrastination" could be "comfortable with comfort" or "there is safety in stagnancy.") Attempt to work with banishing both the internal basis and the external symptom(s).

Clarify if you will be calling in any help from ancestors, guides, your higher self, planets, deities, etc. If it is a particular goddess, such as Venus, or a planet, such as Saturn, that you will be working with, you may wish to cast your spell on the day (or even the hour) that is associated with them, while under the waning moon.

Clarify what sacrifices you will have to make to release the energies and protect yourself from future incidents. If you are letting go of procrastination, you may have to sacrifice always having an excuse, being stressed out always/addicted to cortisol, or having an unconscious attachment to psychological self-harm. Affirm that you are clear on what you are letting go of. If your spell is focusing primarily on protection, affirm what protection will feel like, and what acts will support you in strengthening your protection.

If working with a deity or other energy to aid you, clarify how you will show your appreciation and devotion for their aid. How will you thank them?

You will want some chant or affirmation around what you are letting go of. Feel free to write it out ahead of time. It can be a poem, a letter: whatever makes you feel powerful and sure.

Spell set-up:

Combine herbs and salt in a bowl to make your cleansing mixture. One-third of a cup of this mixture should be more than enough.

Cut a circle out of a piece of paper. (You may wish to trace around your bowl as a template.) You will want enough room on this circle to write down what you are banishing and/or what you would like protection from. In the center of the circle, draw a personally meaningful symbol of what will help you with this. (What is a symbol that makes you feel safe?)

Around the circle, write down what you are banishing, what you are releasing. Put the paper circle on the altar. Put the candle in the middle. Arrange the rosemary and your protective crystals around your paper. Have your rosemary and salt mixture at the ready.

Cast your circle, or begin your spell how you usually do.

Light your candle. Chant your spell.

Connect with what you are releasing or banishing. This will provoke sensations of unease or grief. That is okay. Bring this all up into your consciousness. With your breath, bring this up into your body as a tangible form—as visualizations, colors, shapes that have a tangible beginning, end, boundary. They might have a color or a temperature to them. They might originate in a certain place in your body. Continue to breathe through any contraction. This is hopefully the last time you will be feeling the emotions around this specific situation, so let yourself feel.

Imagine the unwanted forms beginning to release from your body and mind. This could take a while. Imagine returning them to a field of golden energy to be transformed for good. Try to release any ill will, blame, or grief that comes up again, out of your body with breath, or sobbing, or venting. Do this until you feel a shift in your energy. Take as long as you need.

As soon as you feel a shift, sprinkle your salt and rosemary mixture on top of your paper circle. You will want to slowly and completely cover your words. Some witches go counterclockwise to banish.

Focus on restoring and protecting your aura. Imagine your energy being completely protected, completely safe. You now have a new, very strong color surrounding you. Place your protective imagery all around your aura. Connect to the earth, and affirm that you are supported and protected.

Thank your helpers, higher self, all elements involved. Close your circle.

Let your candle burn through. (Never leave a candle burning unattended.) When your candle is burned down, smother with the salt mixture. If your candle is in glass, fold up your circle paper, put it in your candle, throw some salt in it, and throw away/ recycle in a trashcan that is not yours.

For at least three days after the spell, ground and protect your energy. In the coming weeks, carry out any and all additional sacrificial work you must do—in waking life, or for your helper deities/spirits. Whenever you feel pulled to an old behavior, thought, person, or pattern, bring up your protective symbol as a deflection and a reminder. Go put your attention and energy somewhere else. Be very mindful of putting your thoughts and actions on positive thought forms and behaviors for at least the next few days.

UNCROSSING RITUAL

 This is a great ritual to do whenever you feel "off." When you can't pinpoint who or what might be affecting you, but there seems to be stagnancy or a stuckness in your life. Maybe you've been dealing with a series of unfortunate events, and feel like you can't catch a break.

You will need approximately two to four hours for this ritual, or, if you feel called to really dive in deep on cleaning, you may wish to spend about a few hours a day, for a few days, decluttering and cleaning before doing the ritual.

You will need: a yellow candle, water, salt, a bowl, a bell or chime, dried hyssop, dried agrimony, dried angelica, a loofah or body scrubbing sponge, a broom, and/or other cleaning supplies, and a dried plant bundle to clear the room, if that is in your practice.

Part 1: Clean at least one or more rooms in your house. If you don't know where to start, pick your bedroom, and/or pick the room you do the majority of your spell work in. Get rid of what you don't need, dust and mop, and then move a couple of items around so that the energy moves differently in the room, or it looks slightly different. Shift the energy by moving art around, or changing the set-up of your room.

Part 2: Set up your altar. Dress your candle with the hyssop and angelica. Place water in your bowl, salt in the water, and the candle in the bowl.

Light the candle.

Center yourself and raise some energy. You could do this by fire breathing, by clenching all the muscles in your body and releasing them, and/or moving your body, chanting, or focusing on energy flowing all around your body like a fountain. Imagine yourself moving any energy inside of you that you no longer need or no longer want.

Say: "I release any and all stagnant energy, any and all unhelpful energy, and any energy that is not mine, now, and in all futures."

Ring the bell.

Say: "I release any and all curses, hexes, or workings against me, whether I am aware of them or not. I release any and all contracts made in this life or others. They are gone now, never to return."

Ring the bell.

Say: "I release any and all unconscious attachments to stuckness or stagnancy for now, for ever, for always." (Or name whatever it is you are releasing.)

Ring the bell.

Take the broom, and start sweeping the room. Sweep the air, sweep any and all stuck energy out, out, out. If the room has windows, open them. You may wish to say, "Begone! Do not return!" You may wish to burn dried plant matter, like rosemary, or lavender, to cleanse the air. You may wish to stomp, bang on a pan, or chase all unwanted energy out of your home. When you feel the energy has shifted in the room, re-center.

Say: "I welcome any and all positive energy."

Ring the bell.

Say: "I welcome in love, joy, and movement."

Ring the bell.

Say: "I do everything in my power to center movement, luck, and joy."

Ring the bell.

Say: "Fresh starts, new opportunities, and clarity come my way, today, forever, and all ways! My mind/body/spirit are protected now in all ways, in all futures to come!"

Ring the bell.

Part 3: Draw a bath. Put salt, hyssop, agrimony, and angelica into the bath. Pour the water all over you; dump it over your head with a cup or a bowl, if possible. Soap up your entire body and scrub it with your loofah. Imagine all fear, accumulated unwanted energy, and stagnancy draining into the water. Once your entire body has been scrubbed well, drain the tub.

Part 4: Aftercare. Dispose of the spell workings, such as the herbs and burned-down candle. as soon as you can. Make a pledge, in the coming week, to do at least one thing to let go of more old energy, such as cleaning out your fridge, and one thing to get energy moving, such as visiting a place you've never been before, reaching out to friends to do something fun, or adjusting a part of your daily routine. It is also suggested to change your appearance in some way: get a haircut/new style, switch up your fashion or makeup in some way. Changing your energy up and changing your appearance makes it hard for old energy to reattach!

A TAROT PULL TO CONNECT TO THE LESSONS OF THE WANING MOON

Get into a clear, calm space with your cards, some water or tea, and a notepad and pen. Leave your phone in another room and dim the lights.

Go through your deck and pull out a card that right now is an accurate reflection of you. Put it in the center. This is card 1.

Pull out a card that best reflects the main theme of this lunar cycle for you. Place it to the left, below card 1. This is card 2.

Pull out a card that best reflects where you'd like to go next.

Place it to the right and next to the last card you pulled. This is card 3.

Pull out a card that best reflects a card you feel drawn to, but don't fully understand right now. Place it to the right and next to the previous card. This is card 4.

Now, shuffle the rest of the cards in your deck.

Ask: What lessons am I learning? What did I start healing during this cycle, whether or not I feel it? Pull a card, and place that card underneath card number 2.

Shuffle the cards.

Ask: What is the secret superpower I'll need to keep moving? What is my energy and heart ready to put into motion for future cycles? Pull a card, and place that card underneath card number 3.

Ask: What is the truth about my current situation? Something I may not be able to recognize completely, but need to see or know, in order to progress? Pull a card, and place that card underneath card number 4.

Shuffle your cards.

Ask: What does my inner power, or source, or my other helpers want me to know about where to focus my energy and efforts in the next lunar cycle? Pull a card, and place this card above the very first card you picked.

JOURNALING PROMPTS
FOR THE WANING MOON

How can I invite in even more gratitude for all my blessings?

Do I feel called to share my knowledge? How will I do so?

What behind the scenes work do I feel ready to do?

If this is an energetically balanced time for me, how can I take advantage of it?

What are my current blocks?

What are my subconscious narratives?

What is draining my focus or energy?

What can I do to consciously slow down?

How can I protect my energy?

How can I develop better boundaries?

What are the self-imposed limits I must rewire or reject?

Where is my shadow telling me I am ready to start healing?

How is an aspect of my shadow actually my superpower?

What have I put off dealing with?

What must I clear away to begin a new cycle?

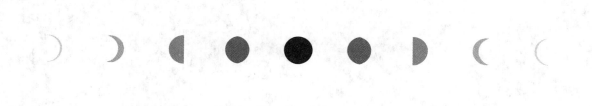

The Dark Moon

Transformation in the Void

The last three days of the lunar cycle are the dark moon period. This marks the end of a lunation. At this time, the moon is not visible to us on earth. Even the moon needs to hide away sometimes.

During the dark moon, the Great Mother creator archetype of the full moon morphs into the Dark Mother destroyer. Intense, insubordinate, mysterious, and difficult to define, the energy of the dark moon slithers out of any hands that try to grab her. Some of the most powerful goddess deities and archetypes in the pantheon that possess a dark moon quality—Hecate, Medusa, Inanna, Baba Yaga, Ixchel, Lilith, the archetype of the Witch—have morphed from all-powerful, self-actualized wise ones to deities who inspire fear. Many of us are now interrogating those narratives, reclaiming these goddesses, and tapping into these aspects in ourselves. In doing so, the liminal beauty and power of the dark moon is also reclaimed.

The dark moon assures us that periods of depression, rest, illness, rage, grief, sorrow, withdrawal, rebellion, and unbridled creativity are completely natural. Often, finding our own unique ways to stay with and transform these intense experiences into visionary meaning is what heals us. To embrace the unknown or mysterious aspects of who we are is to enter the portal of the void. If the full moon is the wild known, the dark moon is the wild unknown. The dark moon helps us destroy, vision, reawaken, and go beyond.

The dark moon is the most mysterious phase of the lunar cycle. Because we cannot see it, our imaginations make up all kinds of quixotic possibilities. It is where desire and liberation wave to us through the other side of the mirror. It is where we are forced to reckon with that which has held us down, and decide to wriggle out of its knots. The dark moon is a site of liberation.

For so long, we have been taught to ignore or repress dark moon aspects of ourselves and our lives: the divine feminine, queerness, death, sex, kinks, subversion, rage, power, transmutation, intuition, and dreaming. The more we resurrect and explore these themes, the more we understand the treasures buried within them.

The dark moon is the waning moon amplified. Finality and endings coincide with this time period. This is the end of the end. The shadow's source. Rock bottoms and breakthroughs. Destruction is enacted in order to create. After the loss is thrown in the fire, new life stirs in the smoldering ashes. Our inner North Star magnetizes us to rise up into different realities. In this way, the dark moon is about envisioning faraway futures.

If one has been working through an entire lunar cycle, the dark moon is the period in which the main themes of the cycle may come back around again. If this occurs, release and integration work is imperative. Clear whatever debts, past life patterns, and long-standing emotional wounds that are associated with the themes of this specific lunation. Take accountability, express gratitude, then decide to move on for good. Vow to step into a different time line that is now activated with your clear intentions and actions.

Dark moon energy is seeding energy. During this time we begin to conjure the qualities of the seeds that will be planted at the upcoming new moon. When we garden, we are often dismayed when a plant has gone to seed. (This state is also referred to as "bolting.") The plant no longer yields fruit. Its energy has switched to the creation of seeds. The original plant has to die in order to offer up new life: a transformation must take place. Seeds gestate and grow in the dark. All of creation begins in the dark.

The dark moon is a wildly generative space.

It is where we make friends with the unknown.

It is where we make friends with *our* unknown.

When we revel in the beauty of the dark, we access our own spiritual secrets.

Within the dark moon are the seeds of a new world.

DARK MOON TIMING

The dark moon rises around 3 a.m. and sets around sunrise. The moon follows the sun closely at this part of its orbit. The length of time the moon *appears* dark to us, however, varies from one and a half days to three and a half days.[1]

There are a number of ways to observe the timing of the dark moon. One way is to observe the dark moon during the time of the technical "new" moon—as we cannot see the moon, it is "dark." The "new" moon is then observed when one can see the first shimmer of light on her face, technically at the waxing crescent stage. A lot of folks observe the dark moon time period as being the three days just before the astrological/astronomical "new" moon.

How you wish to observe the dark moon is up to you and how you feel. Experiment with honoring the three days before the new moon as the dark moon time, the next cycle try honoring the dark moon period during the "official" new moon. If it's the "new" moon and you feel full of rage or exhausted and you don't know why, the "new" moon may be your "dark" moon. Over time, you will figure out when your own dark moon time tends to fall.

Similar to the new moon, your dark moon may consist of different actions for each day. On the first day of the dark moon, you may wish to touch base on what is coming up for you and journal. On the second day, you could try casting a spell or holding a ritual around that information. On the third day, you may wish to rest or do any activities that would best prepare you for the upcoming new moon.

IF A DARK MOON IS HARD FOR YOU

It is no wonder that the dark moon period and energies are challenging for some—intangibilities, endings, death, and unknowns are grueling to navigate regardless of where we are in our lives. If dark moons are especially taxing for you, you may have been born during a full or new moon phase—or you might be *in* a waxing or full moon phase: resonating very deeply with building, with growth. Resting or getting mystical can seem beside the point. If that is the case, your dark moon work is simply to pause. Take stock of all you have accomplished so far.

If you are someone who has a lot of ego work to do, it may be difficult to soften here. The unbalanced ego has a pathological need to protect itself, and that need comes with a lot of constrictions. Examine why you need to feel safe even when it comes at a cost, to feel protected even when it blocks opportunities. Can you accept that often you do not have the control you would like to have? Can you accept that everything always comes to an end, in some way?

If a dark moon is difficult for you, it could be because your relationship with the shadows is already very intimate. Once we've lived through tragic situations and survived, there can be a very understandable fear that anything negative that surfaces again will take us under. Those of us who have mended destructive patterns and recovered from trauma tend to be preoccupied with peace, quiet, and calmness (for good reason). If this is the case, you can double down on your coping skills or prioritize pleasure. One way to define healing is an ability to get through intense challenges and still love ourselves. Even when the weather outside is stormy, we can still treat ourselves with compassion, still be our own safe container.

The dark moon is the time to touch base with our inherent power. With power comes accountability and responsibility. Cutting ourselves off from our own power, or denying that we have any power whatsoever, is a behavior we enact to avoid ego death. Manufacturing chaos, procrastinating, overscheduling, engaging in numbing or escapist behavior, being passive-aggressive, having loose or leaky boundaries, engaging in dramatic relationships, waiting for permission from others or for outside validation to do or try something meaningful to us: these are just some of the ways in which we abdicate personal power. All of us engage in some of these types of behaviors at certain times in our lives. But if many of these behaviors seem to be your default, it might be time to use this part of the process to eradicate any over-attachments to serious energy distractions—energetic and literal—you create.

When we confront these complicated aspects of self and attempt to transform them into fertile landscapes of possibilities, we are supported by our own dark moon energy. The act of conscious destruction facilitates growth. Pain made into meaning shows us the lessons of loss. Within the dark moon lies the knowledge that we can do the hardest things. It is a symbol of our survivorship and resilience, which is also our power and self-actualization. The gifts gleaned from the diamond depths offer up the widest possibilities.

WHEN YOU ARE IN A DARK MOON PERIOD

If you are in a dark moon period you may want to get rid of everything you own. Feelings rush in quicksilver hot; you want to rage, to burn it all down. You may experience uncontrollable pangs of sadness, hold a deep longing to grieve—but not know exactly what it is you are mourning. There could be the inclination to rise, phoenix-like, into another brilliant and glittering phase. Incredible visions and huge bursts of creativity may rattle around in your aura, potent psychic downloads may be your loudest conversations. This time is intense, itchy, inspiring—any shedding cycle is.

The experience of living through a dark moon period could be described as undergoing a profound spiritual awakening and transformation. Otherwise known as a spiritual crisis, a healing crisis, or an identity crisis. This process is disorienting and also isolating. It is beyond language, more immense than mere words. How to explain a death that is also an awakening? There is no going back. Once we've gone through a dark moon period we are irrevocably transformed. There are now greater inclinations toward the service of humanity. The personal becomes collective.

If you are in a dark moon period, you might not know what your style is anymore. You might be in between identities. Take the time to get to know who it is you are becoming. You will find yourself positively allergic to pettiness, trifling situations, and other time wasters. You want the truth. You want depth. Good-byes will be necessary. Not every person is meant to be invited into your next chapter.

When you are in a dark moon phase, you've met many makers and many masters. Mountains have been scaled, nightmares have been survived, and these encounters have shaped your evolution. Titles, approval, and the trappings of the material world become drastically less important. You've gone beyond false constructs in order to create a world where your true self and spirituality will blossom.

THE DARK MOON IS WHERE
WE JOURNEY IN THE UNDERWORLD

The waning moon is where we begin to pull inward into the descent. The dark moon is the active journey in the underworld. In many ancient cultures, the afterworld was the underworld—not heaven. Folks would travel down into caves and caverns for ceremony and shamanic journeying, pantomiming an approach toward death. Obsolete aspects of self were left there in the underworld so as to return to an awakened life more whole, more holy.

Underworld travel requires bravery and an interest in excavation. The descent is into the vast interior; our own personal fairy-tale realm where we must slay our own dragons and dance with our own demons. Who we have become when we return from these depths will be different than who we were when we initially set off. The future self is the destination.

The descent myth of Inanna, the ancient Sumerian goddess, offers us insight into the healing opportunities of the dark moon descent. Before there was Persephone, before there was Isis, before there was Aphrodite, there was Inanna, the "Queen of Heaven." She was the goddess of sex, fertility, justice, and war. She was also known as "the First Daughter of the Moon."[2]

Inanna descends into the underworld to visit her sister, Ereshkigal, Queen of Death. Unhappy about her sister's visit, Ereshkigal tries to keep her out. Inanna, at first lavishly adorned in her finest garb, must pass through seven gates, or challenges, where she finally ends up completely naked at her sister's throne. Ereshkigal orders her death and has her skewered onto a meat hook for three days. With the help from her adviser, two genderless beings, and her father, Inanna is resurrected and rescued. When she returns to her throne, she finds her husband on it. Instead of mourning her he has taken over her kingdom. She banishes him. After so much hardship, Inanna returns to her life more whole and more powerful than ever. She has known rejection, betrayal, and death. She has been stripped in every sense of the word. She has surrendered completely. Inanna now becomes Queen of Heaven and Earth.[3]

The myth of Inanna predates any masculine god's descent tale. In this myth, women are the central figures. In many myths where goddesses enter the underworld, they are dragged or pulled against their will—usually by a masculine figure (see Hades and Persephone, or any number of other Greek myths involving non-consent). Inanna *willingly* travels down into the underworld, curious and ready to experience her shadow self.

Inanna dies for three days and three nights. The experiences of her own dark moon period are initiated by a yearning to visit the mysterious underworld. In the process, various relationships are completely changed—most important, the one with herself. Once she is so naked as to lose her skin, her death rebirths her.

This myth can act as a guide for our own descents. Inanna passes through seven gates, removing an item of clothing at each one. This can serve as a metaphor for our own journeying. Habits and beliefs form layers of distractions that hinder us from living authentically. What falsities do we cling to as if they were real? What has been distracting us from important work? What stories keep us ensnared in the trance of unworthiness?[4]

This myth also illustrates how much honesty and vulnerability is required in order to facilitate growth and healing. At the dark moon, dare yourself to get honest about who you really are. Admit how incredibly strong, brilliant, and genius you are. Believe that you possess the courage to meet your own demons and dragons in order to transcend them. Envision what will be possible when you connect with your own personal power completely.

Descent is either a willing or unwilling initiation. A willing process often begins when we are called to make an enormous change. If we can parse out how we are ready to expand, we first pay attention to all that blocks us and clear those blocks away. The healing process around an old wound may commence. We are ready to unite once again with our intuition through subconscious or dream world exploration. We are Inanna, paying a visit to the underworld to meet our sister self. We know that she might be angry, resentful of our intrusion. Underworld selves prefer to rule unbothered, perched on their jagged thrones from deep inside our psyches.

Willing descent requires a commitment to interior work. Therapy, support groups, journaling, meditation, dialogues, forgiveness work, unabashed self-observation, nervous system healing, facing hard truths.

Often, we are dragged into the descent unwillingly. Depression, illness, profound loss, breakups, addictions, uncomfortable revelations, and other deeply painful situations will often initiate a descent. If this is the case, the number-one rule is to give ourselves oceans of compassion. So often, we blame ourselves. Almost always, though, we are doing the best we can. All of the ways humankind grapples with the unfairness of life will surface. Unfortunately, gentle reader, life is not balanced; bad things happen to wonderful people. If possible, seek outside help in as many forms as you can. Dress your wounds and give yourself buckets of compassion. In time, try to identify what this situation is teaching you.

Think about what resources the situation is asking you to tap into. What does this challenge want you to get clear about? What are your coping skills? Is there a way to make this situation an ally? Reflect on how this hardship has helped you focus in on what is most important to you. This descent has scraped away all that is frivolous; in time, this will be a gift. Make an action plan about what must be done differently, moving forward. Be clear about what must be done now.

Enlightenment occurs through the journey into the different areas of the psyche, from the subconscious to dream states to the ego to the conscious to imagination to super-consciousness. There is much light to be found in the underworld, we need only learn how to look. The visions collected in the dark will bring forth future revelations.

THE DARK MOON IS THE TIME TO DEAL WITH THE HARD STUFF

Suffering is too often accompanied by shame; shame is often the instigator of much suffering. Shame can be found virtually everywhere: in the media, advertising, in our family of origin's beliefs and patterns, in our workplaces, in the spiritual community, as well as in the world at large. The consorts of shame are humiliation, silence, and self-hatred. The accomplices of shame are racism, fat-phobia, classism, transphobia, capitalism, and sexism. The ropes keeping shame upright are guilt, blame, embarrassment, and paralysis. The enforcers of shame are perfectionism and competition. Shame also often takes the shape of "shamers"—other people who enforce your feelings of unworthiness. Sometimes we are the shamers, whether or not we know it.

Shame is one of the most pervasive emotions there is. Shame could stop you from moving forward on your dreams. Shame silences us and leads us to believe that whatever abuse we experienced was our fault. Shame renders us powerless no matter how high we climb.

Shame is a hex that takes hold in both apparent and intangible ways. It is a hex that, if left to fester, will feed on itself. There are ways out of the curse of shame. Vulnerability and connection are antidotes to shame. Silence is shame fertilizer; voice your truth and watch shame wither. Laughter, humor, fun, silliness, and joy make shame run away. Focusing on all you have until your heart feels warm and glowing snuffs the flame of shame. Connections to your own unique creative expression or spiritual practice alleviate shame, as does surrounding yourself with a positive support network.

Separate your actions from your intrinsic value. Yes, maybe you made a mistake. Maybe it was truly horrible and hurt others or yourself. Maybe it was just slightly uncool. But that doesn't make *you* any less awesome, or any less valuable. If you need to take accountability, take accountability. Apologize, make amends, and understand how not to repeat the mistake. Take action around your misstep. Realize that others might not be ready to accept apologies or be quick to forget. Move on with the wisdom you've gained.

I have found that shame in my life tends to pop up when I am about to get more expansive, when I'm ready to take up more space. Because my background has abuse in it, my subconscious and my ego have told me that to stay small is to stay safe. I have found that it is when I am about to level up in some fashion that shame and doubt will actually sting and stick around. My subconscious is looking for proof that I'm meant to hide, that I'm unworthy or undeserving of my hard work, and it comes out in shame spirals. Be mindful of *how* and *when* shame turns up for you. Use it as information, not as a reason to quit.

During the dark moon time, as part of your moon mapping, you may wish to check in and see if shame is holding you back. Where do themes of shame pop up in your life? Where do you weaponize shame, to punish yourself, or others? What are some recurring limiting thought patterns related to shame that hold you back? Reflect during the quiet of this time in order to gain a different perspective or more information around how shame may pop up, or hold you back.

Forgiveness Is a Gift You Give Yourself[5]

Forgiveness is a worthwhile practice when dealing with the hard stuff. Sometimes, if you've done a lot of other work, tried a lot of different things, and something still seems stuck, it could be that forgiveness is in order.

Some folks think forgiveness is the same as welcoming someone who wronged you back into your life. It isn't. It is about dropping a burden you may not have even realized you were carrying.

Some of us are waiting for an apology that will never come. With all fibers of our being we believe that we are owed this—and truly, we do deserve one. But it never comes. So resentment grows like mold on our insides. Underneath the resentment are complicated emotions. Longing. Abandonment. Anger. We need to direct our attention to those subsurface emotions and be open to feeling them and giving them love. This awareness serves as an indicator of where we can alleviate the stress we've put ourselves under.

The power of forgiveness is such that it releases energetic cords and brings more tenderness and compassion into one's heart. Rather than remain stagnant in the past, the act of forgiveness places us into the present.

We slip into patterns of being our harshest critic. We hold so much against ourselves. Usually no one is harder on ourselves than us. Even if you can't quite name or place why you might have to forgive yourself, it is important to have a consistent self-forgiveness practice. Sitting down once a month and having a longer forgiveness meditation around the waning or dark moon is a fruitful habit to practice. Forgive your past self. Forgive your present self. Whisper, "I forgive you. I love you," and set those parts of yourself free. Let go of what is no longer yours to carry. It most likely was never yours to drag around in the first place.

Another related piece of healing work is to not forgive, but accept. Compulsory forgiveness may feel activating, and isn't always appropriate. If there was abuse or violence, or horrific mistreatment, maybe that isn't even an option, nor should it be. Maybe being able to tap into anger and own it feels empowering to you, which is in itself a gift. The point of forgiveness is to reclaim precious energy. Another way of doing this is to try acceptance. Acceptance is not approval. It is not condoning awful behavior, it is acknowledging it. It is understanding and accepting what happened, or understanding and accepting what kind of person someone is, in order to make the decision to untangle one's energy and to move on. Acceptance is a powerful healer. As Lily Tomlin said, in reference to forgiveness, it is giving up all hope of a better past.

THE DARK MOON IS
WHERE WE DEAL WITH DEATH

There are levels and layers to death. There are subtle deaths: when a phase of inquiry or interest ends. There are deaths that leave you numb: processing the particular wound will unfold over time. There are deaths that are exuberant: orgasms, bonfires burning pages and pages of "no mores" and "see you nevers!" There are deaths that are a long time coming: a pronoun change, a name change, the end of a toxic relationship, the release of an identity that no longer fits.

Part of what makes these types of more metaphorical deaths so incredibly anxiety-producing in real time is that we truly do not know what awaits us on the other side. Our consciousness may react to our circumstances in a defensive way. Figuring out how to soften while these metaphoric deaths occur helps us rewire our systems. When we stay present with ourselves through shock, this supports our ability to be flexible. We bend instead of break.

There is the literal death most of us recognize as primary: the end of life, the permanent cessation of an organism's being. It is my belief, based on visitations by clients' loved ones and my own, that the consciousness of a human goes on after their body ceases to function. Our bodies return to the earth from where we began, back to the source, while consciousness lives on in different forms in different realms.

Energy cannot be destroyed. Energy can only be transformed. Death is not the end of a person's legacy. It is not the end so long as we have people who remember us, and those people have others that remember them. If you are grieving a person, this means that you have been blessed by someone's love. We create legacies that live long after our bodies have passed on. We live on through the acts of love we undertake, in the inventions we offer, in recipes we share, and through the families—biological and chosen—we create. All the more reason to be careful and exacting with your intentions, your words, and the energy you bring to a space.

In her monumental book *Women Who Run with the Wolves*, the scholar Clarissa Pinkola Estés presents the concept of Life/Death/Life.[6] This is the idea that time continues on: nothing living ever really dies. States of being are transmuted constantly. Matter is transformed. Our periods of dormancy, of death morph into life. The moon dies each month so she can be reborn.

If metaphoric deaths are painful for you, it might be useful to meditate on the idea of life, of rebirth. What new life will this death dissolve into? Remember all the times that when something left, another way of loving came along. Life/Death/Life is a circle, not a straight line.

We weave in and out of death and life, out and in. Sometimes with others, never quite alone. Even in death, we are not alone. We enter the realm of the ancestors. The remembrance of our actions weaves into the loving memories of those we have influenced. As long as there is love, no one ever dies.

Our Harmful Ego Must Die So We Can Be Reborn

The dark moon energy is one that facilitates ego death. Everyone has an ego and everyone needs an ego—a *healthy* one. Unfortunately, not a lot of us were taught what a healthy ego looks like. A lot of us weren't given tools to feel safe and so our ego stepped in to become a shield, a defense mechanism, leading to an unhealthy ego that acts as a separation device. Not being controlled and constrained by the harmful parts of our ego is a struggle for many.

Try to locate what your ego "feels like" in your body and when it tends to flare up, becoming protective at the cost of openness and growth. It could be around money stuff, it could be around criticism, it could be around being acknowledged. (Most of us have multiple ego activation points.) Usually, the only way the ego knows how to keep us safe is through avoidance, defensiveness, or denial.

For trauma survivors, for folks whose agency has been taken away from them on repeated occasions, change can often feel like ego death. For those of us who have been abused, once we've broken free from harm and gained agency, we sometimes wish to reinforce the boundaries of all our choices. Saying *no*, sticking to routines and the known, is a reclamation. Doing so reinforces our autonomy and safety. I am in no way suggesting that folks who need safe and secure arenas threaten that. If you feel called to rebirth, there is something that must die in order to facilitate that. The gentle suggestion is to seek out changes in small, safe-feeling increments. Change up the order of your daily routines. Change up what you do for fun. Change up how you meditate. Meditate *on* change.

One way we must actively seek death is through the death of fixed identities. We are always changing, always growing into multiple identities at all times. All of the ways in which an ego is tested—embarrassment, disruption, humiliation, vulnerability, rejection—threaten to strip off the masks we have constructed. The walls we have painstakingly built—to keep us separate, keep us isolated, keep us safe—come tumbling down when we face a death of any kind. During these times, we are reminded that safety is not a given. The illusion of safety can prohibit our growth. One reward of dissolving our over-attachment to a constrictive identity is the sense that we can be anyone, we can become whatever we would like.

The death of unhealthy aspects of the ego promises us an experience of self that is far greater, enduring, and more meaningful than if we had kept our defenses erected. The essence of who we are—our core consciousness—has space to chime in. With our authentic selves laid bare, we get real. When we get as real as we can, we name and focus on what is most important for our reinvention. Another self emerges. And then another. The death and rebirth, Life/Death/Life cycle goes on as long as we do.

Grief Is a Part of All Our Ongoing Life and Death Processes

Grief is not something to be fixed or ignored. Grief is to be worked with, listened to, and allowed to take up space. Grief is to be engaged with, another teacher in the classroom of life.

All of us sit and converse with grief at some point. We grieve those we lose. We grieve the past, whether through nostalgia, or if stolen from us by cruelties. We grieve our ancestors' pasts—what they had to go through to get us here. We grieve violence, injustice, and needless suffering. We grieve for whole peoples, mistreated and exploited. We grieve for the earth and her flora and fauna, polluted and ravaged.

We grieve what we never had. We grieve what no one gave us. Who we were told we were. We grieve the fear and scarcity that were dumped on us by society, or by our families.

Grief can also be existential. It can feel both vague and nameless, and yet also deeply entrenched in bone and blood. If you come from a group of people who have experienced persecution, remnants of grief are passed down through your DNA.[7] If you are part of a diaspora, there is grief that comes from that deep grief accompanying people who have been colonized, with all of the violence and erasure that it includes.

Once grief sets in, it will not go away until we acknowledge it. Grief is bitter molasses, there is no rushing through it. Grief is an ongoing process, and we must treat it as such. Expecting that we will wake up one day finished with the feelings that keep company with loss only sets us up for more pain. Only when we accept that grieving will be an ongoing part of our existence will our pain transmute into deeper healing.

Grief shows up in unexpected ways. Sometimes after experiencing a great success, we may find ourselves numb or sad in some way. The time line of grief is not logical. Witnessing and working with the timelessness of moontime, the timelessness of magic can help us embrace this. We can return to a painful scenario, reframe it, and leave certain attachments behind. We can still include our loved ones in our lives even if they have passed. Speak to them, write them letters, and share our lives with them. Remember that many of our ancestors, blood or not, want us to carry on and create lives that are a testament to the lessons they've taught us.

Grieve what you need to and when you need to. There is no grief hierarchy and no grief handbook that will be completely tailored to you. (The books of Elisabeth Kübler-Ross are a start, as is *The Year of Magical Thinking* by Joan Didion, *The Smell of Rain on Dust: Grief and Praise* by Martín Prechtel, and *Bluets* by Maggie Nelson.) Grieving is a somatic process: it must be experienced through the body. It must make its way through your nervous system and out of your tear ducts. It must be experienced viscerally; do not hold back from expressing emotions. Do not force yourself to "get out there" or be the same person you were before the traumatic event. Let grief hold you as it needs to hold you. Let yourself be in a relationship with your grief until you are holding it. This helps loosen its grip. Eventually, the holding moves into integration, and the integration gives us more insights and a more spacious quality of life.

Looking to archetypes of grief—symbols of sadness, sorrow, and rage—can help us better understand or empathize with our pain. There are the Harpies: those wailing winged soul-snatching creatures of stormy winds. There is Lilith, the original grief-stricken woman, her pure expression rejected by her husband, punished by god, losing thousands of children a day, all alone in an empty world. Hecate glides over the expanses of the liminal world and the underworld, her black cloak gliding over headstones, her hounds gnashing their teeth, her torches lighthouses in the night. She is a solace to those who exist in between worlds. Indeed, over time, Hecate was demoted from being the ruler of all worlds, to the ruler of Hell, to a sub-deity forced to roam; she expresses a particular form of feminist grief—the grieving of a power repressed, stolen, and shunned.

These images of pain-ravaged femininity present to us the ways that pain literally mutates us. Made out of claws, teeth, monstrous parts, and too many heads, grief transforms us into surrealistic pain bodies. These archetypes speak to how we are physically and psychically augmented by grief and trauma. Look to tales and stories from your own culture and background to see if there are any teachings in your ancestor's archetypes of feminist grief. Listen to various examples of grief personified through art: the music of Nina Simone, Alice Coltrane, Nick Cave.

Pay attention to how grief comes up for you and what it needs you to know. Let your grief inform your life. Let it change you. Let it break you open. Let it pull you through. May your suffering make you softer and stronger. May your grief inspire you to demand justice, connect to others, and help you to protect your joy.

THE DARK MOON IS THE ENERGY OF THE VOID

Death is scary to us because it lies outside the limits of our imagination. Beyond death, there is what we truly cannot conceptualize. This is the void. The void is infinite.

Where there is the infinite, there is joy. "There is no joy in the finite," the Chandogya Upanishad reminds us.[8] The finite can be controlled; the finite is exact and thus is limited. The finite does not acknowledge the endless beyond from which our consciousness springs. The infinite is chaotic, the infinite is messy. There are only possibilities, beyond laws, beyond money, beyond linear time.

In much of Eastern thought, the 0 is a strong symbol: it cannot be destroyed, it is a stand-alone. It is the numeral between the positive and negative; it is a balanced base. Zero is the tunnel, the portal, that cosmic spiral that occurs in nature: the earth, the orbits, the moon. The void is a fruitful place.

Nothingness is like the nothingness of space, which is actually everything.

Magic Loves a Void

Even though embracing the void can run counter to our impulses, doing so will completely enhance our magic. The most potent magic takes place in the void. In the liminal space.

Non-attachment can stimulate growth. Detachment from a very specific outcome in our magical workings gives the energy more opportunities to flourish. Clear the mind of concrete expectations and even more fantastic results will occur.

Generally, we avoid the void. Humans really like space to be filled in, schedules to be packed, and goals to be stacked five miles high. The machine of capitalism tells us this is the path to success: this is what success *is*, what worthiness *is*. That spell gets broken when we accept that we must float in the land of the unknown for periods of time. Embody the unknown in order to create imaginative groundbreaking art, ideas, and liturgy.

New combinations are activated in the unknown. When we don't know what is next, or even what we wish to be next, clearing out space and time, and allowing ourselves to get comfortable in the void is some of the most important work we can do.

Build a bridge from a finite place to an infinite space. Restructure our mindset so that we are in a relationship with our desires, not controlled by them. Radically accept where we are: the pain, the chronic illness, the disappointment, the avoidance. Whatever the block is, it is also the information that leads us into a more generous space. A place of no-thingness. A place to begin.

When we practice having healthy detachment, our spiritual and magical life tends to grow. Our magic is more alluring when we meet the universe halfway, not when we are chasing her down with a butterfly net. Treat your magic as you would like to be treated. Give your desires the space they need to take. Let the shapes they make best teach you the lessons you need to learn along your path of infinity.

Make time for play. Play is anything that is enjoyable and doesn't rely on an outcome to be worthwhile. Anything that doesn't have a "should," "have to," or due date attached to it. Activities that are solely for pleasure, connection, and expression. Make a list of those activities. Do more of them.

Create something, then destroy it. Do some things that are invisible to everyone but you, every day for many weeks. Remember a time when many things were unknown to you. What came out of that phase? What is mysterious about yourself, to yourself?

In the void, we discover what works for us and us alone. What that is will not be the same thing as it is for anyone else. It may not even be the same as what worked for you a year ago. But it will be exactly what you need to take with you on the next leg of your journey. In the void, we learn to float. We meet our future crone, our wisest self—and listen carefully to what they want to impart.

Every path is unknown. Even the ones that appear tried and true have a destination we cannot fully know. Even if we get the "good" job, even if we do what is expected of us, even if we make the "right" choices, life will continue to throw us cosmic curveballs. Even when we try to play it safe, things fall apart. This is why it is important to work with the energy of the dark moon to ask the important questions.

What do I want to accomplish, spiritually, before I die? What do I wish to accomplish, creatively, before I die? What am I healing? What are the most important things in my life? What are my emotional, physical, and spiritual needs? How can my unique gifts flow through me? What wisdom am I searching for in this lifetime?

When we can answer a few of those questions truthfully, we've gained real intimacy with the self. There's a bedrock of trust and understanding. To enact the lessons of the dark moon is to follow our own wisdom, to apply all we have learned, while leaving some space for some unexpected wonder.

The dark moon is the part of the lunar cycle where we step into our own authority. There is meaning to be made of the accumulation of patterns, time, and dreams. Within this authority is power. This power is built on trust. As we complete and close our own circles we come home to ourselves.

Little Activities and Rituals to Try During a Dark Moon Time

Learn to see in the dark. If the outside is safe for you, find someplace very quiet, and go outside in the dark alone. Sit in the darkness and stare at the stars. Lose yourself in poetry, in fairy tales, in children's stories. Hold a funeral for your self-hatred. Write down one thing you need out of your life by next dark moon on paper and watch it dissolve in a glass of vinegar. Eradicate the word *sorry* from your vocabulary. Focus on what is most important more often than you focus on what is not important at all. Make a list of activities that consistently drain your energy and eliminate at least one of them forever by the last day of the dark moon. Turn your phone off: for hours, or days. Go on a detox: from all that you think you know, from all that you think you are. Meditate on nothingness. Connect to the various elders and wise ones of the cosmic pantheon—or the ones in your neighborhood or family. Connect with your inner crone. Connect with your outer crone. Encourage yourself to vision in the void.

Dark Moon Magic

Dark moon magic is of a piece with waning moon magic. Any spell work you do around traditional waning moon themes during this time will pack an extra punch. However, dark moon energy, spells, and ritual are also their own compendium. It is that time where we cut the tether to the old in order to construct radical creations. Cast your dark moon spell accordingly.

Traditionally, dark moon magic is synonymous with banishing spells and release work.

If we're being honest with ourselves, much of the time when we cast a spell what we are mostly seeking is to change the way we feel. We wish for peace, or at the very least, neutrality. Going nuclear against anyone or anything you perceive to be imped-ing your goals, if it isn't actually the case, is a sign that it isn't a banishing spell you need: it is therapy. If you are resentful and annoyed at the majority of people in your life, then it is time to figure out why you feel this way.

When you are ready to be done with something once and for all, it's time for a banishing spell. As always, put your focus on your thoughts and behavior. After you untangle from the energy you wish to banish, you can enact your ceremony or spell. Afterward, always, always, *always* take care to seal and protect your energy. Seriously commit to stop thinking about the person or situation. Stop going places or engaging with anything that will stir that energy for a while. A banishing spell is a fundamentally altering spell: it is radically changing a relationship you have had in your life, whether that be to an ex or the patriarchy. Think of your energy field like a healing wound. Treat it tenderly and with proper protocol.

Personally, I prefer to conduct release or integration work during a dark moon. Release work requires less energy, for one. Release work is like slowly driving away from a place you know you'll never see again, giving yourself space to cry, hash out old memories, and process as you depart. Banishing is similar, energetically, to suddenly shoving someone out the door of your house, dead bolting all the entrances, and lighting all that they've left behind on fire while vowing to never speak to them again. (Which, while dramatic, is sometimes a needed action!) A banishing spell could look like going through your house and discarding any reminder of the person/situation, energetically clearing all the conscious and unconscious imprints of the situation, and mentally and psychically transforming it—destroying it and changing it into something better. Then, you very effectively protect your house, your vehicle, and your person so that your energy is airtight and will be so for at least a lunar cycle. That's banishing. Banishing is to be used when you never, ever, *ever* wish to see or experience something ever again. Use it to quit smoking, or when leaving an abusive relationship. In my experience, banishing takes quite a bit of skill, quite a bit of energy, and even more discipline.

Integration is softer. Integration can be shadow work, but it can also be love work, and rest. It is allowing space for the feelings about the situation to be recognized, and extending compassion to that aspect. In doing so, we stop repeating harmful thoughts and patterns. This takes practice. Often, this takes eradicating all punitive impulses and rigid edicts. The self will shrink, will disconnect, will freeze, will run if given more messages that it is wrong, or that it should or must or has to. Sometimes our perceptions need to be examined and altered through pausing and inquiry: What if I stopped doing this? When does that mood surface most? How can I move this energy, this emotion? What does my body need? Do I need to turn my brain off and just breathe for a while? Integration allows us this spaciousness.

Dark moon magic encompasses creativity, generative practices, and deep visioning work. It is a very fruitful time to cast spells you would like to be planted deep inside your psyche. This is the energy of the Fool card in the tarot: you are about to take a great leap, so what instincts do you want guiding you? Spells for connecting to intuition or the subconscious, support around taking risks or new expressions, illuminating dreams, and new muses all are supported at this time. Spells for reinvention and rebirth correspond to this time. Pull those glimmers of your next best self out of the ether by beginning to dream about what could be. The dark moon time is a beautiful space to experiment with innovative ways of making, expressing, being. Try something you've always wanted to. Do meditations to connect you with other worlds, other beings, the planets. Creating states always begins with unbridled imagining.

Your Dark Moon Altar

The shape your dark moon altar could take could vary wildly. This is the unknown, the wild zone. Your dark moon altar could be moments spent in the cradle of a large root system of an especially alluring pine tree you find in your forest wanderings. It could be screaming in your car. You may wish to especially rely on your intuition in this phase and follow what bubbles up.

If you are in a dark moon life phase, you could take advantage of this phase by constructing an altar that you decide to leave up as a sacred space to connect to this energy. As with all of the lunar phases, your altar could exist solely in your mind. Your altar could move through you like a rattlesnake shake, delivering you closer to abandon through interpretative dance. Your dark moon altar may symbolize anything you are ready to offer up to the void to be transformed in generative ways.

Some Magical Correspondences of the Dark Moon

It is important for any practitioner to develop their own set of correspondences depending on how they personally interpret each phase of the moon. Below are some suggestions that might resonate with you. Feel free to leave what does not resonate, and add your own. Some of the correspondences of the dark moon also overlap with the correspondences of the waning moon. Violet, datura, thorns; volcanic ash, pumice, charcoal; shungite, jet, hematite, vanadinite, lepidolite, rhodonite, black moonstone, merlinite, Dumortierite; black salt, salt water, vinegar; bones, vintage leather; black holes; Death, Temperance, the Tower, Judgment cards in the Major Arcana, and the 10's in the Minor Arcana.

Deities that correspond with the dark moon: Shiva, Kali, Hecate, Baba Yaga, Medusa, Lilith.

Archetypes that correspond to the dark moon: the work and lives of Nina Simone, Toni Morrison, Diamanda Galás, Hilda af Klint, and Pamela Colman Smith.

Animal guides that correspond to the dark moon: the phoenix, cat claws, cats, shark teeth, sharks, snakeskin, snakes, leopards, lobsters, horseshoe crabs, katydid shells, cricket symphonies, ravens, crows.

DARK MOON SPELLS

A Spell to Banish Confusion and Doubt

You can use this spell as a template for the banishment of anything you'd like. Commit to making the behavioral shifts that will ensure that this spell will be successful.

You will need:

- At least two hours' time, true resolve, and committed focus
- A pen
- A small black candle that will not burn for more than a few hours
- A small pin with which to carve the candle
- A small bowl or cup filled with water
- Five very small pieces of paper
- A small piece of black tourmaline
- A small piece of quartz crystal

Before the spell:

Get very clear on what you are banishing. Examples could be: behavior that is time wasting, dependence on being disorganized, self-punishing behaviors like staying up too late, reliance on misogynist notions of success, etc. *Pick one thing and one thing only.* You can always do this spell, or a spell you create similar to this one, once a month at the waning or dark moon.

Spell set-up:

Write down the thing you are banishing on the five separate pieces of paper, one for each element. Place your candle in the center of your altar, with each stone on either side of it.

Casting the spell:

Get centered and cast your circle, or begin your spell in your usual fashion. Carve the word or a symbol of what you want banished on your candle.

Charge the candle with the energy of the thing it is you wish to banish. Feel it leaving your body and going into the candle. Take as many deep breaths—with an emphasis on your exhale—as you need in order to feel some of the energy detaching and moving into the candle.

Light the candle.

Say: "I banish _____ with the power of fire! Fire, burn this energy off me and turn this energy into good!"

Cross the writing out on the paper until you cannot see it, and burn it, using the lit candle.

Say: "I banish _____ with the power of water! Water, wash this energy off me and dissolve it into something cleansing!"

Cross the writing out on the paper until you cannot see it, and then put it in the bowl of water.

Say: "I banish_____with the power of air! Air, clear away this energy and replace it with peace!"

Cross the writing out on the paper until you cannot see it, and then tear it into tiny pieces, and breathe on it.

Say: "I banish_____with the power of earth! Earth, absorb this energy and turn it into something nourishing!"

Cross the writing out on the paper until you cannot see it, and crumple it into the tiniest ball.

Say: "I banish_____with the power of my center! I conjure my will to keep my promise!"

Cross the writing out on the paper until you cannot see it, and then poke it full of holes with your pin.

You may wish to add a chant you made up, or yell, "Begone begone begone! I banish you I banish you I banish you! Go away go away go away! Never to return never to return never to return!" until you feel like the energy has retreated.

As the candle burns, take time to imagine moments when the energy you are banishing might come back in. Imagine yourself dealing with that energy. Imagine yourself ignoring it, or walking right past it, or allowing it to have no control over you. Do this at least three times.

Touch base with where you feel it in your body. This might be the area that needs extra love, release, and attention. Place your hands over the body part and send it love and neutrality. Clench your entire body up and release it. Take some very deep breaths. Move energy around and out of your body.

Conjure up a feeling of joy or harmony. Maybe you think of a color that you love. Allow this energy to fill your entire body.

Imagine your mind being wiped clear of the clutter and replace it with a grounding object or word.

Now imagine yourself with a new energy. This energy comes as a result of allowing what is banished to be gone. Take time to imagine yourself doing things you want, communing with folks you love, in this freer state. Imagine yourself in specific scenarios that are healthier, that are more in line with your soul. Do this at least three times.

Take time to thank every element that has helped you, and your other helpers, the universe, source, your higher power.

Close the circle.

As you step out of the spell, imagine vibrant parts of your soul flowing into you; you are stepping back into yourself with more clarity. This is a person who is powerful, this is a person who is not distracted. Promise yourself you will no longer engage in chaos, confusion, conflict, or drama.

Bury or burn all the pieces of paper, as well as any remainders of the candle, somewhere far away from your home.

Carry your tourmaline with you for at least a week to remind you to put up your protection shield.

Once a day, meditate with your clear quartz.

Direct your energy toward what is true for you when you are at your most neutral or calm. When you get frazzled or derailed, take deep breaths, close your eyes, and imagine the color, word, thought, or visualization that makes you feel calm.

A Spell to Strengthen Intuition

 This spell fosters a greater intuitive connection between yourself and a chosen tarot card, infusing you with the specific intuitive gifts of the card archetype. You can do this spell at any day, at any time, at any point on the lunar cycle.

Spell set-up:

Choose a tarot card that communicates power, confidence, and clarity. Maybe it is a card that reflects the ability to easily receive information. You could pick the High Priestess, for example—the card that directly corresponds to psychic ability or intuition. Other cards associated with psychic ability and intuition include any of the Queens, the Star, the Fool, the Empress, the Hierophant, the Chariot, the Hermit, the Hanged One, the Moon, the Aces—feel free to use any you feel attracted to.

Make your altar. Place any objects around the card that resonate with the energy you have chosen to ignite.

If you are working with the High Priestess, some of its magical correspondences are: moonstone (all kinds), selenite, clear quartz, Herkimer diamond, lumerian quartz, lapis lazuli, silver, coral; mugwort, motherwort, datura, chamomile, jasmine, lavender, rose, ylang ylang; water, dolphins, whales, any animals that live in the sea, any animals that transform or shed, such as snakes, frogs, and toads; black, all shades of blue; pomegranates.

If you feel called to use a candle or candles in your spell, white, black, blue, or silver all work.

If you are using another card, you can use some of these ingredients, as all of the above correspond to elements of intuition, or you can make up your own that correlate with the card you are working with.

Before you cast the spell, write specifically about what the card can help you with. Turn that into a spell chant, or a petition to the archetype of the card, or a song you will sing in your spell.

Cast the spell:

Cast your circle, create your safe container. Allow your body to get relaxed and open. Light your candle or burn your incense, if that is part of your ritual.

Pick up your card and really drink it in. What do you love about it? That is what you love about yourself. What does this card excel at? This is what you excel at. Accept these wonderful things about yourself. This is the truth. Your intuition picked the card, and your intuition is the truth.

Invite in any messages from the card. Listen, notice. Take note. Put the card back on your altar.

Read your spell, chant, or sing your song. Do this until you feel energy move. Now try to move like the archetype of the card would. Change your posture, pose as the card. Take deep breaths and move the energy of the card into your body. Maybe it is the colors of the card. Maybe you bring the symbols of the card into your aura or mind's eye, maybe you imagine yourself eating pomegranate seeds, flirting with the moon, talking to stars. Really place yourself energetically in the realm of your card.

When you feel energy move or shift, you know that you have integrated the energies of the card on some level. Thank the energies of the card.

Promise to carry out the energies of this card in small or large ways every day. Dialogue with the card. Journal as the card. Research the symbolism of the card; dig up mythologies of the card—look for any tales or myths or deities from your culture, or even from your family history, or your personal history, that resonate with the energies of the card. Pull the energies of the card into your cells and intertwine them with your actions. Make the card your helper for at least two weeks.

A Ritual for Nothing

This ritual requires nothing other than a calm, quiet, comfortable space. You may wish to have the following read to you, or you may wish to read it out loud. A recording of this meditation can be found at: themoonbook.com. It is meant to evoke the void.

Focus on your breathing. There doesn't have to be a particular rhythm, just allow for your breath to take up all the space it needs to inside yourself, inside your lungs, moving from the soles of your feet to the top of your head. Spend time connecting yourself to your breath, its ins and outs, and the spaces between. Explore where your breath wants to go, and where it may be tight. Explore where your breath needs to go, and what happens as a result. (Pause.)

Now imagine a circle around you. It is a circle of energy. It is a circle that protects you. It is a circle that keeps all your energy inside its boundaries and everything else out. As your eyes close, can you feel how far away from your body this circle needs to be? Just notice this. (Pause.)

Make sure to fill your circle with your breath. With every exhale, expand your breath out past the skin of your body, into the circle of protection, the boundary around you. With every inhale, imagine fresh energy from the sky coming into your body and filling you up.

You may imagine your breath as colors. You may imagine your breath as a sound. Notice what your breath needs from you. Notice what you need from your breath. (Pause.)

In your circle, allow all your thoughts, all your dreams, wishes, mental chatter to fill up the space. Have it all out there, all around you, all inside you. Take the time to see what pops up. Notice if it has weight, if there is an overriding energy there. (Pause.)

Then imagine a big gust of wind blowing it all away outside your circle, outside your body. Imagine everything leaving your body, and with it, you suddenly have all the space you need. You feel very clear. You have now entered the nothingness of clarity. (Pause.)

Your body slowly and easily sinks into the earth. You find yourself magically in an underground tunnel, full of crags and pockets and curves. The earth is alive, and you feel grounded, concrete, and tangible.

You are safe here and you explore. You find yourself in a small dirt room, made naturally by a cave. In a niche in the dirt wall, there is a secret object. See what it is. Hold it. Listen to it. The dirt room becomes a tunnel becomes a portal to the outside. You follow the light that leads you out of the ground. (Pause.)

You break ground, and as you leave the earth, your body begins to get lighter. With each breath, you rise higher and higher and higher, until you are in the sky, floating like a cloud.

Imagine your consciousness dissolving so that you are aware that the thoughts you are thinking are of you and not of you. Imagine yourself connected to sources inside of you and outside of you. Imagine any resistance to the idea that you are actually part of everything and everything is part of you; fade away. You are actually everything, and everything is part of you.

The more everything you become, the more nothing you become. You are actually nothing, and nothing is actually you. Both things are true. The more this is true, the more true you are. As you allow yourself to become very, very still, notice any new awareness you have. Keep breathing. Keep filling your lungs with air. (Pause.)

Your consciousness slowly leaves the sky, you slowly rise through the atmosphere and into deep space. You see stars, and nebulae, and planets. You see the sun, the moon, and realize that just as you are a part of yourself, just as you are a part of earth, just as you are a part of the sky, you are also a part of space. You slowly allow yourself to dissolve. You see yourself, and all your thoughts and your actions and your pain and suffering and love, turn into the tiniest particles of matter and float away.

A gentle sense of calm washes over you. Tell your subconscious that after you wake up, any downloads, any messages will be enacted in your life following this dark moon period. Thank everything for showing you nothingness. Thank nothingness for showing you everything.

Take three deep breaths. Count backward from thirteen. Open your eyes, stretch your body, come back to yourself.

Death Doula Tarot Card Pull

This tarot pull is designed to help you facilitate, name, and enact the parts of the process that create room for the transformational qualities of death. Give yourself at least forty-five minutes to do this spread and process it.

You will need: a tarot deck, a notebook, and a pen.

Get into a cozy position in a quiet area. Take some slow and calming breaths. You may wish to shuffle between each card pull, or just shuffle once for as long as you like and then pull all the cards one after another. Place all the cards in a row.

Card 1: What needs to leave.

Card 2: What the resistance or grief is around.

Card 3: How to work with that resistance or grief.

Card 4: What spirit wants to tell you; another perspective.

Card 5: The healing that waits on the other side.

Journaling Prompts for the Dark Moon

What have been my major accomplishments this season or lunar cycle?

What is my pain teaching me?

How can I change my relationship to pain and suffering?

What is dying in my life? What will this death clear out space for, in the future?

What must I surrender?

How do I deal with transitions?

How do I stay hopeful in the dark?

Who am I ready to be now?

What is the work of my life about?

What are the major themes, patterns, and energies of my life?

What are my wildest, most exciting dreams for my future?

What are my wildest, most exciting dreams for the collective?

Lunar Lore and Literacy

Eclipses, Blue Moons, and More

ECLIPSES

What Is an Eclipse?

An eclipse occurs whenever the sun, moon, and earth are lined up in such a way that the sun or the moon is obstructed temporarily. There are two kinds of eclipses: solar, which can only happen at a new moon, and lunar, which can only happen during a full moon. The word *eclipse* comes from the Greek *ekleipsis*, meaning "failure to appear" or "cease to exist."[1] In this case, the reference is to light being obstructed, or augmented, which is essential to life and vision. *Eclipse* also means to leave, to pass over, to move past.

Eclipses come in pairs: there will always be a solar eclipse at a new moon and a lunar eclipse at a full moon, about two weeks apart. (Sometimes, the order is reversed; the lunar eclipse comes first at the full moon, and the solar eclipse follows at the new moon.)[2] This time period, from about a week beforehand to a week after, is referred to as "eclipse season." Eclipses are frequent, occurring between four and seven times in one year.

Some Historical Background
of the Interpretation of Eclipses

From the beginning of recorded history, eclipses have inspired wonder, fear, and awe. How could they not? Even though a solar eclipse cannot last longer than about eight minutes, and a lunar eclipse cannot last longer than four or so hours, time seems to stand still while we are transfixed by the visual spectacle high above our heads.[3]

In ancient times, humans would look for reasons for wars, deaths, famine, and other extraordinary events on earth. Often, they would attribute such events to eclipses—even if one was a week, a month, or even a year afterward. Eclipses *are* extraordinary to witness—it is understandable that our ancestors would attribute specific events with them.

Humans also avoid accountability. They wish to assign greater cosmic meaning to tragic or tumultuous happenings. Over time, eclipses became synonymous with the death of kings and popes, the removal of dynasties, and other chaotic upheavals like sickness, famine, coups, and revolutions.

There's also the astrological connection. Many European kings and rulers looked to astrologers for insight on when to make major decisions, when to wage wars, when to predict deaths; their own demise, and the demise of other important rulers, such as popes. During that time, eclipses were often the predictors of deaths of powerful people. (The sun, especially, was correlated with kings and other powerful masculine rulers.) In Vedic astrology, Rahu and Ketu are charged mathematical points: nodes in the sky where the sun and the moon cross each other. In Persia, it was a monster that ate the moon. In Tibet and China, it was a dragon eating the sun and the moon.[4]

Eclipses were also used to control others. Astronomers were able to chart when eclipses would happen, and humans would use this information in nefarious ways. Before a solar eclipse, ancient Egyptian kings and priests would chastise their people, and ask for atonement for their sins and misdeeds. People would offer sacrifices and contributions, hoping to get in the good graces of the sun god Ra. An eclipse would occur, and the people would double down on their efforts, and strengthen their loyalty to the priests and kings as sole intermediaries to their god.[5]

Much of the current-day fear around eclipses comes from this long history of the correlation between chaos, punishment, and eclipses. It is also corresponds to the patriarchy's—and some ancient astrologers'—view of the moon as a malefic entity. The literal view of an eclipse can be frightening. At a solar eclipse, if you stare at the sun too long, you may injure your eyes; even Socrates warned Plato about this.[6] A bloodred moon, a common visual during a lunar eclipse, appears ominous. The Bible interprets eclipses as being a sign of the end times: "The sun shall be turned into darkness, and the moon into blood, before the great and the terrible day of the Lord come" (Joel 2:31). It is no wonder humans have been alarmed about eclipses!

Not all religions associate eclipses as evil. Muslims have a special prayer to recite during them. Tibetan Buddhists believe that any activities performed during an eclipse are greatly amplified, and emphasize undertaking healing and supportive practices directed at the self and others.[7]

Attitudes around eclipses are absolutely due for a revision. Now that we know what eclipses are, and how often they occur, we can work with them—not just be superstitious of them. They might just have a slightly different or amplified flavor, like a planet going retrograde, a reversed tarot card, or sleet instead of rain. This could cause shock, annoyance, or inspiration. It might give you all the more reason to pause, to think about your patterns, to be present with yourself and the world around you.

Eclipses are always innocent. All celestial events are. It's we humans who feel so out of control so much of the time, who project the good, the bad, the ugly, the fearful onto the cosmic stage. Funny how we see ourselves as superior to those in ancient times and their archaic customs, yet so many of us play out the same superstitions, albeit through crystal screens we hold in our hands.

To be certain, eclipse energy can be intense, and sometimes painful. It is often contrast that wakes us up, makes us look up, and helps us to make needed course corrections in our lives. Anything can always be looked at as a curse or seen as an opportunity.

Eclipses as Blessings, Eclipses as Breakthroughs

Eclipses can be a time of breakthroughs. We can work with, not against, the energy of eclipses. To tune in to eclipse energy, begin as you would with any lunar practice: with tracking and noticing. Pay close attention to your thoughts, your emotions, your energy, and any external events that transpire during eclipse season. What comes up for you physically, emotionally, intuitively, symbolically? Are there any out-of-the-ordinary external events that pop up? Write them all down in your journal. If any downloads or epiphanies occur to you while you are going about your day and living your life, write them down in your note section of your phone, or record a voice memo to yourself.

Your experience around eclipses may be similar to new or full moons, just with the energy greatly amplified. Emotions may feel extreme. Your energy could be depleted or boosted. Note your experience for at least one eclipse season, and up to a year, to try to understand your eclipse patterns. You can connect the eclipses over six months, one year, or eighteen-month periods, which are usually related in terms of greater themes or patterns. If you follow astrology, you can track what happens when an eclipse occurs in your sun, rising, or moon sign, or what it is specifically activating in your chart.

Emotional healing is available to us at eclipses, especially full moon eclipses. We must collectively reframe healing trauma and processing painful emotions as worthwhile, constructive, liberating work. Because that is what it is. Eclipses can help us with our change work, by showing us our shadows, and shedding light on where we need to heal.

Some questions to ask yourself during eclipse season:

Where am I deciding to no longer self-sabotage?
What neglected part of me am I ready to care for?
What behaviors of my own, and others, are no longer acceptable to me?
What do I really need, that I must give myself?
What patterns are occurring right now, and where does that relate to where I
    must make a decision or take action?

Eclipse Energy Is Amplified Energy

The amplified energy can be utilized as a boost to help you make bold moves. Initiate important wrap-up processes and end bad habits. If you choose to pay attention, these times can aid you in developing your metacognition. In doing so, perspectives shift and mindsets change.

Eclipse season will intensify what is already present. It shows us what we must deal with in order to move on. It is best to think of the entire pair of eclipses—the time a week or two before them, the time between the solar and lunar eclipses, and the time up to two weeks after them—as a distinct period, and be ready to slow down or speed up accordingly.

Energetically, eclipse season may leave us exhausted. Our physical bodies may be affected. We might get the flu, get headaches, or have more trouble sleeping than usual. Pay attention to what your various bodies—emotional, physical, spiritual—need.

Eclipses are about shadows, and so our shadows will be shown to us. By tending to our triggers somatically, and giving ourselves space for our nervous system to process, we can stay in our body. In doing so, we can snap out of the trap of our subconscious programming.

Make eclipse season work for you by recognizing and acknowledging your needs. Then center them and communicate them clearly. Listen to and respect the needs of others. Do something for your inner child. Start a new way of thinking or begin a much-needed self-care habit.

An eclipse could provide you with answers or deliver information that you need in order to move forward in some fashion. Even if it is painful, such as catching a friend in a lie, or not getting a promised raise at work. Eclipse season can provide you with deep, rich insights about yourself: your needs, your fears, most vulnerable places, and your boundaries. It can also feel harrowing, overwhelming, and like many deaths traveling through your nervous system at once. Encounters with the truth can be intense. What is most important is how we treat ourselves.

Eclipses can be portals. They can speed up processes if we get very clear and make the appropriate decisions and moves. If we are focused on what needs to be dealt with and followed through on, eclipses can help us—a positive, albeit turbulent rocket boost to a different reality.

It can take several weeks, six months, or up to a few years to see the lessons and blessings of eclipses. Some astrologers see eclipses as tied to six-month periods. Most eclipses in the same sign families happen about six months apart, with a lunar and solar eclipse happening in opposite signs. For example, if there is a solar eclipse in Leo in August, then a lunar eclipse in Leo would happen about six months later. Around the time of a solar eclipse, think back to six months prior. What themes and patterns were surfacing in your life? Are any of the same themes coming up for you now? What are some new beginnings you'd like to make? What endings must happen in order to clear space?

Endings and beginnings are synonymous with eclipses. If the urges around starting new chapters are long overdue, eclipse season is the time to stop lingering and make the appropriate decisions. Even if you don't, the eclipses might come in and clear some no-longer needed parts of your life away. Ways that these endings and beginnings can show up are deciding to move, actually moving, breakups, loss, or conflict. Getting to the point of getting sick and tired—of your own bullshit, of being sick and tired—definitely fall into the categories of beginnings and endings. The encouragement is to use the situations as educational experiences. Let them help you make decisions that have been a long time coming.

People around you will have breakdowns and breakthroughs. People can be especially ungrounded during eclipse season, and when people feel insecure and disconnected they are especially reactionary. Be gentle with yourself and others. Do not leap to conclusions around this time. When in doubt, pause. Assess if you need to gather more information. Avoid making projections or assumptions based on nothing. Ask questions first, instead of flying at someone with accusations. (This is also general life advice, courtesy of eclipse season experiences!)

We can also utilize eclipse season as a time to "catch up to ourselves," in one or more areas of life. Because they generally take place about six months apart, this is an opportune time to look back, review, and reflect. Recollect everything meaningful that has transpired for you since the last eclipse season. Try to connect the dots.

Eclipses collapse time lines. The past, the present, and the future are all woven together at the time of an eclipse. That makes it easier for us to unravel certain threads from different chronologies. We can unknot these and choose the most golden one to take with us. The magical ability to access the past, present, and future all at once also helps to tie up loose ends. Much of how we use this time depends on our belief in free will. We can just as easily get sucked backward as catapulted into an unbound future. Sometimes, we have to look backward in order to move forward. Every so often, there is the encouragement to take the leap, don't look back, and travel into uncharted territory. Within the future/past/present of eclipse season is great potential to heal specific time lines and create the change you seek.

SOLAR ECLIPSES

Solar eclipses can only happen during a new moon. There are three different kinds of solar eclipses: a partial solar eclipse, an annular solar eclipse, and a total solar eclipse. A partial solar eclipse occurs when the moon does not pass directly in front of the sun. The sun is still visible and generally looks like a crescent. When the moon passes directly in front of the sun, either an annular solar eclipse or total solar eclipse takes place. An annular solar eclipse is when a ring of sunlight can still be seen. This occurs when the moon is in the farthest part of its orbit, and so it appears slightly smaller than the sun. Most eclipses are partial. A total solar eclipse is when the sun is completely covered. This happens when the moon is closest to the earth in her orbit. At least two solar eclipses happen a year. As many as five can occur, though that is rare.[8]

At a solar eclipse we have the sun (a star, our consciousness), not quite aligned with the moon (our closest celestial body), not quite aligned with the earth (our home, our world). That's what creates the shadow that affects our perception. Our consciousness is influenced. Our brains remain elastic; the pathways can always be rearranged. Different sources and spaces can be tapped into at any moment. It just takes a little experimentation, a suspension of wanting to control outcomes. It just takes listening to new music, learning another language. Plugging into a different outlet. Plugging back into yourself.

At a solar eclipse, the moon—our emotions, psyche, magic, and subconscious—is obstructing the sun—our consciousness, our actions, our identity, our ego. At a solar eclipse, insights might occur from within that end up profoundly affecting our behavior. A solar eclipse can mix things up externally in order to wake us up. Be ready and willing to be open to anything different and aligned that comes your way at this time: it could be an open door.

The astrologer Dane Rudhyar believed that at a new moon solar eclipse, the present is obscured by the past. This allows us to see something important from our past clearly and confront it. Heightened awareness allows us to move on.[9] In general, solar eclipses tend to be related to action taking, decision making, rebirth, and creating anew.

Some questions to ask yourself at a solar eclipse:

How can I respond differently to whatever obstructions are thrown into my path? Is this connected to another ongoing issue in another area of my life? How will I change my energy, my emotions, and my behavior around this? How can I get another perspective on this? What needs to be left in the past? What bold choices am I ready to make? What actions must I take?

Little Ways to Work with a Solar Eclipse

 Meditate on the sun. What is your relationship to it? What does clarity of consciousness feel like? Widen your perspective. If you zoomed out on the movie on your life, what are the most interesting parts? What scenes would be left on the cutting-room floor? Be clear about how you will make one important behavior change. Clarify if it is time to quit, or if a break is needed. If you are stuck, keep asking questions until you can come to an answer that reverberates in your bones as true. Clean. Clear. Sign up for the class, tell the friend you are sorry, make that proclamation of love. Create a ritual dedicated to healing a specific issue. Craft an altar to your inner child.

SOLAR ECLIPSE MAGIC

In general, many practitioners will advise against spell making during eclipse season. The energy is thought to be too chaotic and unpredictable. As always, I encourage you to tune in to your intuition. I have found that eclipse energy works well for healing old wounds, clearing, as well as for gaining different perspectives. In my own life, eclipse season has coincided with moves, contracts, endings, breakups, and bright new chapters. Eclipse magic can help us master change and teach us how to surrender. Magic is the ability to shift consciousness or energy. That does not just include spell work. Solar eclipse magic can be the decision to see yourself more inventively and with more kindness. It can correlate with moves, literal or metaphoric. With specific relationships changing. Solar eclipse magic could simply be preparing to take supported, healthy steps forward.

A couple of days before a solar eclipse, start making some lists. Get honest with yourself. Where do you want to be, in a month, six months, or a year? If this is hard for you, try to envision your best day. What would you be doing on an ideal day? If your life is already fairly magical, think about what you are working on to gain more intimacy with self or the world.

In what ways are your gifts, your soul's expression, needing to come out? What needs to be cleared out of your life? What activities, actions, and behaviors can you focus on in order to integrate more of yourself into your world?

 Pick a couple of key words to meditate on. Focus on one or two actions you can take, beginning during eclipse season, to bring those themes into your life.

Pay attention at the solar eclipse. Is anything coming up inside of you or outside of you? Does it relate to any of your higher visioning?

 Invite in all the love you need, all the connection you crave, all the peace you are ready to cultivate, all the visibility you are ready to embrace, all the creativity ready to bubble up from inside of you. Show up for yourself in those ways. Imagine your entire life, from sunrise to sunset, as a ritual designed to keep all that you have invited in supported. Your daily activities serve as reminders of your intentions.

Getting Out of Your Own Way Spell

 Sometimes the most potent magic is getting out of your own way. We all put up internal and subconscious roadblocks to feeling and acting as our best selves. You may wish to do this spell under a solar eclipse to move energy and start making decisions that are in alignment with where you need to go, with who you need to become.

You will need: a small piece of carnelian, a red, yellow, or orange candle, a letter-size piece of paper, a small piece of paper such as a sticky note, a tarot card that embodies movement, such as The Knight of Wands, The Chariot, or The Sun.

Set up your altar so the tarot card is between the middle of the candle and the crystal.

Cast your circle.

Light your candle.

On a large piece of paper, write down three daily habits or routines you will begin after you cast your spell. These represent smaller breakthroughs of discipline that will support this new phase.

On the small piece of paper, write down an affirmative word you need to remember when you experience resistance or doubt. Examples: *Courage! Love! Action!*

State all of the qualities you are embodying. Say: "From this moment forward, I promise to get out of my own way."

Stare at your tarot card and imagine yourself in the card, or becoming the energy of the card. Imagine all of the things you want to do, all of the ways you wish to be. Place the crystal in your hand and meditate here as long as you need.

Close your circle. Never leave a candle burning unattended.

Commit to your three routines for at least one lunar cycle. Remember that the beginning is always the hardest. If you can't do it one day, start again the next without punishment. Carry your carnelian and your affirmation word with you as encouragement amulets.

Solar Eclipse Tarot Spread

This is a simple tarot spread to try around a solar eclipse. You may wish to shuffle the cards just once, then pull cards, or shuffle in between pulls. Lay your cards left to right, or bottom to top.

Card 1: The Sun: What must I move toward now?
Card 2: The Shadow: What block from the past must I address?
Card 3: The Moon: What inner gifts will help me?

LUNAR ECLIPSES

Lunar eclipses occur only at the full moon. A lunar eclipse happens when the earth blocks out the rays of the sun. The earth's shadow cast upon the face of the moon has a darker, central area referred to as the umbra, and a lighter, outer area called the penumbra.[10] The darkening of the usually bright moon occurs, which often appears red, orange, brown, or even yellow. This is why folks sometimes call a lunar eclipse a "blood moon" or a "red moon." The color is due to light pollution, and other variables. There's a color scale called the Danjon Lunar Eclipse Scale that charts the different colors.[11] Sometimes, the full moon gets almost completely blacked out—a total eclipse. Lunar eclipses can only happen three times a year at the most. Every eclipse will be different, however, the characteristics of one eclipse is repeated every eighteen years—this is called the Saros cycle. These eclipses take place at the same distance from earth at the same time of year.[12]

There are three kinds of lunar eclipses: a penumbral eclipse, a partial eclipse, and a total eclipse. There is the penumbral eclipse, which is a kind of partial eclipse. This is when the moon is only in the secondary shadow of the earth, the penumbra. This is the most subtle visually—sometimes these types of eclipses are not visible to the naked eye.

The second kind is a "regular" partial eclipse. This is when the moon enters the main part of earth's shadow, the umbra. Color on the face of the moon changes visibly. Penumbral and partial eclipses are the most common types of eclipses.

The third kind is a total eclipse. This is when the moon is completely inside of the main shadow of the earth. The shadow doesn't completely obscure the moon, but this is when we see some of the most striking coloration on the face of the moon. This is also the longest kind of lunar eclipse; the moon can stay completely in the umbral shadow for as long as an hour and a half, and the movement through the penumbral part of the shadow can take as long as an hour.[13]

A lunar eclipse can be a particularly potent opportunity to nourish your moon. Tend to your emotions, your water, your wildness, your feminine-ness, and your inner child. Prioritize feeding those parts of your moon. If you aren't sure what nourishes these parts, then a lunar eclipse could be a wonderful time to explore this.

Emotional healing is another use of a lunar eclipse. Eclipse season could spotlight what wounds and shadows are ready to be tended to. Call upon your guides or higher self or ancestors. Ask for any guidance or messages to come through in a way you can really see and feel in the coming days.

Astrologer Dane Rudhyar theorized that at a full moon lunar eclipse the past is obscured by the present.[14] Deep-rooted patterns from the past—our emotional hooks and defenses, our earliest or most profound woundings—can be acknowledged and accepted. The time has come to no longer be controlled by past stories. What we do in the present moment is accentuated by lunar eclipse energy. Our actions and intentions will create a new time line.

A full moon lunar eclipse might heighten your psychic abilities, or make you feel more connected with a universal consciousness. It could also make you feel much more on edge, wired, and anxious.

Eclipse season is a great time to zoom out on your life. If you've been run ragged by putting out endless fires, if the mundanity of your life is starting to make you feel like it's *Groundhog Day*, this could be an opportune time to start to get unstuck. Identify what you enjoy and what you don't. It could be time to cut out whatever drains your energy. Emotions are energy. What is stealing your precious energy? You don't get your time back.

When I facilitate circles or lead classes, I often begin by inviting everyone to name what they most need in this moment and embody that over the course of our shared time. This can often be the opposite of how the person frequently behaves, in their "regular" life. If someone is shy but wants to experience what it feels like to speak up in a group and be heard, I invite them to try that. At a lunar eclipse, name what you'd like to try that might be different from your automatic response. Bring it into the circle of your reality and receive the benefits of other ways to be.

Little Things to Try During a Lunar Eclipse

Spend at least an hour on the day of the lunar eclipse doing something for other people. Put bad habits in the past by using the past tense. *I used to make assumptions about other people, I don't do that anymore. I used to shut down in conflict, I'm working on staying available and curious in the present moment.* Look back in order to see if it's time to pick up forgotten, but still worthwhile dreams. Look back to figure out how you'd like a particular journey to end. Name what you need to do in order to gain closure around a painful relationship. Imagine new time lines opening up to you. Call your people and tell them exactly why you love them. Rest. Show up, vulnerable and willing in all your soft power. Fully commit to stepping into a paradigm of miracles.

LUNAR ECLIPSE MAGIC

As with solar eclipses, ask a group of witches about what to do with spell work and eclipses, and you'll get a much different answer from person to person! Traditionally, the advice is to not practice spell casting at an eclipse, but I think it is important to widen out what magic means and work with the lunar energy in ways that are supportive. Below are some suggestions.

Shadow Work

Shadow work and shadow magic were discussed earlier. Underworld journeying, trance work, and examining our demons all count as this. Mirror magic: looking at yourself in the mirror for a long period of time as a form of gaining messages, and as a way of bolstering self-love. Shadow work creates inner breakthroughs.

Divination

On lunar eclipses, you may wish to embark on divination activities like tarot cards and pendulums, as a way to tap into your intuition. Mix up the way you engage with your divination tools: gaze into a transparent crystal and see what world you enter. Read the coffee grounds at the bottom of your mug, make your own set of runes. Ask your pendulum something you've never asked it. Focus intently on your favorite tarot card in order to notice something new.

Breaking Curses and Uncrossing Spells

Eclipses are a great time to break curses and to facilitate unblocking spells. A curse can be defined as a heavy feeling you have about yourself, or a stagnant or thick energy. A curse can be a harmful pattern that holds you back from living in expansion. It could also be an uncanny repeating block that seems to accompany some theme around what you deeply desire in life. In most cases, curses come from within and must be released from the inside out. Break any and all curses holding you back. Unhex yourself. Uncord yourself. From the past. From dependence on fear and self-punishment. One way to break curses is to learn how to love yourself. Another is to step into your power. Another is to prioritize joy and pleasure.

 Create your own curse-breaking spell. Break a tomato or an egg at a crossroads during the evening of the eclipse. Take a knife or an obsidian blade and cut any and all energetic cords that attached you to that curse. Write a letter detailing all of the ways you are no longer tied to the curse. Petition your higher self, any guides, or helpful deities, for help to detach from the curse. Burn and bury the letter.

Uncrossing spells are spells designed to neutralize your energy and get you unstuck. Even if you can't think of anything or anyone "crossing you," an uncrossing spell enacts a cosmic and energetic reset. It clears your energy and recharges you. Think of it like erasing a chalkboard. An uncrossing spell can be very specific: "to uncross any creative blocks for the next year." Or it can be more open: "I uncross any and all barriers to loving myself completely."

You can design your uncrossing spell however you'd like. I'll give you a suggestion for a very thorough uncrossing spell that takes time, effort, and energy, but is designed to work. It will require prepping over the course of a few days.

You will need: time, household cleaning tools, clear quartz, tourmaline, one candle with a color that resonates with you, such as a rainbow candle, or white, black, blue, or silver candles. Optional: a loofah, salt, rosemary, agrimony, hyssop, or other cleansing and protecting herbs.

First, clean your home. In doing so, you'll want to clean more than one or two drawers, cupboards, or closets. Do some decluttering. If you can't clean your entire house, then at least clean and declutter the room in which you'll be doing your spell and your bathroom, as you'll be taking a ritual bath or shower as part of your spell.

Set up your altar: You may wish to put out quartz crystals for clarity and black tourmaline to soak up negative energy and protect you.

Cast your circle and center. Carve an uncrossing symbol on the candle, such as a cross. Witches sometimes use a circle, with many different lines coming out of it, like a sun's rays, to signify new roads being opened on every level. You may draw onto it with a needle or with a pen. Charge your candle with your intention and light it.

State what you are uncrossing, and write it down on paper. You may wish to speak or yell it out loud. Then burn it up on the flames of your candle.

Spend time breathing and focusing on the flames. Imagine any and all stagnant energy leaving your body and space, to be moved into the flame and transformed.

After you close your circle, take a bath. You may wish to put rosemary, salt, and clear quartz in the bath. Bring up any fears or doubts related to your uncrossing intention. Then, scrub your body vigorously with soap or salt, with a loofah or scrub mitt. Imagine any stagnant energy leaving your body, and as the water goes down the drain, the past goes with it. When the water has been drained, stand up in your bath and turn the shower on, dousing yourself in cool water.

After the spell, drink lots of water and get lots of rest. If any situations arise that are symbolic of what you are trying to uncross, ignore them completely or engage in a totally different way.

Lunar Eclipse Exercise

One way to collaborate with a lunar eclipse is to work with the tarot as symbols of autonomy and choice. Take out the tarot card or cards that resonate with the qualities you feel that you need to embrace right now. What tarot cards symbolize what you are ready to work with in order to feel most safe, most held, most loved? Pick a color in one chosen card and dress in that color. Maybe find a symbol in the card that you can use as a magical talisman, to serve as a reminder of what you are able to receive now. Leave the chosen cards out on your altar and journal about them and engage with them for at least a couple of minutes every day. Let them help you tell a new story.

Lunar Eclipse Tarot Pull

This is a spread designed to get you thinking about bigger pictures. Give yourself a calm, quiet time to spend with your cards.

Shuffle your cards until you feel called to stop. Place the cards in a circle, going counter-clockwise. Put card one at the top.

Card 1: What does the moon want me to know at this time?

Card 2: What healing opportunities are available when I trust my inner voice?

Card 3: How is my shadow currently appearing?

Card 4: What is the gift of acknowledging this shadow?

Card 5: What is a useful teaching of my current life lessons?

Card 6: What help and support is available to me at this time?

Card 7: What must I leave behind?

Card 8: What do my higher power, source, or my guides want me to know about where to focus my energy now?

OTHER LUNAR LORE

Supermoons and Micromoons

Supermoons happen when the full or new moon is the closest to the earth in its orbit. This moon appears 14 percent larger and can appear up to 30 percent brighter than an average full moon.[15] The closest the moon can get to the earth is 225,662 miles. For comparison, the farthest away the moon can get from the earth is 252,088 miles away.

Supermoon is an astrological term—not one common in astronomy. The term was first mentioned by astrologer Richard Nolle in a 1979 article for *Dell Horoscope* magazine.[16] He defined a supermoon as a full or new moon that occurs within 90 percent of its closest approach to earth. In the past ten years, as astrology has garnered more interest, the term has caught on in general use, mostly in North America.

Of the twelve to thirteen full moons we generally have in a Gregorian calendar year, and about as many new moons, about three or four can be categorized by this classification. Whether or not you feel energetically affected depends—you'll have to tune in to the energy of that particular supermoon.

A micromoon is when a new or full moon coincides with the point in its orbit farthest away from the earth, known as apogee. This results in a full moon that appears approximately 14 percent smaller than usual. Also called an apogee moon, these occur about once a year.

Blue Moons

Blue moons have taken on several different meanings. The original phrase "Once in a blue moon" was coined about four hundred years ago. It expressed disbelief, rarity, or a sense of unlikeliness, akin to "When pigs fly!" Over time, it began to take on the meaning of a rare occurrence.[17]

The original definition of a blue moon is a third full moon in an astronomical season with four full moons. A year regularly has four astronomical seasons with three months and three full moons. A "blue moon," by that definition, would be the addition of one: the extra moon of the season. This is sometimes referred to as a seasonal blue moon, and it occurs about every 2.5 years, according to NASA. The origins of this definition are most likely agricultural.[18] The "blue" in "blue moon" may be a mispronunciation of the old English word *belewe*, meaning "to betray," the idea being that an additional full moon was a betrayal of the standard lunar cycle.

A more recent definition has morphed this original definition. Now, you likely hear folks refer to a blue moon as the second full moon in one calendar month. This is because in one article from 1946, an author named James Hugh Pruett declared it as such. The definition stuck, and folks began using that definition more widely, especially when that (mis)information was picked up and used in a nationally syndicated radio program in 1980.[19] An astrological blue moon—as opposed to a calendrical one—is one that occurs for the second time during the period that the sun is in the same zodiacal sign.[20]

Which definition to use? Language and definitions are always evolving—as evidenced in the etymology of the blue moon. A seasonal blue moon is an anomaly, a beautiful wild card to use how you'd like. And the newer definition of blue moon also makes sense. I've personally experienced an amplified feeling when there are two full moons in one calendar month: the entire time period feels extra charged! Remember that all of these categorizations are constructs designed to help us observe. Use what works for you, leave what does not.

Black Moons

There are two different definitions of a black moon, both of which refer to a type of new moon. Depending on who you ask, a "black moon" is either the third new moon in an astronomical season with four new moons, or it can be the second new moon in one calendar month.

Either way, a black moon is fairly rare: When defined as a second new moon in a single calendar month, it occurs about every twenty-nine months, and can occur only in thirty-one-day months. If defined as the third new moon of four in a season that usually only has three, it is even rarer: these black moons occur about every thirty-three months.[21]

Witches sometimes use them to harness more powerful new moon energy around beginnings, fresh starts, and goals. One thing that is particularly nice with black moons is that they generally fall on the last day of the calendar month, so if you can tap into the new moon energy, you can begin your next month—usually the next day or so—with a boost of correlating energy from the lunar cycle.

Void of Course Moon

When the moon is said to be "void of course" this refers to a time when the moon is not in any astrological sign. This can last anywhere from a few minutes to hours to a few days. The "void of course" moon, according to astrologers, is not a recommended time to start anything new, or to make decisions around anything that will have lasting repercussions. Many say it is a time for resting or doing nothing. Some witches advise doing no spell work during a void of course moon, if you time your spells astrologically.

During this time, activities that include wrapping up or are restful are recommended. Napping, resting, organizing, revising, editing, finishing projects, meditating, or hanging out with friends.[22] In my opinion, a void of course moon is so common it doesn't make sense to stop everything while it occurs. I've not felt any different energy, personally, when the moon is void; the idea that the moon answers to anything or is impacted by the lack of being in a sign is dubious. Our ancestors didn't know when and what sign the moon was in, or if it was void of course, and they survived. So will we. My favorite interpretation of a void of course moon is by the artist and tarot reader Eliza Swann, who conceptualized this time as the moon not being "owned" by a sign, or by anything—a space to be unencumbered and free.

Putting It All Together

The Work of Love

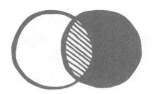

This book has offered you an overview of some of the ways there are to interpret and work with the moon. By now, hopefully you've begun tracking your energy and noticing what each lunar phase feels like for you. Maybe you've made a moon map and have begun your own process. Perhaps you've tried some of the suggested spells, rituals, or tarot pulls for each phase. Maybe your relationship with all things moon ebbs and flows, comes and goes. And that's absolutely perfect too.

And also: You are here now because you want results. Powerful, lasting results. You are ready and willing. If you want results, you must be consistent. If you want internal and external transformation, you must put in the effort. And if you want the most stellar results possible, you must engage with one entire lunar phase from start to finish. At the bare minimum.

Committing to an entire lunation through taking some of the recommended actions presented will benefit you greatly. The process is designed to consider all aspects of a shift. If energy, mindset, internal blocks, behaviors, and habits are not addressed, we may find ourselves repeating the same patterns that have held us back from achieving self-actualization. For many of us, trust in self has been eroded or severed. Commitment to a solid self-practice is one way to restore trust.

Usually, we work through the same large themes over the course of many lunar cycles. Deprogramming takes time, reprogramming takes time, and building trust takes time. It is also recommended to revisit a theme through a different lens: as we grow and evolve, so does the nature of our self-inquiry. Moon mapping and doing lunar work around scarcity, for example, will look very different when you are trying to make enough to support yourself, versus when you've been able to meet your income goals. Similar to reading the same book once a year, or seeing a movie repeated times, you'll be aware of different things each time you use this process.

Even if one is not necessarily interested in undergoing huge changes every luna- tion, understanding your own energy patterns is incredibly helpful. Giving yourself space to follow your intuition and natural inclinations within the moon's phases offers us a way to ground. This gives us the relief of acceptance. If we feel full of sorrow, we cry without judgment—the need for analysis isn't always necessary. We don't always need to figure out the why: sometimes, we cry because for us personally, the dark moon correlates to emotional release.

Everything is a relationship. We define ourselves by relating. In the past, humans existed in an intimate relationship with nature—much more so than most of us do now. This was in part because our survival depended on it. Our brains have been hardwired to notice patterns, and this attribute is one of the reasons of our species' growth. This noticing led to agricultural technology and astrology, for example. This noticing also led to an enhanced relationship with our surroundings, which in turn led to spirituality, religions, cultural traditions: all ways in which humankind finds meaning. Turning to a practice of noticing connects us to the present. A re- lationship with cosmic cycles assures us that our own cycles are part of an ancient natural order.

Moon work can be daunting, because we are meeting our hopes and fears while dwelling in the in-between. Through my own work, and work with hundreds of people, I've witnessed that painful emotions like fear and grief will inevitably surface. Finding a toolkit of healthy resources and additional support systems is key. (And is also another great benefit of this work.) Sticking to the decision to choose yourself and your goal, day after day, in some way, despite boredom or doubt, will be one of your tasks. Internal blocks and resistance are often a sign that you are doing the work. Find ways to stay motivated and continue investing in yourself.

Following are some things to remember about the process of lunar magic. As you embark on your own particular path, take note of the ugly, the unexpected, and all the untamed beauty you encounter. After working closely with the moon for a few cycles, you will be able to come up with your own list of reminders.

THINGS TO REMEMBER DURING THIS PROCESS

1. **If this was easy, everyone would do it.** Committing to a spiritual path is not easy. Under the white supremacist patriarchy, committing to yourself and your dreams can feel like actual treason. This is a nonlinear process filled with victories *and* challenges of all sorts. You will come head-to-head with your demons. Mindsets will need to be examined and re-patterned. Habits and behaviors will have to be fundamentally changed. Certain relationships may have to be shifted, or you may have to leave them behind altogether. You will be asked to find and come back to yourself, over and over. This is difficult work—anathema to the quick-fix culture we are immersed in. But you **can do it**, absolutely. You are fully equipped to step into your power and to experience the authentic expression of your soul. In actuality, that's what you were born to do!

2. **You will meet resistance.** Countless times. Day after day. There will be lying voices in your head trying to fill you with doubt. Voices that will tell you change is impossible. That you are an imposter; that you don't deserve to take up space; that you don't even know what you know. That you are too old; your desires are too unattainable. Every person will meet resistance. Resistance is proof that you are undertaking something important. One sign that a breakthrough is imminent is when everything seems impossibly hard or scary. I dislike telling people *in it* this, but it is true. Factoring in resistance as part of your process will help you move through it. Address resistance and find ways to keep going. (Rest is absolutely one way to keep moving.)

3. You will meet grief. During any humanifestation process, you will also encounter grief. You may mourn "lost time" or a past self. This is normal. This happens because the brain has not yet caught up to the soul. This also is a symptom of "survivor's guilt," the conflicted emotions one feels when you exceed the expectations or achievements of your family, your peer group, or your initial self-regard that was primarily forged out of self-protection. When we heal a certain pattern it can, at first, leave a hole in our life like a ghost. Our animal body and emotional body interpret this as a loss. Grief isn't necessarily something you need to analyze or interpret. Grief *is* something that needs to be named and processed. Hold space for your grief and do not judge it. Do not use this as a reason to stop moving forward in your process.

4. You will need to build a container for your desires: one that is more flexible and larger than you think you need. The container you build will be forged from the qualities of your desire. This container needs to be adaptive, not rigid. There might need to be multiple containers you spend time in. Use your intuition to allot energetic containers, emotional containers, and containers of time to your goals and process. There always needs to be extra space to let in whatever magically wishes to grow inside them. Consider yourself a container too. Try being responsive, yet having a specific, beneficial structure. Consider what it would look like to let things pass in and out of you, without clinging to any of it. To be a crystal-clear channel, ready to receive and transmit. This is a trick to living in the moment and it is most certainly a trick to manifesting. Part of this practice includes letting go and surrendering. It is difficult to overcome controlling, scarcity-based programming, but let the rewards entice you enough to try. It is completely possible to become a clear channel. The kind that no one owns and that is a gift of the universe.

5. Expect to embrace a lot of complexities. This process requires you to suspend certain expectations, while also being present for and attuned to your deepest desires every day. You must toggle between panoramic vision and granular detail. During one lunar phase, you may be blown away by the depths of your magical power, then emotionally leveled during the next.

Knowing that no one state lasts forever will make it easier to make it through the hard times. In this culture, we are often programmed to believe in profound scarcity. In order to achieve success or victory, someone else must not achieve. Even without overt capitalism, competition still pops up in different ways: comparison, judgments, sabotage. Humans look for metrics of acceptability and "goodness" everywhere. Those who operate outside of the metric, refuse to play the game, or who possess a form of unacceptability are threatening to those within the matrix.

We then perpetuate those ideas within ourselves. We put limits and caveats on our very soul. We can have one thing, but it has to come at a cost to another. We can be one thing, but we've got to stifle or shove down another aspect of ourselves. Showing up whole—allowing ourselves to be complex, at times contradictory—is one of the greatest presents (presence) we can give ourselves. You are allowed to be: successful, neuro-divergent, happy, messy, timid, fierce—all at once. You are allowed to be depressed and still have desires. You are allowed to have thoughts of self-loathing yet still hold an enviable job and have a partner that adores you. You are allowed to be wildly successful and wish the same for everyone else. You are allowed to grow out of certain identities while still enjoying fundamental aspects of self. You are allowed.

This process disrupts either/or thinking and the binary by accepting all the parts of self, including the parts that may never be reconciled or healed. It encourages self-acceptance and goes beyond the problematic gaze of the meritocracy. Learning how to hold, and accept, various complexities simultaneously is an invaluable skill set you will learn as a result of this process.

6. **Finding clear metrics of success will be imperative, as will ways to stay motivated.** This entire process also needs discernment around what success will actually look like. What is the ultimate outcome you want and what will be the indicators of that? This is doubly important for goals that are more interior or healing focused, such as finding self-love or happiness. Find a metric with which to measure your success. Staying motivated will be another vital part of your plan. Humans gravitate toward instant gratification. There will be discomfort. (See numbers 1–3 on this list.) A part of your plan must be coming

up with ways you will reward yourself for keeping your promises. Thinking of the process as an experiment is more useful than seeing it as a means to an end.

7. **You may not recognize yourself afterward.** Who you are will absolutely change. You may find you do not know yourself during, or after, the process. Try to refrain from labeling yourself too quickly. Take note of what you feel drawn to and what you are no longer interested in. Let yourself discover another—also temporary—identity. Allow your natural intelligence to guide you into the gardens and scenes in which you now feel engaged. There can be an inclination to grant others the authority of your own results. It was this person that helped you, it was this book, it was this, it was that. Of course we do not operate in a vacuum; as relational beings we need support and help from others, and we need to thank and reference those helpers accordingly. Ultimately, *you* are the author of your own results. Underneath any doubt, anxiety, or confusion, you are the one who ultimately knows what's best for you. Try to view this version of yourself with intrigue. Let getting to know this different version of yourself be pleasurable.

8. **Trust the blessings that come.** There will be extraordinary success and unexpected gifts that come as a result of your work. Results beyond your wildest wishes will blossom. Things you never even knew you wanted, but absolutely needed, will be offered. When betrayal and hardship is what we've come to expect, because that is what we've been living with for much of our past life, we think the good is a fluke. Common survivor responses are hypervigilance, constructed caveats, and waiting for the other shoe to drop. It is normal to not believe or trust the love or grace or ease coming in, but staying closed off will help no one. Try to trust the gifts and blessings. Try to normalize them. Try to expect them. These are yours to enjoy and there are even more on their way.

MY STORY: A SPIRITUAL PRACTICE

The above reminders can serve as a guide—and a dose of truth—through our experiences with lunar living. It is also helpful to share other actual examples of the tangible results of this work. Below are some stories from myself, my clients, and my students that illustrate some specific processes and the results. While all of our paths are our own, there is universality to this specific kind of lunar work. The goals can sometimes be a Trojan horse into a deeper healing process: as belief in one's capabilities expands, previously compromised life force is restored. Chasing material or more superficial desires leads to subconscious pattern reprogramming and profound spiritual connections. My story might be similar to yours or you might be inspired by one of the other shares.

I initially came to working with lunar cycles the good old-fashioned way: I was a baby witch who was unhappy. I desperately wanted results. I would cast spells here and there, in an unfocused manner. My desires were deeply unrelated to my reality—I was not working with my sphere of influence. My actions in the real world were quite unrelated to the efforts of my spells. There would be little to no follow-through around what I wanted after the spell was cast. As a result, very little would change. Or enough would change to make me believe in magic, but then my own behavioral backslides would leave me back where I metaphorically began. I was ready to break self-harming patterns. I was ready to know abundance and tap into my own power. I then began to time my spells with the moon. The results were much more effective.

Through the years, I began to pair my psychological, behavioral, emotional, and subconscious efforts with the suggested magical and practical correspondences of the moon phases. I decided to work through one major desire around the phases of one lunar cycle. The results were remarkable.

In 2012, after four years of fine-tuning the work I had developed, I began teaching what I had learned all around the country. A few years later, in 2015, the moon told me to write real-time, channeled workbooks, giving the readers suggestions on how to work with each phase. So I did. Even though I wasn't a writer, even though I never wanted to self-publish self-help or magical books, I channeled, designed, wrote, and distributed six Many Moons workbooks over the course of three years, on top of running my existing business.

My lunar work has brought me a lot of joy and a lot of abundance. I've also had to face a lot of the pain and sorrow that accompanies healing through this process. Boundary work, saying good-bye to certain influential relationships because they were not supportive, investing in trauma therapy, and needing to make time for deep grief have all been aspects of this process that have been brutal but necessary. I have made vast improvements in many different aspects of self: work, creativity, self-worth, self-esteem, mindset, and more. This is where the ripple effect comes in. Directly healing the root of an issue generates greater energy and ease for positive change in related areas or themes. That in turn affects other aspects of our existence. When I was able to understand that scarcity issues were at the root of what I thought were "just" issues around work or money, doing work around that root not only changed the actual aspects of my work and bank account, but how I fundamentally valued myself. My healthy self-regard and the abundance philosophy I live by have been priceless consequences of this approach.

There's a mysterious aspect of lunar work. The specific outcome will be unknown. This requires active listening on many different levels. In doing the work, we must pay attention to our intuition.

Our intuition is here to help us heal. When we listen to our intuition, in part, we are receiving information on where to go next in service of our healing. The steps we take toward our intuitive yearnings facilitate this healing. Healing doesn't always feel good. It doesn't always line up with our culture's definitions of success. One by-product of listening to our intuition can be encountering loss, trials, and tests. Ask yourself: What is available now for healing? Define what that would look like for you, and for you alone. Proceed accordingly.

When we enter into the spiral that is moontime, we see how many different aspects of our lives are connected. All rivers that flow into the same ocean. Our intuition gives us more clues on what to focus on, what healing is available to us, or what thread to follow next.

I wouldn't do this work if I was not witness, over and over again, to the positive effect it has on people. Over the last six years, I've been fortunate enough to hold space for and to guide thousands of folks on how to work with the moon in order to self-actualize in various ways. What follows are some of their stories. These narratives all describe a six-week period: the length of time of my Moonbeaming classes—two weeks of teaching and goal setting, and then moving through one entire lunar cycle.

Participants focus on a specific theme or goal. Their stories include self-love, managing physical pain, honoring creativity, finding meaningful work, and shifting fear and anxiety around money. Hopefully these stories will inspire you and give you greater insight into what collaborating with the moon consists of and looks like. Please note that because I conduct my classes at different times of the lunar cycle, some of the testimonials begin at different lunar phases. This proves that you can start at any phase you wish, and still see results!

SILAS'S STORY: PRIORITIZING ART AND CREATIVE ABUNDANCE

Silas's goal was to focus on his art practice. He wanted to have more time to work on his art, outside of his day job, and wanted to prioritize energy for it. Silas kept a moon journal of his physical, emotional, and energetic states. He meditated daily (which was already part of his existing practice), though he shifted to doing so at the lunar altar he changed up for each moon phase. As he journaled, he got super clear on what he wanted his art practice to look like.

New Moon: In the new moon phase, Silas wrote down all his dreams for his art. He planned studio visits with artists he knew. He identified three specific finished pieces he wanted to make. He also determined that two days a week, he would work on his art for three hours minimum. Interestingly, he was often traveling for work during this time and did some of his most productive visioning work ten thousand feet up in a plane!

Waxing Moon: During the waxing moon phase, Silas spent his time working on the art itself. He applied to a residency and though he didn't get it, the process of doing so clarified his work so strongly that he ended up taking a staycation and doing his own "residency." This gave him time to make the work he had been conceptualizing at the new moon. Having work he believed in led him to reach out to artists he admired; this ended up leading to a studio visit with an artist who was also a critic at the residency he did not get into! This was also when Silas realized that everything he does is his art—his design, writing, poetry—because he is an artist, no matter what.

Full Moon: At the full moon, Silas celebrated abundance. He did a deep gratitude ritual. This coincided with a profound run-in with a former teacher of his, who is a prominent leader in the field his day job is in. She asked to put his work in a lecture she was giving. She then inquired about a book he designed, which he happened to have with him. As he gave it to her, she asked him to sign it. Silas interpreted that as a really potent, full circle, full moon moment.

Waning Moon: During the waning moon phase, Silas focused on letting go of limiting beliefs around his art practice. He also just coasted and rested. Focused on enjoyment and meditation. He enjoyed the feeling of being an artist. Silas noted that he ended up being the most productive with the least amount of effort here. He also earned the most money he had ever earned in one month. He gave a profitable talk and won several new clients in his business.

There was a lot of challenging stuff for Silas to acknowledge. Making time for his art alongside his already busy life was tough. A lot of imposter syndrome resistance came up. He was also tracking his money very closely during this cycle, which brought up complex emotions. Silas met fear and self-doubt mostly at the dark moon and waning moon. The dark moon was also where he noticed that he was most drained, which is useful information for him moving forward. He also had regret and sadness that he had not done this sooner.

Engaging with a lunar practice changed Silas's life financially, emotionally, physically, and spiritually. He connected and became close with many working artists. He feels more connected to his partner, family, friends, and ancestry. Silas feels more present to his own needs and to his own higher self. Most important, he knows he is an artist and art witch in ways he didn't know before.

DEYANDRÉ'S STORY: DEEPENING INTO DESIRES AND CREATIVITY

DeYandré's goal for her lunar cycle manifestation work was to kick-start her fashion-styling business. DeYandré challenged herself to live what she wanted to inspire: to adorn her energy, to have fun getting dressed, and to appreciate self-expression. Through this intention, DeYandré opened herself up in a public way.

New Moon: Behind the scenes, she created a "moonifesto" and planted future seeds for her personal growth and her business. DeYandré set an intention to post an outfit on social media every day of the lunar cycle that coincided with her mood and was inspired by the current moon phase.

Waxing Moon: During the waxing moon, DeYandré committed to her intention and consistently shared her outfit daily alongside growing the social media presence of her business. Fear, resistance, and insecurity came up during the new moon and waxing moon phases as DeYandré worked toward her goal. Doubt and discomfort around feeling not ready and exposed arose during these phases, as did fighting the feeling of imposter syndrome.

Full Moon: At the full moon time, these struggles became illuminated as lessons. She celebrated her progress at the full moon. As a woman of color, she allowed herself to be seen and take up space. DeYandré embraced the act of receiving this gift and recognized how valuable it was to be vulnerable.

Waning Moon: At the waning phase, anger surrounding old habits, patterns, and limiting beliefs were harder for DeYandré to tolerate. She translated these struggles and resistance into reminders to continue showing up for herself and her personal growth.

DeYandré recognized that Black beauty is a radical act and needs to be shared in an authentic way. DeYandré reclaimed self-love through the act of investing time and energy into a personal goal, and felt supported by something bigger than herself—allowing her to chip away at her ego and contribute to the collective. Through the process, she gained courage, confidence, and peace. As a self-identified highly sensitive person, lunar work is now invaluable and ingrained in her daily practice. Since the first moon cycle DeYandré worked with, she has launched a determination project inspired by both fashion and the moon. She has also been presented with multiple opportunities that remind her of her purpose. She now also has her own spiritual toolkit. Through working with the moon, DeYandré has created a practice of self-care, meditation, and writing.

CHELSEA'S STORY: SOFTENING INTO HEALING PHYSICAL PAIN

Chelsea utilized lunar work to alleviate pelvic pain she had been suffering from for several years. She wanted to create healthier practices to better take care of herself physically and mentally; specifically reevaluating her relationship with social media and drinking. When starting her lunar work, Chelsea initially struggled to give up these crutches. By reframing and adjusting how she consumed both, she was able to focus on her self-work as well as help heal her body.

New Moon: Chelsea created a morning routine of meditation, tea, journaling, dream work, and physical exercise. At first, shame surrounding Chelsea's past relationships, and how she allowed people to treat her, came bubbling to the surface. So did feelings of shame around her body not functioning correctly, and fears of never being loved because of it. These forms of resistance emerged right away, as they had been festering for a while before she began the process. This helped Chelsea realize that she needed to focus on a lot of self-love and forgiveness activities throughout her lunar work.

First Quarter Moon: During the first quarter moon, Chelsea focused on her physical therapy exercises and external core strength exercises, while making an effort to do yoga three times a week. In this phase, Chelsea cast a protection spell around her sacral area and practiced self-love by receiving and accepting compliments.

Full Moon: The full moon brought celebration around the milestone she achieved: no social media usage since starting this cycle! Her morning routines were also going strong.

Last Quarter: As the moon entered the last quarter phase, Chelsea reflected on what had softened in her body and in her mind since deciding to focus on her physical and emotional healing. She performed a cord-cutting ceremony to bring back her own energy and block those relationships that were draining to her energy. Chelsea also practiced forgiveness work around a past relationship that she still held shame around in order to let go of energy that was hindering her healing.

Dark Moon: The energy of Chelsea's cutting ceremony continued during the dark moon: she cleaned out the physical spaces of her home and made her bedroom a sacred area and removed all objects from past relationships and thus their lingering ghosts.

After the lunar cycle—and the class—ended, Chelsea continued to work on resolving her physical pain, but was able to accept, through lunar work, that the healing process would not be a quick fix. For Chelsea, the most exciting and tangible results were the shift in her mindset surrounding her healing path. Before this lunar work, Chelsea had a lot of shame and guilt around dealing with discomfort in such a private area of her body. The work allowed her to find self-acceptance, to process her health more holistically, and to find trustworthy and supportive people to talk about it with. In working with the moon and its phases, Chelsea was able to carve out specific time to plan, work, and rest and created more ease and connection to her inner self.

Chelsea writes: "I definitely feel more at ease and connected to myself through this work. My confidence in general has grown, to the point where I've had friends mention that they can tell there is a difference in the way I present myself. I've always felt connected to my intuition, but only to a point. This work has made me more comfortable in listening to that intuition and following what she's telling me without making excuses. It allowed me to realize that I purposefully wasn't listening to the messages I was receiving. It allowed me to define my magic."

JAIME'S STORY: EMBODYING THE DEATH CARD TO FACILITATE NEW BEGINNINGS

Jaime's goal for her first lunar cycle was to begin to cultivate trust in her intuition and in the universe. Throughout the lunar phases, Jaime's goal shifted to become about self-acceptance, and ultimately about embracing the void. Jaime utilized the tarot to help enhance her lunar cycle work, creating structure, guidance, and prompts for each lunar phase. Jaime started at the waning moon, a potent time to clear away obstacles.

Waning Moon and Dark Moon: During the waning moon, Jaime cast a tarot magic spell and chose to embody the Death card. In doing so, Jaime embraced the process of release and the prospect of new beginnings, internally and externally. For the dark moon phase, Jaime continued to embody the Death card energy while implementing breath work to help release fears.

New Moon and Waxing Moon: Jaime cast a new moon attraction spell and repeated this spell for three days in a row. Jaime began this spell when she could see the first sliver of the moon, and so this spell was also part of her waxing moon work. Jaime called in new beginnings, new opportunities, and new relationships that would increase her financial, emotional, mental, and physical prosperity. Jaime challenged herself to do things that scared her. This included promoting a new class she was teaching despite her fear of being seen. Jaime also started a daily gratitude journal to remind herself how abundant her life was.

Full Moon: Jaime completed a full moon expansion spell from my Moonbeaming class during the full moon to bring in expansion in four different areas of her life, based on the elements. This time also brought tangible change: Jaime decided to quit a job she no longer enjoyed, chased new job opportunities, and embraced trust in herself to create space for necessary growth and new beginnings.

Jaime writes: "Working an entire lunar cycle proved to me I can trust and rely on myself. I started to see my life reflected in the lunar cycles. The course was a new moon period of my life where I planted the seeds of what I see budding and blossoming around me today.

"Trusting myself and the Universe felt challenging. Figuring out how to implement my goal was a challenge because after setting my intention I realized trust had many layers to it. Committing to the daily practices was often challenging because it required self-discipline and relentless self-love. Accepting the changes, even the changes for the better, was a challenge and definitely brought up grief. Doing so many spells in one lunar cycle was also a bit of a challenge, but I really wanted things to change!

"A series of synchronistic events occurred, some things ended abruptly and painfully, and some amazing opportunities came my way. Ultimately my partner and I both quit our jobs and started a business that has afforded us the opportunity to travel and live in different areas, be with our dogs nearly 24-7, and set our own schedule, all while making more money than I ever have in my life.

"I'm trusting the Universe without the same resistance I once had. I have a stronger relationship with my intuition and have been able to more easily understand and receive when an intuitive hit comes in. It has been freeing to step further into my personal power."

ERYN'S STORY: CONJURING WORTHINESS AND LOVE

Eryn utilized working through a lunar phase to work on self-love: specifically to deeply know herself as worthy of receiving love. When going deeper in the moon-mapping process, Eryn felt challenges in acknowledging how she had abandoned herself and denied herself love, and her inability to be herself in her quest to garner approval and acceptance from others. To help work through this, Eryn decided to lean on a toolkit of self-care, particularly breath work and prioritizing self-compassion and understanding.

New Moon: Eryn wrote a new moon moonifesto (from a suggested exercise in my course), which outlined all the ways she was committed to practicing self-love. She practiced making decisions from a place of love, rather than from fear of losing love. She also cast a new moon attraction spell from my Moonbeaming course, for gratitude and love.

Waxing Moon: Eryn scheduled self-care and created more firm boundaries around her needs. She pulled tarot cards to help her identify that the root of her belief was she was unlovable. She spent more intentional time with herself. She ended up connecting with a new spirit guide who came through to help with this work.

Full Moon: At the full moon, Eryn received clarity about some unloving and unhelpful patterns she had. She wrote herself a love letter and did an embodied spell for self-love based on giving herself pleasure and honoring her body.

Waning Moon: Eryn connected with some times that she had abandoned herself, and worked on self-forgiveness and self-compassion. She did a suggested class tarot pull for shame that was incredibly powerful for her. She did a clearing spell to release shame around being alone and the belief that her worthiness is conditional. She reframed beliefs about herself, mostly around the conditions under which she had believed she deserved love. She created more unscheduled time/free space for herself and slept more.

Eryn shared: "It was challenging to see the ways in which I had abandoned myself, the ways in which I had denied myself love, the ways in which I had tried to make myself different in order to be more acceptable to and receive love from others. Grief and anger both came up, mostly toward myself.

"The process absolutely changed my life. Some things that have come from the process: More honoring of my desires without apology. Less people-pleasing. An ability to be more vulnerable and let myself be more seen. Taking up more space in my authentic expression of self. More self-compassion, and a kinder voice in my head.

"From that place (along with other work through other lunar cycles), my external world has certainly shifted—my work has expanded, my intimacy in relationships has deepened, I've been able to set some needed boundaries (something I have always struggled with), and I've made more money in my work."

THE MOON WILL HELP YOU
BREAK UP WITH THE PATRIARCHY

In the stories just shared, we see themes of empowerment, healing, and self-actualization. These are all the through lines of lunar work. This is profound work that helps the collective. The world needs more aware and empowered people than ever before. When we create our own compassionate paradigms, the archaic oppressive ones fall away. As we model resilience, soft power, and strength, others gravitate toward collective models of care and liberation. As our own cups of care get filled, we are able to better offer up resources to others who need them. This is all threatening to patriarchal systems. Lunar work helps to dismantle oppressive systems. Maybe that's the reason why the patriarchy is so afraid of the moon.

The white supremacist capitalist patriarchy has us back bent and twisted in mind-body-soul to standards that are impossibly violent as well as impossible to achieve. This is reflected in the media, in discriminatory and violent laws and policies, in the impossible standards that people who are not cis, straight, white, thin, and able-bodied are expected to conform to in order to be allowed to exist without violence and abuse. By patriarchal standards I am a failure. I have a weird job that isn't easily explainable at a dinner party, I'm queer, I struggle with ADHD and a serious chronic illness, I live my life intuitively, and am committed to spiritual growth. I focus on what I can do to aid the collective. Organizing my life around pleasure, connection, and healing often makes me feel like I am a psychedelic-colored salmon swimming upstream.

Having a different code of ethics and value system than most often leads to disappointment. There isn't a lot of external reward for making decisions based in values and integrity, such as turning down lucrative offers, or needing to end relationships with folks who are behaving in abusive ways. Listening to my body and slowing down goes directly against the busier-than-thou culture. Yet my very thriving depends on defining success in a very personal, very lunar, very magical way. Knowing my inherent worth outside of what I can do for others, or based on what I can produce, is the North Star that brings me back into my energetic alignment.

Ultimately, the moon helped me undertake one of the most priceless gifts of my entire life: honoring myself and getting free of abuse. It will be a lifelong process to heal from the abuse and trauma I've experienced in my life. The ideologies, self-acceptance, and messages I've received as a result of investing in my magic and spirituality have been the foundation of my healing process. Investing in this work continues to give me hope and faith during the days that threaten to plunge me into despair. Time and time again, the practices I've shared here with you have worked. And so, I keep sharing them and utilizing them.

The moon helped me break up with the patriarchy. Helped me to live by my own set of ethics and values. Helped me to honor my intuition and my own unique talents. Helped me to detach from abusive ways of treating myself that I internalized. This is a lifelong effort that I will be preoccupied with. It is a nonnegotiable one. To allow space for our imaginations to bloom and commit to support others in their processes is to steadily re-enchant the world.

THE MOON LEADS US
TOWARD THE WORK OF LOVE

Lunar work reminds us that it all begins with the self, and it all begins with love. As bell hooks taught us, love is an action, first and foremost.[1] Expressions of love change as we grow. As we gain versatility in the ways that we process our emotions and connect with our intuition, we enact a homecoming of the self. Our influence on the world around us increases as we understand and tap into our power.

We must feed ourselves before we starve. A self-care practice requires constant consideration, as it is the practice of continuous nourishment. A self-care practice is not selfish. If you don't prioritize yourself, who will?

Love yourself enough to let yourself be loved. In the exact ways you require. You can always decide to go where the love is. In quiet moments, you can show yourself, with actions, how you need to be loved, and become love itself. The work of love helps us do the work of life.

There is so much work to do. There is priceless nature, animals, and humans to fight for, so much to resist, so much organizing to join and do, so many dollars to donate, so many signal boosts to amplify and petitions to sign, artwork to make for protests. Love helps us focus where we put our energy, helps us hold on to our visions, and helps us put one foot in front of the other in the scariest moments.

And there is so much beauty to take in: so many books to read, so many sunsets to behold, so many songs to listen to or play or write, so many dogs to meet and pet, so many wise teachers to learn from. So many opportunities to close our eyes, gently smile, and turn our cheek toward the sun. If we don't enjoy our lives, if we don't drink in as much sheer awe and sweetness as we can, then the sadness and the sorrow we all will face becomes utterly unbearable.

Our lives are very, very short.

We get to put our energy into sweet connections, mutual care and support, loving conversations, and all the things that light us up and inspire us and excite us.

It is my hope that returning to a space of reverence in your practice will invoke a reverent spaciousness for all the aspects of yourself. Whether or not you decide to continue on with the moon as your sole guide, or incorporate other practices into your toolkit, you can always call on her to be an anchor. A reminder that it is okay to change, to evolve, to explore different sides of yourself. To keep going and trying. An affirmation that the spiral of your life is a natural and blessed one. That the work of love is worth every second.

Epilogue

On Writing a Love Letter to the Moon

Not surprisingly, I spend a lot of time with the moon. I look for her and find her in the sky, trace her shape. Remember where it lies on the horizon each day, peeking through power lines, framed by branches. She doesn't always look the way I think she will. Sometimes her line of light is on a diagonal, sometimes she appears craggier than I've last remembered. Other days she appears dim, filtered through the pollution in the sky. It's a weird exercise to go by moon calendars or apps, because while her overall phases are predictable, trying to match her real-time semblance to the icons on a flat surface requires imagination. Sometimes she's only there to be caught after the fact, in the net of our memory.

You could draw the moon a thousand times and not be able to quite capture her likeness. Maybe that is why so many still try.

Science says that the moon is composed of minerals, four different types. They show us satellite photos, paparazzi photos of her gray surface, the drabbest dress at the cosmic ball. We know what she is made of: basalt and cooled volcanic eruptions. And yet, she remains magnetic, a beacon for witches, a supernatural friend. Something to pray over. Something to believe in. Something that affects and reflects the literal tides of our lives. Knowing the what of the moon doesn't stop us from enjoying the mystery of her. That is called magic.

I wrote a book about the moon knowing it would be impossible. And to write it knowing that part of the process would not just be running toward that particular failure, but finding a way to joyfully splash about in the ocean of it, reveling in the futility of such a vast project.[1]

A book about the moon needs to be never-ending, spun out of holographic spiderwebs installed inside of a suspended orb carved out of selenite by hundreds of ravens. A book about the moon has to be approximately three thousand pages, made out of datura and motherwort, moonstone and silver. A book for the moon isn't supposed to be a book at all. A twenty-nine-day opera unfurling over every continent, involving every earnest warbler who dares to dream—winged, hooved, or human—would be more fitting. A video of births and deaths and snakes shedding their skin and jasmine seeds unfurling under the earth and live footage of whales migrating, all spliced together on loop, projected on the dark ocean water at night, with plankton and manta rays rising up to meet the surface light in an underwater ballet would be more appropriate.

I wrote this book because collaborating with the moon helped to save my life. How to repay a priceless gift? There are countless lessons the moon has taught me, and I've tried to fit as many of them as I could here. One of them being to pass it on. Share, frequently. Put radical generosity into practice as much as possible. And also, that each person's experience with lunar energy and their intuition is incredibly specific, titillatingly intimate. To wish for others to love how they want is a lesson in the pursuit of joy.

A project about the moon is a project about a lot of other things. Magic or magik or magick: the spellings don't really matter, unless you need them to. Witches and worshippers and seekers. How humanity is trapped by our inability to accept ourselves as part of the collective. How civilization, in the colonialist sense, tries to cut us off from our intuition. How we make up stories about the sky to reflect ourselves back to us. How we treat others and how we treat ourselves. How in spite of the inexplicable abuse we've enacted on one another, we also create whole structures and communities of care and protection. Always. How in spite of the unspeakably tragic distractions of debt and capitalism, in spite of the horrifying violence and brutality we've bizarrely enacted on one another to keep us all starved and uncreative, art still blooms. Our perfect songs and hymns still manage to find a way out of the mud and onto the piano's keys.

The moon will always be inside of, and simultaneously outside of, the conversation. What she thinks? We won't ever know. No matter. She rises in front of us boldly: the Queen of the Night. That emotional dominatrix reminding us that though the suits prize logic, it is our intangible desires, fears, and wounds that determine the fates of countless lives. If only we'd really take the time to consider her most brilliant reflections. Our own perceptions. If only we'd crumple on our knees before her, before one another, crying out all the ways we most need to be nurtured, most need to be embraced, most need to be seen.

I regard the moon as a metaphorical lover. A mother and a friend. A guide and a teacher. Something so sacred that I could never dare to think about trying to translate such magic, trying to explain vibrant mystery with mere words. Who am I to speak on such wonderful wildness? Most days I let life pass me by. Many other days it simply pummels me. The moon pulls me out of my trance, out of my automatic defaults of unengaged living. I could write endless poems, pen stacks of letters, open my mouth to sing a forever harmony, paint an unimaginable amount of canvases, and still just barely be able to express a fraction of what the moon is to me.

How do you pour eternity into an hourglass?

How does one encapsulate infinity into a beginning and an end?

What is more mysterious than the moon? Maybe it is our selves. At first, I thought I'd write in codes and strict metaphors, a way to imprint the deep violet of unknowing inside of your mind's eye. But then, as one does, I tumbled into the unknowing so deeply I became a shipwreck of words. I could only find land through concrete sentences, anchors through the examples of human experience. As one does.

The moon is beyond human-constructed language, out past the ozone, orbiting around a language beyond a language. That doesn't mean we don't write haikus of appreciation to her. That doesn't mean there aren't a million different ways to describe her: all of them fingers, pointing at the moon.[2]

This project has been a challenge because my understanding of books is that, often, they are a nail in the coffin of a concept. A finite, enclosed talisman to a subject, to life, to love, to learning. Nothing is finite, everything is in a constant state of fluctuation. Rivers flow into the ocean, waves roll out and back, different each time. Even the ice caps, which we thought would always be frozen, are melting.

The moon is poly. The moon is somehow enough for everyone. Sometimes I wonder, how does she do it, with so many eyes on her, for so long. Isn't she exhausted?

Doesn't she get performance anxiety? But the moon is so naked and honest so as to have nothing to hide; what you see is what you get. She's good at privacy and boundaries. She makes sure to take space, to leave and then come back. Her identity changes hour to hour, from day to day. Just like ours.

When my heartbreak threatens to overtake my soul, I turn to the moon. She is Sappho, she is Selene. She is the wolf howling, she is the spider spinning. She is every lusty woman, hunting in the forest for a shred of her own self.

On her most resplendent full moon evenings, particularly during the extreme seasons, winter and summer, she is breathtaking, almost too much to behold. Her opaque crystal-ball nakedness almost too graphic to witness, she needs a taffeta ball gown as a cover-up, at the very least. The Drag Mother to us all, shining, vibrant with charisma, uniqueness, nerve, and talent.

Other times, I get mad at her: I rail against her shuttered face, her facade a silent, silver gate. Whenever I'm grasping for the clearest answers, she won't budge. I'm frustrated when she won't speak to me, petulant that she didn't warn me, didn't give me the information my very human ego had wanted to know. But to expect her to always mother me, always help me, especially when I'm not mothering or helping myself, is hypocritical. She's always teaching me about exchanges and boundaries. She leads by example.

On full moon nights, I'm absolutely exhausted by her—praying to her and to the goddess of sleep furtively, to please just let me sleep. Yet when she is dark, when I can't see her, I feel slightly lonely. I must sink into the trust that even if I can't see her, she is with me: even when I can't always see myself. That I never have to own anything to love it.

She's there as accomplice to my joy and to my breakthroughs. I use her phases as affirmations and personal commemoration days. *Of course I feel exhausted and ready to scream: it is a dark moon. Of course I feel ready to accomplish twenty tasks today: it is an April waxing moon! Three days after a raw October full moon, my beloved familiar died, the moon made my heart begin to grieve early. Two days after the June new moon, we opened the door to our first home together, filled with jubilance and excitement.* When I find myself in brief moments of total abandonment, total exhilaration, she cheers me on. When I waver around feeling solid or deserving of my joy, I ask her:

"Who am I, to feel so free?"

The moon bares her teeth, throws her head back, laughs, and says right back:

"My life is long. Yours is short. Who the fuck are you *not to*?"

I gaze at the moon, my body so tiny, yet so shot through with the sharp agonies of grandiose injuries. Her face is so massive, made out of collisions. Her eyes huge craters; Mare Imbrium and Mare Serenitatis. The shadows making up mythologies. The impacts creating stories, the pain leading to art we all can understand.

What do you call a lover that you keep chasing after, knowing even with their reciprocity, you'll never reach their essence, never quite touch, and yet they also live inside of you, always? I call this the moon. Others call this love.

My hope for you is that this inspires you to write a love letter to the moon. A love letter to *your* moon. Take all the spiral time you need to take. Let it feel impossible and joyful and holy. Offer it up freely with precision and surrender. Let your experience shape you as much as you shape it. Allow your future to blossom into the most true reflection of your ocean heart.

Acknowledgments

To my love, the sweetheart of my dreams, the one who is my rock, my support system, my best friend, and my fantasy come true: this book, my business, and so much of my healing and of course my entire life would not exist in the way it does if it weren't for you. Oliver, you love me so perfectly in so many different ways. You are the most generous, wisest person I have ever met. You hold me up and keep me going. What you give me allows me to give to others. You are my sounding board and give me the truth I need. Our conversations, and your astute insight, end up helping strangers. You sat down and edited a 500-page book about the moon—and you don't even really care about the moon or even like to read. That is just one tiny example of the unconditional support you never hesitate to share. Getting to be with you is the gift of a lifetime. Thank you, I love you, thank you, I love you, thank you, I love you.

To my other family members, Gigi and Sacha: Neither one of you read, but you sat next to me for countless hours as I bent over a keyboard, often frustrated. Even though I didn't walk you as much as you wanted me to during this time, you still give me solace, joy, and always show me unconditional love. You served as comic relief, the professional cuddle committee, and official break-taker accomplices. I love you.

To my family, who has shown me so much support: Mom, the love and work you poured into your family is the love of a million moons and suns. Dad, thank you for doing all you did. Seth, your discipline is inspiring. Nana, you are love personified and thank you for helping raise me (and almost a dozen children and grandchildren). Papa, you've taught me so much, been so helpful, and been such a model of what doing the work can look like. Gramma, you have passed on, but your grit and guidance lives with me every day. I appreciate all the sacrifices you made for all of us. Those, and your love, will always be remembered.

To my extended family: Aunty Sandy, Holly, Matt, Missy, Laurel, Amanda, Haley, Austin, Ellie, Meghan, Samantha, T. J., Abra, Lee, Ellen, Jeff, Ben, Noah, Eli, Norah,

Mimi, Adam. All of you have taught me so much about family ties and kinship, about life and humor. Thank you. I love you.

To my in-laws, especially Barbie, Suzy, Amy, and Gumma: Thank you for your warmth and openness in welcoming me into your lives, and for raising the stellar human I adore.

Kara Rota: Thank you so much for all of your help and for believing in me. This book would not be in the world if not for you. If not for your effort and energy, this book would have never gotten the opportunity to exist. I'm lucky to know you.

Meg Thompson: For your kindness and patience, thank you. I have nothing but gratitude for you and your mission. Thank you so much for all of the help and advice during this truly glacial journey.

Madeline Coleman: How can I express my thanks for the amazingness that is you? You make *so* much of what I do possible! You are brilliant and patient and so, so beloved and appreciated. Your efforts with the manuscript helped make this book what it is. As always, you go above and beyond. In everything. *Thank you* can't express what I feel in my heart.

Libby Edelson: You saved this project. My gratitude for your intellect and care is enormous. Thank you.

Gina Young: You helped this book (and me) so much. I love our talks, I love our truth, and I love you. Thank you for being my friend and being inspirational in all the ways.

Rhiannon Flowers: So much of my earliest introductions into feminist queer magic were from you. For over a decade you have also taught me about friendship, sweetness, humor, and queer femme magic. I love you and can't wait to read all of your hilarious, gay books.

Jenstar Hacker: I love you! Your lunar work impacted mine profoundly! You were one of the first folks to introduce me to queer magic, so many long years ago. Your friendship has been one of the gifts of my life.

Lago: I'm squeezing your arm right now. It means I love you.

Jo-Ná Williams: You are the best. Thank you for everything you do. Words can't express how lucky I am to know you.

Russell Brown: I love you. Thank you for all the encouragement and for just being one of my favorite humans. Also thanks to Backpack and Marc J. for cuteness and commentary.

Marlee: For so much of the depressive and rough period of my life that included the writing of this book you were a nonjudgmental space holder. Kindly giving me space to process a Very Hard Year. I will always appreciate your support. Thank you, bun. I love you.

Much of my lineage has been cobbled together from writers sharing their work—not necessarily about magic or witchcraft, but priceless information about how to live. Pema Chödrön, bell hooks, Rabbi Gershon Winkler, Audre Lorde, Rachel Pollack, Mary K. Greer, Laurie Cabot, James Baldwin, Thich Nhat Hanh, Starhawk, Elizabeth Pepper, Mary Oliver, T. Thorn Coyle, Kate Bornstein, Tara Brach, Robin Rose Bennett: all of you have influenced and impacted my life and my magic profoundly. Thank you for sharing your work.

I have been lucky enough to know, respect, be taught by, have healing sessions, and have expansive dialogues with many exceptional practitioners. Shayne Case, Syd Yang, Dori Midnight, Allison Carr, Rash Tramble, Brandie Taylor, Adee Roberson, Liz Migliorelli, Diego Basdeo—thank you for your readings, your support, your teachings, and for just being. Your authentic being-ness and the sharing of your gifts has been inspirational.

Vanessa: Thank you so much for showing me what exceptional therapy really looks like and what it can do.

To all of the folks who bought and read the original Many Moons workbooks and sent me kind messages: Your support kept me going through that three-year project.

To all the stores who carry my work and support me and my business: Thank you.

To my wonderful tarot clients, if you are reading this, thank you. Your vulnerability and willingness to show up in the service of evolution always offers me hope in humanity.

To my incredible students: Teaching you is a gift. You are my teachers. I learn so much from you. Thank you for trusting me and believing in this work.

Thank you, Rahn, and my other spirit guides who have given me universal source energy and all the messages that supported me and so many others. Thank you for loving me.

To all the queer witches: Thank you for existing. Don't stop. The world needs you.

Notes

What Is the Moon?

1 Nola Taylor Redd, "Was the Moon Formed?" Space.com, November 16, 2017.
2 Ewen A. Whitaker, *Mapping and Naming the Moon: A History of Lunar Cartography and Nomenclature* (Cambridge, UK: Cambridge University Press, 1999).
3 Kim Long, *The Moon Book: Fascinating Facts About the Magnificent, Mysterious Moon* (Boulder, CO: Net Library, Inc., 1999), 89.
4 Monica Sjöö and Barbara Mor, *The Great Cosmic Mother: Rediscovering the Religion of the Earth* (San Francisco, CA: HarperOne, 1987), 151.
5 Hanne Jakobsen, "What Would We Do Without the Moon?" sciencenormay.no, January 12, 2012, at https://sciencenorway.no/forskningno-norway-planets/what-would-we-do-without-the-moon /1433295.
6 Matt Jackson, *Lunar & Biodynamic Gardening: Planting Your Biodynamic Garden by the Phases of the Moon* (New York: Cico Books, 2015).
7 George Got, "Weird Things That Have Been Left on the Moon," *Futurism* (2017), at https://vocal. media/futurism/weird-things-that-have-been-left-on-the-moon.
8 *The Old Farmers' Almanac* (Almanac Publishing Company, 203 edition, 2020).
9 Carolyn McVickar, *In the Light of the Moon* (New York: Marlowe & Company, 2003).
10 *Ryokan: Zen Monk-Poet of Japan*, Burton Watson, trans. (New York: Columbia University Press, 1992).
11 Sjöö and Mor, *The Great Cosmic Mother*, 169.
12 Ibid., 156.
13 Sung Ping Law, "The Regulation of Menstrual Cycle and Its Relationship to the Moon," *Obstetrics and Gynecology*, January 11, 2011, at https://obgyn.onlinelibrary.wiley.com/doi/abs/10.3109 /00016348609158228?sid=nlm:pubmed).

Witches, Magic, and the Moon

1 Margot Adler, *Drawing Down the Moon: Witches, Druids, Goddess-Worshippers, and Other Pagans in America Today* (Boston, MA: Beacon Press, 1986).
2 Silvia Federici, *Caliban and the Witch* (New York: Autonomedia, 2014).
3 Robin Rose Bennett, *Healing Magic: A Green Witch Guidebook to Conscious Living* (Berkeley, CA: North Atlantic Books, 2014).

Living in Moontime

1 "Sky Tellers—The Myths, the Magic and the Mysteries of the Universe," Lunar and Planetary Institute, accessed February 10, 2020, at https://www.lpi.usra.edu/education/skytellers/moon-phases/.
2 "Lunar Phases and Eclipses," NASA, accessed February 5, 2020, at https://solarsystem.nasa.gov /moons/earths-moon/lunar-phases-and-eclipses/.
3 Charlie Rainbow Wolf, "The Eight Phases of the Moon," *Llewellyn Worldwide*, June 14, 2016, at https://www.llewellyn.com/journal/article/2583.
4 "Moon-Related Words & Phrases: A Glossary," NASA, accessed February 10, 2020, at https://moon .nasa.gov/observe-the-moon/viewing-guide/glossary/; "Sky Tellers," Lunar and Planetary Institute.

5   Joshua J. Mark, "Wheel of the Year: Definition," Ancient.edu, January 29, 2019, at https://www.ancient.eu/Wheel_of_the_Year/.
6   Ibid.

Ways to Work with the Moon

1   Dane Rudhyar, "A New Type of Lunation Guidance," Rudhyar Archival Project | Astrological Articles, December 31, 2007.
2   "How Long Is a Typical Menstrual Cycle?" Womenshealth.gov, March 16, 2018, at https://www.womenshealth.gov/menstrual-cycle/your-menstrual-cycle.
3   "Do Periods Really Sync with the Moon?" *Clue*, February 13, 2020, at https://helloclue.com/articles/cycle-a-z/myth-moon-phases-menstruation.
4   "Planetary Rulers of the Zodiac Signs and Final Dispositors," Astrology Club, at October 28, 2016, at http://astrologyclub.org/planetary-rulers-zodiac-signs-final-dispositors/.
5   David Frawley, *Astrology of the Seers: a Guide to Vedic/Hindu Astrology* (Delhi: Motilal Banarsidass, 2004).
6   Steph Yin, "What Lunar New Year Reveals About the World's Calendars," *The New York Times*, February 5, 2019, at https://www.nytimes.com/2019/02/05/science/chinese-new-year-lunar-calendar.html.
7   John Matson, "Ancient Time: Earliest Mayan Astronomical Calendar Unearthed in Guatemala Ruins," *Scientific American*, May 10, 2012, at https://www.scientificamerican.com/article/xultun-mayan-calendar.
8   Geoffrey W. Dennis, *The Encyclopedia of Jewish Myth, Magic & Mysticism* (Woodbury, MN: Llewellyn Publications, 2016), 291.
9   Jules Cashford, *The Moon: Myth and Image* (London: Cassell Illustrated, 2003), 258.
10 Ibid., 113.
11 Daniel Foor, *Ancestral Medicine: Rituals for Personal and Family Healing* (Rochester, NY: Bear & Company, 2017).
12 Tara Brach, "Relaxing the Over-Controller ~ Part 1," presented on April 26, 2017, at https://www.tarabrach.com/wp-content/uploads/pdf/2017-04-26-Relaxing-The-Over-Controller-PT1-PDF-TaraBrach.pdf.

The New Moon: The Seed and the Stage

1   adrienne m. brown, *Emergent Strategy: Shaping Change, Changing Worlds* (Chico, CA: AK Press, 2017).

The Waxing Moon: Doing the Work, Following Threads

1   Gary Forsythe, *A Critical History of Early Rome: From Prehistory to the First Punic War* (Berkeley: University of California Press, 2006).
2   Eknath Easwaran, *The Bhagavad Gita* (Berkeley, CA: Nilgiri Press, 2007), ch. 2, verse 47.
3   Octavia E. Butler, "Positive Obsession," in *Bloodchild: And Other Stories*, 2nd ed. (Seven Stories Press, 2005).
4   Jennifer Moon and Mook Attanath, *Principle 1 of the Revolution: Definition of Abundance*, 3rd ed. (Eindhoven, Netherlands: Onomatopee, 2017), 10.

The Full Moon: The Alchemy of Consciousness

1   Hal Arkowitz, "Lunacy and the Full Moon," *Scientific American*, February 1, 2009, at https://www.scientificamerican.com/article/lunacy-and-the-full-moon/
2   Kim Long, *The Moon Book: Fascinating Facts About the Magnificent, Mysterious Moon* (Boulder, CO: Net Library, Inc., 1999), 31, 36.

Full Moon Magic

1 Jules Cashford, *The Moon: Myth and Image* (London: Cassell Illustrated, 2003), 272.

The Waning Moon: The Gateway into the Unknown

1 Vigdis Hocken, "The Waning Gibbous Moon," timeanddate.com, accessed February 10, 2020, at https://www.timeanddate.com/astronomy/moon/waning-gibbous.html.
2 Dane Rudhyar, "A New Type of Lunation Guidance," Rudhyar Archival Project | Astrological Articles, December 31, 2007.
3 Patricia L. Barnes-Svarney and Thomas E. Svarney, *The Oryx Guide to Natural History: The Earth and Its Inhabitants* (Phoenix, AZ: Oryx Press, 1999).
4 The Nap Ministry has been doing activism around resting since 2016, positing that it is especially imperative for people of color to rest. Find out more at https://thenapministry.wordpress.com.
5 Katie J. M. Baker and Jane Bradley, "Tony Robbins Has Been Accused of Sexually Assaulting a High Schooler at a Summer Camp," at https://www.buzzfeednews.com/article/katiejmbaker/tony-robbins-accused-sexual-assault-teenager-supercamp.

The Dark Moon: Transformation in the Void

1 Kim Long, *The Moon Book: Fascinating Facts About the Magnificent, Mysterious Moon* (Boulder, CO: Net Library, Inc., 1999), 33–34.
2 Diane Wolkstein and Samuel Noah Kramer, *Inanna: Queen of Heaven and Earth: Her Stories and Hymns from Sumer* (New York: Harper & Row Publishers, 1983).
3 Ibid.
4 Tara Brach, "Awakening from the Trance of Unworthiness," *Inquiring Mind* 17, no. 2 (spring 2001).
5 Suzanne Somers.
6 Clarissa Pinkola Estés, *Women Who Run with the Wolves: Myths and Stories of the Wild Woman Archetype* (New York: Ballantine Books, 2003).
7 "A Painful Legacy," *Science Magazine,* July 18, 2019, accessed December 20, 2019, at https://www.sciencemag.org/news/2019/07/parents-emotional-trauma-may-change-their-children-s-biology-studies-mice-show-how.
8 Abbot George Burke and Swami Nirmalananda Giri, "Narada," *Original Christianity and Original Yoga*, December 15, 2013, at https://ocoy.org/dharma-for-christians/upanishads-for-awakening/the-chandogya-upanishad/narada/.

Lunar Lore and Literacy: Eclipses, Blue Moons, and More

1 Fred McDonald, *Folens Combined Thesaurus and Dictionary* (Dublin, Ireland: Folens Ltd., 1999), 121.
2 "Why No Eclipse Every Full and New Moon?" *EarthSky,* July 1, 2019, at https://earthsky.org/astronomy-essentials/why-isnt-there-an-eclipse-every-full-moon.
3 Kim Long, *The Moon Book: Fascinating Facts About the Magnificent, Mysterious Moon* (Boulder, CO: Net Library, Inc., 1999), 31, 36.
4 "Rahu and Ketu—The Invisible Planets," Sri Deva Sthanam, March 1, 2014, at http://sanskrit.org/rahu-and-ketu-the-invisible-planets/.
5 Grady, "When the Dragon Ate the Sun." full ref. needed.
6 John Dvorak, *Mask of the Sun: The Science, History, and Forgotten Lore of Eclipses* (New York: Pegasus Books, 2018), 117.

7 "A Total Solar Eclipse Was Once All About Fear, but It's Still an Awe-Inspiring Event," *Public Radio International*, August 14, 2017, at https://www.pri.org/stories/2017-08-14/total-solar-eclipse-was-once-all-about-fear-it-s-still-awe-inspiring-event.

8 Dvorak, *Mask of the Sun*, 244.

9 Demetra George, *Finding Our Way Through the Dark: the Astrology of the Dark Goddess Mysteries* (San Diego, CA: ACS Publications, 1995), 113.

10 Deborah Byrd, "What's a Penumbral Eclipse of the Moon?" EarthSky, January 9, 2020, at https://earthsky.org/astronomy-essentials/what-is-a-penumbral-eclipse-of-the-moon.

11 Fred Espenak, "Danjon Scale of Lunar Eclipse Brightness," NASA, accessed February 13, 2020, at https://eclipse.gsfc.nasa.gov/OH/Danjon.html.

12 Long, *The Moon Book*, 33–34.

13 Flint Wild, "What Is an Eclipse?" NASA, June 1, 2015, at https://www.nasa.gov/audience/forstudents/5-8/features/nasa-knows/what-is-an-eclipse-58.

14 Dane Rudhyar, *The Astrology of Transformation: A Multilevel Approach* (Wheaton, IL: Theosophical Publishing House, 1980).

15 "What Is a Supermoon?—NASA Solar System Exploration," NASA, April 28, 2019, at https://solarsystem.nasa.gov/news/922/what-is-a-supermoon/.

16 "Astrologer Who Coined the Term 'Supermoon' Is 'Delighted' Everyone Uses It," *The Atlantic*, January 31, 2018, at https://www.theatlantic.com/science/archive/2018/01/why-is-it-called-a-super-blue-blood-moon/551831/.

17 Tim Sharp, "What Is a Blue Moon?" *Space*, November 15, 2018, at https://www.space.com/15455-blue-moon.html.

18 "Supermoon, Blood Moon, Blue Moon and Harvest Moon," NASA, September 30, 2019, at https://spaceplace.nasa.gov/full-moons/en/.

19 "What Is a Blue Moon? Is the Moon Ever Really Blue?" Library of Congress, accessed February 13, 2020, at https://www.loc.gov/everyday-mysteries/item/what-is-a-blue-moon-is-it-ever-really-blue/.

20 "Types of Blue Moons Explained," Blue Moon Information ~ Lunar Living Astrology, accessed February 13, 2020, at https://www.lunarliving.org/moon/bluemoon.html.

21 Aparna Kher, "What Is a Black Moon?" timeanddate.com, accessed February 13, 2020, at https://www.timeanddate.com/astronomy/moon/black-moon.html.

22 Jenni Stone, "Understanding the Void-of-Course Moon." The Mountain Astrologer Editor's Choice Articles, 2003, at https://www.mountainastrologer.com/standards/editor's choice/articles/void_of_course.html.

Putting It All Together: The Work of Love

1 bell hooks, *All about Love: New Vision* (New York: William Morrow, 2018).

Epilogue

1 Running toward failure is a concept by the poet Eileen Myles. I read about it here: Eileen Myles, "Being Female," *The Awl*, February 14, 2011, at https://www.theawl.com/2011/02/being-female/.

2 "Don't mistake it for the truth itself. A finger pointing at the moon is not the moon. The finger is needed to know where to look for the moon, but if you mistake the finger for the moon itself, you will never know." Thich Nhat Hanh, *Path of Compassion: Stories from the Buddha's Life* (Berkeley, CA: Parallax Press, 2008).

Index